PET LOSS

AND

HUMAN EMOTION

Pet Loss

and

Human Emotion

Second Edition

A Guide to Recovery

Cheri Barton Ross
Jane Baron-Sorensen

Routledge
Taylor & Francis Group
New York   London

Routledge is an imprint of the
Taylor & Francis Group, an informa business

Routledge
Taylor & Francis Group
270 Madison Avenue
New York, NY 10016

Routledge
Taylor & Francis Group
2 Park Square
Milton Park, Abingdon
Oxon OX14 4RN

© 2007 by Taylor & Francis Group, LLC
Routledge is an imprint of Taylor & Francis Group, an Informa business

Printed in the United States of America on acid-free paper
10 9 8 7 6 5 4 3 2 1

International Standard Book Number-10: 0-415-95576-9 (Softcover)
International Standard Book Number-13: 978-0-415-95576-8 (Softcover)

Library of Congress Cataloging-in-Publication Data

Barton Ross, Cheri.
    Pet loss and human emotion : a guide to recovery / Cheri Barton Ross and Jane Baron-Sorensen. -- 2nd ed.
        p. cm.
        Includes bibliographical references (p.   ) and index.
    ISBN 0-415-95576-9 (softcover)
    1. Pet owners--Psychology. 2. Pet loss--Psychological aspects. 3. Grief. 4. Human-animal relationships. I. Baron-Sorensen, Jane. II. Title.

SF411.47.R685 2006
155.9'37--dc22   2006024045

Visit the Taylor & Francis Web site at
http://www.taylorandfrancis.com

and the Routledge Web site at
http://www.routledgementalhealth.com

*In loving remembrance of the animal
victims of Hurricane Katrina and 9/11,
and their human companions and the
volunteers who worked hard to save them.*

Contents

VIII   CONTENTS

Foreword

"I feel so vulnerable, and no one understands." How many times have I heard this feeling expressed—through sobs, haltingly, plaintively—in my 24 years of helping people through the loss of their loved animal companion. I think one reason people feel so vulnerable when they lose a loved animal is that their relationships with their companion animals are like no other relationship. Animal companions come into and impact our lives in ways that no other relationship can. And when we lose that relationship, the grief is profound.

Contributing to the feeling of utter vulnerability is the perception that people "just don't understand." They "just don't get it"—don't get how utterly bereaved and lost a person is and how long this feeling can last. Additionally, this lack of perception is often experienced from someone who is in the helping role, who is that very person the griever goes to for help. When one is already feeling vulnerable and lost and reaches out for help, only to find the chasm wide between self and helper, a sense of disenfranchised grief occurs.

I've heard this experience described more times than I'd like. I ask myself why it occurs so often. I think one of the reasons is that for some people, there is a perceived prejudice that this type and depth of grief is pathological, it can't be "normal." And it's this very disenfranchisement that grievers experience and describe as intensifying their grief and vulnerability.

When I started working in the area of pet loss counseling back in 1982, to the best of my knowledge there was only one person doing this work—Jamie Quackenbush, a Licensed Clinical Social Worker at the University of Pennsylvania School of Veterinary Medicine. He truly was a pioneer and a leader in this field. I sought him out for assistance—he graciously shared himself and his resources with me.

Since then, thankfully, there have been other individuals making a difference in the field of pet loss counseling. Cheri Barton Ross is one of those persons. Her first book, *Pet Loss and Human Emotion*, helped meet a real need for counselors working with those grieving a death of a loved companion animal. What a contribution she made to our knowledge and practice with that book. Her second book, *Pet Loss and Children, Establishing a Healthy Foundation* (Routledge, 2005), is the first of its kind.

Now she brings us a revision of her original book—a much needed addition. Cheri and co-author Jane Baron-Sorensen help us through some of the challenges—the person who wants to die because life is no longer worth living; the person who feels utterly incapable of making it through another day; the person who doesn't know how to start resolving her anger at the person perceived as responsible for the animal's death; the elderly person whose only family member—her animal—has just died and now, because of age, most likely won't get another pet; the child who saw his animal hit by a car; the parents who themselves are grief stricken and don't know how to tell their children that the family companion animal has an inoperable cancer; a family that has to make the wrenching decision to euthanize a young physically healthy dog because of overly aggressive behaviors jeopardizing the safety of family members and those outside the family; a person who is guilt-ridden and filled with remorse because of the decision to euthanize a pet.

Consider other complicated grief responses a counselor might encounter. Often these are the result of tragic circumstances. An animal is brutally killed by someone taking revenge out on the owner. A family watches as their loved young puppy convulses and dies from having swallowed poison used in a garden. A woman accidentally leaves her medications in her purse on the stairs and her dog gets into them and eats them and is dead within 12 hours. A man accidentally backs over his young dog who is killed instantly. One dog in a family unexpectedly kills another family dog while the family are away from the home. A man helplessly and powerlessly watches as his puppy chokes to death on a chew toy. A cat dies from choking on its collar while outside. Each of these client situations I've encountered, so I know well the complexity of reasons for which clients seek assistance. These experiences allow me to know well why Cheri and Jane's book is so essential.

Most likely, those in the helping field understand grief. Working with grievers is for some a major part of their work. Yet, there can be a real gap in knowing about grief and "getting it" when a person is grieving due to the loss of a loved animal companion. This book helps fill that gap.

If those who are grieving deeply go to see a helping person for assistance, yet perceive the helper as negating the death of the animal and, instead, pursuing those factors in the client's background that have contributed to this "pathological" state, the result is often anger and rejection from this "therapeutic relationship."

Therapists assist individuals through "normal" grief responses as well as particularly challenging and complex situations related to the grief of a much loved and adored animal. "But is this really any different from any other kind of grief? If I know about grief, shouldn't I be able to do this?" True, an understanding of the grief process with its manifestations does cross over between the grief for a person and that for a pet. But there is so much more one needs to understand.

Pet Loss and Human Emotion: A Guide to Recovery, helps the reader "get it" that grief related to pet loss can be different because of the relationship one had with an animal. It assists us in recognizing that the pet plays profoundly important roles in a person's life, and when that relationship is over and the grief feels unbearable, that doesn't mean the person is "sick." Cheri and Jane show us that the relationship a person has with an animal companion can be and often is the closest relationship one has—and that doesn't mean there's something necessarily wrong with that person.

Those of us in the helping professions need to comprehend that someone has lost a best friend, significant other, soulmate, baby, and family member. A counselor may have the latest theoretical knowledge and most highly developed skill set with which to help clients. But if the counselor doesn't "get it"—what role or roles the animal had in a person's life and how profoundly important those roles were—then the interaction and effectiveness of the counseling will be limited. The client who is feeling utter desolation does not feel understood. Instead, the person experiences deep vulnerability.

Building on the latest information and growing knowledge and experience in this field, Cheri and Jane bring new information to their revised book. They discuss the options of hospice for an animal at the end of life. Cheri's previous groundbreaking book on children and pet loss has made a major contribution to our knowledge of children's responses to pet loss. Using her experience and knowledge in that area, she incorporates new information about pet loss and children into this revision, with particular emphasis on complicated grief responses in children. She and Jane devote an entire chapter to pet loss from disasters and personal tragedies. They address new therapies which counselors can utilize in their work. They discuss those clients at greatest risk for a complicated grief response.

Cheri and Jane bring to the reader a balance of knowledge and experience that is significant to us multidisciplinary professionals. This will be a valuable addition to counselors, veterinarians and their staff, pastoral care staff, nurses, social workers, physicians, psychologists, and grief counselors, among others. The essence and value of this book can influence and impact the care that is given to those in grief. Cheri writes in a way which models the compassion that those grieving the death of a loved animal are seeking.

Betty J. Carmack, R.N., Ed.D., C.T.,
Author of *Grieving the Death of a Pet*

Preface

Wilbur often thought of Charlotte. A few strands of her old web still hung in the doorway. Every day Wilbur would stand and look at the torn, empty web, and a lump would come to his throat. No one had ever had such a friend—so affectionate, so loyal, and so skillful (White, 1952, pp. 172–173).

This book is a practical introduction into the field of human–animal bonding. It addresses issues and areas of concern encountered by those facing or anticipating the loss of a beloved companion animal. This book will be helpful to grieving pet parents as well as to therapists and others who work to alleviate the stress and suffering associated with pet loss. A variety of therapeutic techniques are described, and case examples are cited, reminding the reader that a multitude of options aimed at resolution of grief symptoms are available. Until recently, people were cautious when discussing their feelings about pet loss with others for fear their feelings would be discounted or ridiculed. It is now becoming more acceptable for people to discuss, in public, their pain and sadness regarding pet loss. Newspaper and magazine articles have addressed the plight of disaster victims who were separated, many permanently, from treasured companion animals during 9/11 in New York and flooding along the Gulf Coast. Stories related to these tragic events have highlighted the role of pet companions as family members and illustrated the heartbreak faced by those who have had the bonds they shared with their pets abruptly broken. In our book, we educate pet parents and the therapeutic and medical communities about the impact of pet loss and strategies for resolution.

The term *therapist*, used throughout, refers to a variety of people in the helping professions. *Animal health care professional* is the broad term we have used to describe the people who work in the animal care professions. *Pet parent* and *pet guardian* are terms that describe those who are responsible for animal friends who depend upon them for food, shelter, and medical care. Once considered *pet owners,* we have found that most people who grieve for departed pets considered them to be a family member. *Pet parent* and *pet guardian* more accurately define the relationship they shared.

Who will benefit from reading this book?

- Allergists
- Animal rescue and welfare volunteers
- Chaplains
- Spiritual leaders
- Crisis intervention counselors
- Daycare workers
- Disaster responders
- Group leaders
- Hospice workers
- Humane Society workers
- Law enforcement officers
- Marriage, family, and child counselors
- Ministers
- Nurses
- Peer counselors
- Pet parents/guardians
- Pet store owners
- Physicians
- Psychiatrists
- Psychologists
- Rehabilitation workers
- School counselors
- Social workers

- Teachers
- Veterinarians
- Volunteer counselors
- Zoo and other animal-habitat workers

Basically, anyone in the helping professions and anyone who has shared a loving bond with an animal companion should find this book helpful.

The material covers a wide variety of relationships humans share with animals and the corresponding bonds that form between them. Grief responses to the termination of those bonds can range from a simple need for support and understanding to full-blown psychotic episodes. Therapists will learn how to guide clients through the phases of the grief continuum.

Because euthanasia is an option for pet parents, they are faced with choices different from those for terminally ill human family members. Pet parents need support and guidance when contemplating this choice. Sometimes the decision must be made immediately, but more often it evolves over a period of weeks or months. It has been our experience that those who receive therapeutic support during this time often resolve their grief and are able to move on in their lives much sooner than those who have had no support.

To give insight into the meaning of loss for specific populations, case examples are cited throughout the book. Those who have emotional or mental health problems often experience extreme responses to the loss of a pet. These responses can include clinical depression, suicidal ideation, and detachment from reality. The loss of a pet for an elderly person can result in loneliness, isolation, and absence of physical and emotional stimulation. Grief education for children can provide them with healthy coping skills that create a solid foundation for future losses in their lives.

In our society, although such attitudes are changing, there remains much denial around the issues of death and dying. This is especially true for bereaved pet parents. Expressed feelings for the loss of a pet often are not validated. Bereaved pet parents are encouraged to "get over" their loss by replacing the pet. They are made to feel silly, embarrassed, and ashamed for displaying emotion over the loss. It is the goal of this book to give therapists and pet parents a thorough understanding of pet loss issues and describe the means for achieving positive outcomes through therapeutic activities and interventions.

We continue to lead a weekly pet loss support group and work with pet parents on an individual basis, as appropriate. In our personal lives and in our counseling sessions, we are continually reminded of the unique bonds that form between people and their pets. It is with great respect that we dedicate this book to all the pets we have loved and lost and to all the pet parents who have shared their private and poignant experiences with us. It is our hope that the material in this book will shed light on a subject that is deeply felt and too often ignored.

In the pet loss group, we discuss how to best express our condolences to bereaved pet parents while avoiding well-intentioned comments that might be perceived as insensitive. Recently, one man discussed the anger he experienced when overhearing someone make fun of the tears he shed over the loss of his dog. He said that pet loss is often trivialized in society in general—but made the point that being male and going through a pet loss often compounds the loss.

I once had the pleasure of meeting and interviewing Marlo Thomas. In Thomas' book *The Right Words at the Right Time*, she discusses how words we speak, and words spoken to us, have the power to change our lives. As a society, we are generally not very good at coming up with the right words at the right time when attempting to offer comfort to someone who's experienced a loss. Imagine the positive impact of using the right words at just the right time. In the example of the gentleman who was angered by comments such as "men don't cry," he shared one of his first experiences with loss—as a child, the death of his grandmother. As he and his family paid their final respects to his grandmother's body, he was surprised to see his "great big, strong uncle" break down in tears at her casket. He asked his father about why his uncle was being so demonstrative with his feelings. His father replied, "Yes, your uncle is a strong man, and he's strong enough to publicly display his deep-felt emotions over the loss of your grandmother." The message that his father gave him was that it's appropriate to display feelings of sadness when faced with a loss.

It is our hope that this book will be a comprehensive guide for therapists and pet guardians in working through this deeply felt and often ignored type of loss.

Acknowledgments

A book is never written alone. Many people have contributed to this book. Thank you to the animal rescue volunteers who bravely saved the lives of unfortunate animal victims in the aftermath of 9/11 and Hurricane Katrina. Work is currently under way on legislative measures to make certain animals are allowed to be evacuated with their human family members. We'd like to extend a very heartfelt thanks to Deborah Antinori, M.A., R.D.T., L.P.C., and award-winning author of the audio book *Journey Through Pet Loss*. In addition, we thank Betty Carmack, R.N. Ed.D, author of *Grieving the Death of a Pet*, for her support, belief in this project, and continued pioneering in this field of study. Thank you to David Grand, Ph.D., Albert Pesso and Diane Boyden-Pesso, for their contributions to the field of psychology. Jay Whitney, our editor extraordinaire, we appreciate your guidance and thank you for believing in the importance of this type of work. A very special thanks goes to Dana Bliss, who has been a source of support and encouragement throughout our relationship with him at Taylor & Francis. Thanks to Charlotte Roh, Stephanie Pekarsky, Dr. Pia Salk, Saskia Achilles, and Laurel Lagoni for their expertise and for their help in supporting this work. We'd also like to thank our agent, Ed Silver, for his continued faith and support. Finally, we thank all the pet parents who have contributed their stories to this book. We hope that pet parents reading this book will realize they are not alone in their feelings for their pets. We also hope that therapists will find the tools they need to help all of their clients who have experienced the loss of a pet.

The Human–Companion Animal Bond

People have the ability to bond with all types of animals and share unique relationships with them. Savannah and Tutti share a loving bond.

A turning point in the way society views pet ownership is occurring. The momentum is swelling and the wave of change is sweeping to the shore. Perhaps it was the unrelenting devastation of Hurricane Katrina, which rocked the Gulf Coast and left thousands of pets and people stranded and eventually perishing. Perhaps it was even earlier than this when another disaster struck the U.S. This time, on 9/11, it was a man-made attack in which pets were abandoned in apartment buildings in New York City. At whatever point in society we can trace the change back to, somewhere along the line the majority of people started to understand and witness the bonds people share with their animals. Pet owners are now being referred to as pet parents or guardians. Journalists acknowledge that the status of the family pet has gone from being a household appendage to a significant family member.

If any good has been derived from such devastation, it is to be found in the endless stories and recounting of tales of just what animals mean to people and how deeply those bonds are felt. People reacted in anger as the media reported the forced abandonment of family pets. Rescue volunteers were not able, not allowed, or perhaps unwilling, to provide for the family pet along with human family members. There was public outrage as people found out that animals were left to fend for themselves, and that many, if not most, died as a result.

People also discussed the very real accounts of how some disaster victims refused to evacuate without their pets, choosing to remain and even die with their pets, rather than abandon them. While some victims did stay, others were forced, perhaps in having to make a difficult choice to evacuate with an aging or ailing parent or child, to leave the family pet behind. The pain and guilt they took with them was yet another affront to what they already had to bear physically, emotionally, psychologically, and spiritually.

It's during this painful period in U.S. history that people are beginning to view pets as family members worthy of being rescued, cared and provided for, because they are loved.

Out of devastation and loss, lessons are hopefully learned. Veterinary medical organizations, rescue workers, and others are re-addressing, developing, and implementing plans to assist pet parents and their pets during a disaster. Some local and state humane and animal rescue organizations are helping to establish emergency policies, protocols, and plans of action to assure the rescue and care of animal family members.

In the eyes of society, the status of pets is forever changed. Ultimately, it is hoped that the loss of a pet will be afforded the same respect as the loss of a human family member and that the validation of, and support for, the loss will be extended to grieving pet parents.

Therapists don't have to look further than the client sitting before them to discover the significant role companion animals play in people's lives. All they have to do is ask. According to the American Pet Products Manufacturers Association's 2005–2006 National Pet Survey, there are 116 million households with pets in the United States. This number has almost doubled since the 1998 survey. The survey included fish, reptiles, birds, cats, dogs, and small animals (guinea pigs, hamsters, mice, rats). It didn't include those who keep spiders, ducks, horses, and other types of animals as pets, so it's safe to conclude that the number of pets people have may be significantly higher than the reported 116 million.

Many of the clients therapists see in their practices share a bond with an animal. Anyone who is a pet parent or who works with animals is in a position to form a deep attachment to an animal. This includes veterinarians, zoo keepers, pet store employees, feed store owners, humane society volunteers, groomers, animal trainers, and people who volunteer for animal service organizations. It doesn't matter what type of pet—bugs to horses and everything in between— deep bonds of attachment can form.

Pets provide people with companionship, protection, entertainment, and stimulus for exercise, social opportunities, and the chance to love and nurture something outside of themselves. When a pet is gone, the guardian often experiences a deep sense of loss and grief. In a recent study on endured stress levels, the death of a pet was the most frequently reported trauma experienced by couples (Lagoni, Butler, & Hetts, 1994, p. 27).

Chances are good that the client who seeks therapeutic services has experienced at least one pet loss in his or her life. Often this is an unresolved loss, as our society is only beginning to recognize the significance of the loss of a pet. Rituals and ceremonies for mourning the passing of a pet are only recently beginning to gain favor in society.

When a client seeks therapy, therapists should include on their initial intake form a question or two about the presence of companion animals in the home. It is important to establish the degree of emotional attachment to the pet(s) of each family member and to determine who takes primary responsibility for the care of the animal(s). An overall assessment of a client's strengths and weaknesses will be incomplete if the therapist fails to list companion animals as a source of support and pleasure, a focus of concern and stress, or even a cause of guilt, anger, and frustration.

Clients may seek support when they experience the loss of a pet, but it is more likely the pet loss will come up when they are working on other, more socially acceptable stresses (for example, at the time of a divorce, the death of a spouse or friend, or the loss of a job). Many clients have been taught not to display their feelings about the loss of a pet. Some have had the wrong words spoken to them at the wrong time about sharing their feelings of loss for animals. Because of this they often are embarrassed at having deep feelings for an animal; they believe that they are wrong, or different, to feel deep sadness over the loss of a pet and they often go to great lengths to hide those feelings.

A History of Companion Animals

Understanding the bonds between people and their animals will help therapists work with clients who are experiencing a pet loss. The only way a therapist can truly understand the bonds is to ask their clients what the pets mean to them. Once their loss has been validated, it is not uncommon for clients to report that the bond they shared with a companion animal was deeper than any they have shared with another person. This is because companion animals give people something that other people are not always capable of giving: unconditional love.

The relationship between humans and pets dates to the beginnings of civilization. Ancient Egyptians kept cats as pets. There are records of dogs being kept as "house pets" as early as 3000 BC (Mugford, 1977, p. 4). A 14,000-year-old skeleton of a human male was discovered in an ancient near-Eastern burial ground, with its arms wrapped around a dog's skeleton. Human–companion animal bonding is not a new phenomenon (Arkow, 1987, p. 70).

Recent years have seen a growing interest in and concern for human–companion-animal bonds. We are only beginning to understand the ties that can develop between people and their pets. The significance of a pet's death can have far-reaching ramifications for the guardian. Because many pets are considered to be members of the family, the death of a pet can alter the entire structure of a family and reshape the guardian's sense of well-being.

The study of the relationship between humans and animals is not new; but the study of the *emotional* and *psychological* bonds humans have with their pets is. One of the first organizations to document the importance of animals to humans was the Latham Foundation, established in 1918 (Levy, 1981). According to Hugh Tebault (1997), its president, the Foundation originated the Delta Group, which was interested in studying the scientific aspects of research in this field. In 1979, the Delta Group became independent, and is now known as the Delta Society. The Delta Society is an international research service and educational center for persons and organizations in the field of human–animal interactions. The Delta Society has uncovered a variety of significant relationships people share with their pets.

Pets provide us with physical, social, and emotional benefits. Most of us are aware of the success of service organizations such as Guide Dogs for the Blind and Canine Companions for Independence (CCI). A vast amount of data has been collected on the difference pets can make in a disabled person's life. Information also is being collected on the therapeutic benefits that pets bestow on humans. Studies indicate that the presence of a pet in a therapist's office can encourage a withdrawn child to open up. Other studies show that a patient's blood pressure can be lowered simply by stroking a cat. No one can dispute the relaxing effects of watching fish in a tank or the positive cardiovascular benefits of walking a dog in the park.

Research also indicates that not all people bond with or even like pets. If a person enjoys having a pet, the human–pet relationship has the potential for positive therapeutic effects on that person's life. On the other hand, a person who has not liked animals throughout his or her life will not find benefit from keeping an animal as a companion.

Finally, it is important to remember that people form attachments to animals other than cats (the most popular pets) and dogs. In Chapter 12 there is a beautiful story about a woman who loves insects and keeps pet walking sticks. She shares the life-lessons she's learned from observing and interacting with these amazing creatures. People can also become attached to wild animals. Susan Chernack McElroy includes poignant examples of interacting with nature in her book *Animals as Teachers and Healers*. Some children and adults will sit for hours in a wooded area to see how many animals will approach them. Many adults like to watch birds or go hiking to experience wildlife.

The Human–Pet Bond

Changes in human mobility and family structure have increased the likelihood that people will form significant attachments to pets.

Studies indicate that, in recent years, pets have become even more important to people. The pet industry reports a large increase in pet expenditures in the past decade, an increase that has skyrocketed in the last five years. Researchers attribute this increase to the fact that people are choosing to have fewer children, and consequently often view their pets as their children. In fact, of the people who share their lives with companion animals, 70% consider their pets to be their children (Ciba Seminar, 1996). Another recent study indicated that 99% of cat and dog guardians consider their pets full-fledged family members (Ciba Seminar, 1996).

A pet can represent many things to a pet parent. Some people view their pets as best friends. Others see them as children. Companion animals can be bridges to our past. They can remind us of happier times or of sad events. A companion animal may accompany a person through childhood into adulthood. A pet can be a source of support during a divorce or other loss. In some cases, the presence of a pet in a person's life can be a lifeline. For many people living with terminal illnesses, pets are not only sources of comfort and support, they are reasons to continue living.

The love and life lessons people experience as pet parents are varied and deep:

- A man living with AIDS said that his three cats kept a vigil by his bedside when he was very sick. When he thought he might die, he was able to reach down and draw strength from his furry friends and feel comforted by their presence.
- A Vietnam veteran whose 17-year-old cat had just been euthanized shared that the cat was the first thing he had learned to love again after returning home from the war.
- A woman who had lost a baby to sudden infant death syndrome (SIDS) acquired a puppy to help her through the loss. When her dog died, she was reminded of the loss of her child as well.
- A woman whose dog died suddenly remarked that his death was more difficult for her to endure than the recent loss of her mother (with whom she'd been close) had been (Petitt, 1994, p. 151).

For a disabled person, a pet not only is a companion but also can be viewed as an extension of the individual. Animals can be trained to be the eyes or ears of a blind or hearing-impaired person. They can provide a disabled person with physical mobility. Animals can be trained to open doors, turn on lights, carry and retrieve items, and even push elevator buttons. They can give the disabled a bridge to the outside world. They can even assist people with emotional and psychological problems by helping them to learn to trust again.

Benefits of Animal Companionship

One emotional or psychological benefit of keeping pets is the very fact that pets are dependent on people. Small animals, such as rabbits, birds, guinea pigs, and rats, require a certain amount of care. Cats reward us with purrs and affectionate rubs. Dogs faithfully greet us at the door. Small tokens of gratitude exhibited by a pet gives one a sense of being needed. Pets also provide us with a focus of attention, something to love and touch. Through care-taking and nurturing of a companion animal, a person's self-esteem and sense of accomplishment can be enhanced.

Play is another benefit of pet ownership. Pets often evoke play behavior in us, and the act of playing has been recognized as one of the most important aspects of social development. According to Mugford (1977, p. 13), "Play provides essential early stimulation for both human and animal young, serving to reinforce social bonds between parents and infant and exercising motor patterns relevant to later adult behaviors."

Finally, pets can be social icebreakers. Someone who is shy or has a difficult time communicating with others can reach out to the world via his or her pet. Studies have shown that people will approach others who are with their pets to inquire about the pet or comment on it. This opens up a safe arena for communication (Ross, 1987, p. 13).

Children and Pets

For a child of working parents, one who does not have siblings to play with, pets can encourage the development of the imagination. Children will make up and play games with their pets. A pet can help a child develop his or her motor skills as well. Babies often crawl after a pet or reach out to grab the dog's tail. Adults as well as children can enjoy interacting with animals.

Dr. Aline Kidd, professor of psychology at Mills College, stressed the benefits of pets for children and their positive effects on the learning process. Young children are not yet aware that they can be hurt or feel pain. The young see other children as objects—like dolls, teddy bears, or plastic toys. Experiencing animals as well as other children helps children learn some of the happier, as well as the more painful, characteristics of life itself. Watching a pet give birth can teach something about the beginning of life. The death of a pet can help teach that life has an end. Both ends of the spectrum, and all the in-between parts, can help a child learn how to cope with his or her own life challenges (Kidd, 1982, p. 8).

A companion animal can provide a child with stability and continuity in the family setting. Especially for those children whose parents have gone through separation or divorce, a pet can remain a dependable family member, someone who silently relates to the child in a constant way in the midst of changes.

According to Levinson (1982), children can develop enhanced self-esteem by seeing themselves in a position of authority when they are permitted to provide care for a pet. In a study of children who sucked their thumbs, Levinson noted that those children who were not raised with pets had a stronger, more intense need to comfort their anxiety than those raised with pets. He concluded that pets can fulfill a child's need for consistency and reduce anxiety for the child, especially when there is a constant shift in caregivers (Kay, Cohen, Fudin, Kutscher, Nieburg, Grey, & Osman, 1988, p. 80). Children are not always able to fulfill parental expectations or receive their approval. A pet can be a nonjudgmental friend to a child, loving and protecting him or her no matter what. In addition, pets provide comfort to children when they are separated from their parents for short periods of time (Kay et al., 1988, p. 80).

Importance of Touch

Touching is another way pets can help people tremendously. The work of Ashley Montagu (1986) has demonstrated the importance of human touch to growth and development. Touching and being touched are important for our feelings of happiness and well-being. In studies with autistic children, contact with an affectionate animal proved to be beneficial in eliciting positive responses; in the presence of a companion animal, in fact, the children demonstrated a connectedness to their surroundings they had not previously been shown (Ross, 1987). Touching helps us feel connected to the world around us, reassuring us of our importance in the world and reminding us that we are alive. This is especially true as we age and our physical beauty changes along with our health.

The Elderly and Pets

Elderly people endure many losses. They lose friends and family, retire from jobs, and often live on limited incomes. A pet can be a close ally for an elderly person, offering affection, companionship, and sometimes protection.

In animal visits to nursing homes, the interactions between pets and residents provide opportunities for conversations, sensory stimulation, tactile warmth, and reminiscing.

A pet also can provide an elderly person with a sense of purpose. An elderly person may center his or her entire day around the care of a pet, and walking and playing with a pet encourages an elderly person to exercise. Pets offer us the best they have to give. When we lose them, we grieve, not only for the pet, but for all the ways in which they enhanced our lives.

In *The Loving Bond: Companion Animals in the Helping Professions* (Arkow, 1987), Dr. Joseph Meeker summed up humankind's need to be close to animals:

> The fulfillment of any given life cannot occur in isolation. Maturity grows from interactions at every stage of life. Although we may pretend that interactions with other people are the only essential contacts that will help us grow, deep within us we know better. Reaching out to other animals is a normal and necessary part of every human life, and it is a rare or deformed person who does not do so in one way or another. There is a voice within us to say that we cannot completely be *us* unless we somehow make contact with all that otherness (p. 64).

Factors Influencing Pet Companionship

According to Lagoni et al. (1994), anthropomorphism (giving non-humans humanlike traits), neoteny (infantile characteristics), and allelomemetic behaviors (animals often appear to mimic humans) all tend to enhance the likelihood of a bond between humans and animals (pp. 10–14). In their book *The Human–Animal Bond and Grief,* these authors cite several theories of how human–animal attachments form:

- One theory suggests that attachment is influenced by our behavioral responsiveness toward pets. Our pets' need to be cared for and nurtured makes us feel needed and wanted. Shared activities such as walking, visiting the park, and playing enhance the bond we share.
- Another hypothesis says that the attachment is based on family member status, shared affection, and companionship. Dominance also is a factor, as a person experiences being the master of a pet.
- A third theory describes the affectionate tie between people and pets that endures over time. Love and interaction between animals and humans as well as joy of pet ownership are factors indicative of attachment.
- A final hypothesis says that attachment occurs from being in proximity to animals.

Therapeutic Benefits of Companion Animals

Conflicting studies have emerged in the past decade over the benefits of pet companionship for both humans and animals. Despite the conflicting data, however, numerous studies, books, articles, and video tapes support claims of beneficial aspects of keeping pets. The importance of relationships shared with animals now is being recognized nationwide. Service organizations are being founded throughout the United States to support pet parents through the loss of a pet, to enable people with AIDS to keep their pets, to provide adoptable pets to the elderly, and to advocate that elderly and terminally ill people be allowed to keep their pets.

Studies have demonstrated that sharing a relationship with an animal can reduce anxiety in hospitalized patients, give hope to people with life-threatening disease, promote self-esteem by giving purpose to inmates of correctional facilities, provide educational opportunities for children, and give meaning to the lives of senior citizens. Other studies have shown that mentally and physically disabled people can benefit from the experience of horseback riding. Pets also can help people with various psychological disorders, including panic disorders and agoraphobia.

Suzanne and Amy. Suzanne was newly married when her husband died in a car accident. Soon after his death, Suzanne experienced her first panic attack while driving. She stopped driving and stayed home after a psychiatrist diagnosed Suzanne as having panic disorder and agoraphobia. She moved in with her parents and began taking medication, leaving the house only to see her psychiatrist weekly. After several months, however, Suzanne expressed an interest in adopting a dog. Her parents thought getting a dog might encourage Suzanne to venture out of the house and might provide her with something to love while she mourned the loss of her husband.

Suzanne chose a golden retriever, named the dog Amy, and developed a deep attachment to her. Because Amy needed to be walked, Suzanne ventured out in front of her parents' house, and then around the block. When Amy needed to have her vaccinations and an examination, Suzanne ventured out of the house to the veterinarian's office. She was able to focus on Amy's needs, and so distracted herself from her fears.

Because of her relationship with Amy and with assistance from the psychiatrist, Suzanne finally felt secure enough to face her fears. She learned to become independent again. After a year, she and Amy moved into their own home and Suzanne began driving again.

Aspects of the Human–Companion Animal Bond

Many studies have been done on our interactions with domesticated and wild animals. Researchers have studied relationships between animals and physically and mentally challenged people, nursing care residents, hospitalized patients, and incarcerated prisoners. A

relatively new field of research in human–animal bonding is pet ownership among people with AIDS.

There is an abundance of information on both the positive and negative aspects of pet ownership for people in a variety of circumstances.
Although many studies have demonstrated the beneficial aspects of
pet ownership, as stated earlier, it is important to remember that keeping a pet is never beneficial for people who are not fond of animals.
Broad-based generalizations that pets are good for the elderly and for
children have been disputed. An elderly person who was not fond of
animals during his or her earlier life will not necessarily benefit from
a pet in later life. The negative aspects of an animal companion for a
child include the trauma of experiencing the loss of the pet and the
various problems associated with playing too roughly or forgetting
responsibilities. All of these can have devastating consequences for
children and pets.

As much as a pet might enhance a client's health, it is important
to note that the responsibility and problems associated with caring
for an animal can hinder a client as well. Therapists should determine
whether current relationships shared with pets are helpful or more
stressful for the client.

Animal Collectors

In recent years, individuals known as "animal collectors" have been
identified and profiled. At the Delta Society Conference in 1990,
Sharon Linda Castro presented a paper on animal collectors derived
from a questionnaire sent to more than 2,000 humane organizations
worldwide to gather data on this type of person.

Occasionally, therapists may encounter a client who falls into the
category of animal collector. These people usually begin with good
intentions of rescuing unwanted animals, but many end up with 30 or
more cats and dogs for whom they cannot provide care.

An animal collector typically displays the following characteristics:

- A need to have many animals
- A refusal to part with any animals
- A return to animal collecting even after being charged with
  animal neglect

- A perception that any life is more important than quality of life
- A love for animals combined with a failure to care for them
- A need to control every aspect of an animal's existence (sometimes refusing veterinary care, socialization, and exercise)
- A hero-martyr complex, personal sacrifices on behalf of the animals collected
- An inability to see that animals need proper care, often insisting that ill animals are healthy and happy (Lagoni et al., p. 19)

Treating Animal Collectors

Animal collectors rarely come to the attention of therapists. They operate from a position of reinforced denial; that is, they truly believe that the animals for whom they claim responsibility would be worse off without their involvement, and they see themselves as saviors and defenders of the helpless against those who regulate, control, or otherwise oversee animal welfare codes. When forced by an outside agency to desist from animal-collecting behaviors, these individuals may have a difficult time redefining their identity and role in society relative to the absence of the large numbers of animals formerly in their care.

Should a therapist encounter an animal collector in practice, the goal of therapy is to identify what purpose the collecting behavior serves in the client's life. The therapist should assist the client in describing both the drawbacks and payoffs relative to the current situation, suggest to the client that the collecting behaviors may be avoidant in nature, and try to determine what the collecting process keeps him or her from doing or being. The client can be asked to imagine activities or relationships that might be available if he or she were not tied down to the demands of caring for so many animals. Therapist and client can research and discuss placement/adoption options within the community, with the therapist reminding the client that reducing the number of animals under his or her care may improve the quality of life for everyone. The option of euthanizing diseased or dying animals should not be discussed unless the client brings it up or after a level of trust between therapist and client has been attained.

Animal collecting is extremely time consuming and expensive, and often is carried out at the cost of the individual's social life. If the client is toiling under the demands of caring for so many animals, or is under a great deal of pressure from neighbors or the authorities to give the animals up, he or she may be willing to look at the overall quality of life of both himself or herself and the animals he or she is struggling to protect. The therapist is cautioned to proceed slowly and gently when pointing out options and alternatives to these clients. Their denial can be very powerful, and anger with regulatory agencies or disgruntled neighbors can run high. Care must be taken so that the therapist is not seen as another enemy; that is, one who is not empathetic to animal rights and is siding with those who represent cold bureaucratic authority.

Conclusion

Recent disastrous events have caused us to pause and consider what pets truly mean to us. Now, more than ever before, people are beginning to understand that pet owners consider their pets to be family members—hence the terms "pet parents," and "pet guardians" gaining popular use in society. When the bond with a pet is terminated, pet parents need support in working through the loss, much in the same way they might for a deceased child, friend, or spouse.

It is important to remember that people can bond with any type of animal. They can gain comfort and knowledge by observing animals and insects in the wild. They can love and care for a duck just a deeply as they would a dog. They can form deep bonds of attachment with horses and goats, just as they might a cat or a bunny.

Clients will seek a therapist's services for a variety of reasons. Often a relationship shared with a companion animal plays a prominent role, positive or negative, in one or more areas of the client's life. It is the therapist's responsibility to identify, understand, and consider the roles of all family members in relationship to one another—including those of companion animals in the home. When assessment includes questions about pets as family members, clients are given permission to speak openly and freely about issues they may have regarding their pets.

Pets represent different things to different people. A pet can be a bridge to the past and a source of comfort and love, and can fill the roles of playmate, sibling, loyal friend, and child. Pets can be symbols of self-esteem and sources of pride and of accomplishment. They provide tactile stimulation and opportunities for socialization.

While studies continue to determine the therapeutic benefits of companion animals, there is much evidence to support the beneficial aspects of animal–human relationships. The role animals play in society should not be discounted. In fact, as our daily lives seem to become even busier, and at times more isolating, the connection pet parents have with their pets takes on a more significant role in society. This is especially true for people who live alone, for children whose daily lives are over-scheduled with school, sports, and other organized activities. Being greeted by your dog or snuggling with your cat, bunny, or guinea pig at the end of a long day can provide pet parents with a sense of well-being and peacefulness.

It is important also to remember there are negative aspects of pet ownership, including around-the-clock responsibility for the care of a pet. As in any relationship, even the best of care can sometimes result in a failure to thrive. In these cases, pet parents can experience helplessness, frustration, and guilt. Because animals' lives typically are only one-eighth the length of humans', pet parents can expect to have to care for elderly and sick pets; and most will experience the death of a pet. Often times, working parents of children can find it a burden to have to care for their four-legged charges at home, too.

If therapists understand the process of human–animal bonding and the importance of the relationships clients share with their pets, they can more completely meet the needs of their clients. This is especially true when the bond is broken and the client needs assistance working through the loss of a pet.

2

WHEN THE BOND IS BROKEN

How deeply we love our pets is how deeply the grief will be felt when the bond is broken. Rituals and ceremonies, such as the funeral these people hold for their deceased pet rabbit, are important in honoring the relationship shared with the pet and in allowing us to say goodbye.

Any time we choose to love someone or something and to receive love in return, we are allowing a bond to form. Part of who we are and how we feel is tied up in that bond. We may derive much pleasure and happiness from the bond, but we run the risk of feeling an equal amount of pain and sorrow when that bond is broken.

Pets make us feel good. They comfort us when we're depressed and share our joy when we're happy. They can be our best friends, our children, physical extensions of ourselves (for disabled people), and someone to share our lives with us.

The bonds people form with their pets can be as deep (and sometimes deeper) as those they form with other people. When a pet loss occurs, clients may grieve more deeply than they would for the loss of a human companion. This can be attributed to the fact that pets give people something other humans are not always able to give—unconditional love. One elderly client summed up the depth of his loss when his dog died by saying, "I cannot believe that I will ever get through this experience. The love she gave me was the purest form of love I have ever known."

There are many types of loss a pet parent can endure. A loss occurs with the sudden or unexpected death of a pet, or when a pet runs away or is stolen. Such a loss can be anticipated if it follows a long-term illness or with the decision to relinquish a pet for adoption. One of the most heart-wrenching types of losses can occur during natural and manmade disasters in which the pet parent often feels helpless and guilty over the known or unknown status of the pet. Regardless of when or how the bond is broken, pet parents who share deep emotional attachments to their pets can expect to grieve. The loss of a pet can make a pet parent feel angry, helpless, isolated, lonely, guilty, frustrated, hopeless, and afraid. The pet parent may experience some or all of these emotions when working through a loss.

Stages of Grief

Dr. Elisabeth Kubler-Ross (1969), one of the pioneers in the study of death, outlined five predictable stages of grief in her book *On Death and Dying*. These stages are widely used to describe the levels of grief a client experiences when a loss occurs. According to the cumulative works of Drs. John Bowlby (1969, 1973, 1980), J. William Worden (1982), Therese Rando (1984), and Elisabeth Kubler-Ross (1969), the typical grieving client passes through three predictable phases:

1. Shock and denial
2. Emotional pain and suffering
3. Acceptance and resolution (Lagoni et al., 1994, p. 37)

In this chapter, we will discuss six stages of grief: denial, bargaining, anger, guilt, sorrow, and resolution. We'll discuss guilt as one of the stages, although it is not so much a separate stage as a pervasive entity that crosses all phases and can hinder progress from one stage to the next.

The process of grieving is not a steady, linear ascent from depression to joy. It can be likened to a roller coaster ride, with ups and downs at every turn. At the end of the ride is a place of acceptance and resolution, where the client is at peace with what went before. The process can be explained as a "two steps forward, one step back" adjustment that occurs in a normal time-limited progression. Therapists should be familiar with the characteristics of each stage in order to recognize where their clients stand in the process. The therapist's job is to facilitate a smooth transition from one stage to the next while alleviating the guilt that is superimposed on the entire process.

Let's look at the six stages of grief through one case study: Mr. Jones and Bruce.

Denial

Mr. Jones and Bruce. When Mr. Jones first noticed that his 12-year-old 15-pound cat, Bruce, had lost interest in eating, he assumed that Bruce was supplementing his diet outside the home.

After two weeks, however, Mr. Jones detected a substantial weight loss. He purchased a high-quality canned cat food to entice Bruce's appetite and became alarmed when another week passed and Bruce lost more weight. Mr. Jones even tried serving Bruce cooked chicken and tuna, but Bruce's appetite didn't respond. Concerned and fearful, Mr. Jones took the cat to the veterinarian for an examination.

After tests, the veterinarian informed Mr. Jones that Bruce was in an advanced stage of kidney failure. She added that Bruce had a poor prognosis for recovery and recommended immediate dialysis treatment followed by a low-protein diet. She suggested that Mr. Jones leave Bruce with her at the hospital.

Mr. Jones was not willing to accept the prognosis. He told the veterinarian Bruce was being a finicky eater in his old age, and he decided to feed Bruce baby food at home until his appetite returned.

It is perfectly normal for the pet parent to first experience a stage of denial when told the pet is dying, dead, or missing. Denial is a coping mechanism that cushions the mind against the sudden shock it has received. Denial may be played out during the first 24 hours if the animal's death is sudden, or for longer if a chronic terminal illness has been diagnosed.

Clients like Mr. Jones need education on the grief experience and help in seeing that their position—although irrational in the face of a veterinarian's assessment and prognosis—is a normal initial response to the fear of loss. Clients need to see that their denial of a pet's failing health is protecting them from the sorrow and loneliness to come. The therapist's job is to reassure them that, no matter how painful, he or she will see them through to the other side of the grief.

Bargaining   Mr. Jones became angry at Bruce when the most expensive foods and vitamin supplements available failed to help him. His bargaining attempts failed and gave way to anger.   Bargaining with the pet or with a higher power for the pet's life is the second response to anticipated loss. A parent may offer the pet its favorite food, force-feed it vitamins, look for alternative treatments and therapies, and make promises to the pet. Bargaining is a way of keeping hope alive while the pet parent comes to terms with the inevitable. When bargaining doesn't yield the desired results, anger is the natural response.

Anger   Bruce became listless and lost more weight. Mr. Jones took the cat back to the veterinarian, who told him that dialysis would be of little use now. The veterinarian recommended euthanasia.   Mr. Jones felt guilty and blamed himself for not accepting the treatment the veterinarian had recommended before. He projected his self-blame onto the veterinarian, accusing her of incompetence and angrily refusing to pay the bill.

When faced with the loss of a pet, a client may become angry—and the anger may know no bounds. The client may lash out at the therapist, a spouse, the veterinarian, children, and friends. If a client is angry with him- or herself for overlooking clinical signs or waiting too long to seek care, this self-directed anger will give way to guilt.

Mr. Jones told the therapist that if he had only taken the advice of the veterinarian early on, Bruce might have been cured before it was too late. "Bruce is going to die," he said. "The veterinarian should have convinced me to do what was right."

Mr. Jones needed to have his anger validated, but he also needed to see that the veterinarian had displayed sound clinical judgment in her assessment and recommendations for Bruce. His projected anger was really about his own inability to accept Brace's diagnosis and prognosis, and his false belief that love and vitamins, instead of dialysis, would reverse the disease process. Mr. Jones needed help to see that his decision was made out of love and care for Bruce, and that no "cure" was available in any case.

Guilt   Superimposed on Mr. Jones's denial, bargaining, and anger was the pervasive presence of guilt. His conversations were littered with sentences that began, "What if I had … ?" "If only I …" "Why didn't I listen?" and "I'm such an idiot." Once again, Mr. Jones needed to see that he had made decisions throughout Bruce's life out of genuine love and concern for his pet. Decisions stemming from love and concern are never wrong; they are simply the best choices we can make at the time. Throughout his life Bruce had received the best of everything; no expense or emotion had been spared. Making decisions in times of crisis and stress is difficult for anyone. Guilt has no place in the scenario when choices are made from the heart. The therapist's job was to help Mr. Jones see all that had gone before and to minimize the trauma of the final weeks.

Guilt is an unproductive, debilitating emotion that often inhibits progress toward resolution. It is the enemy of healing and closure. Clients can find many ways to blame themselves for the loss or impending loss of their pets. It is important that he or she work through all of his or her feelings regarding any real or imagined role in causing the pet's demise.

Sorrow   Mr. Jones chose euthanasia for Bruce. He accepted the fact that Bruce's life was going to end and he did not want his pet to endure any more trauma or pain. Mr. Jones was tearful while thinking of how he would miss his friend. Sorrow, or deep sadness, is the core of the grieving process. Though it can be kept at bay during the early stages through the intensity of denial, anger, and guilt, sorrow eventually settles in and permeates all aspects of life.

Sorrow is, in fact, a healing emotion. This is the time when tears flow freely. Clients feel relief and release from the pent-up emotions of previous days or weeks. Tears may come at work, in the supermarket, or driving down the freeway. Clients may report sleep and appetite disturbances at this time. It's important to remind clients to get adequate rest, limit alcohol intake, and get proper nutrition now.

With time, sorrow dissipates and everyday tasks begin to dominate awareness. Tears no longer break through into daily activities but surface at more convenient times, such as in the evening after work. Clients feel more in control and are able to see an end to the intense pain that is true sorrow. They accept the situation realistically. Resolution has begun.

Resolution   Mr. Jones visited the pet cemetery where Bruce was buried. He sat near the headstone and recalled happier times spent with his pet. Mr. Jones was able to remember the life he shared with Bruce and smile. He was no longer moved to tears when remembering Bruce's antics. Mr. Jones was able to resolve his loss.

In the resolution phase of the grief process, clients realize that the pet is gone, that no amount of wishing will make it different, and that they will survive the loss that previously seemed engulfing. Now they can look at photographs of the pet and smile rather than cry; they can remember walks in the park instead of anxious trips to the veterinarian; anniversaries and holidays can be recalled with tenderness rather than despair. During this stage of grief, clients may consider sharing life with another pet for the sheer pleasure of having something warm and furry to hug again.

It is important to remember that there is no right or wrong way to grieve a loss. While there are some socially acceptable rituals for mourning the loss of a human, the loss of a beloved animal, unfortunately, has not been given the same stature. Many times the mourning can be made more difficult by the lack of rituals in society. People often don't know how to respond to a pet parent's emotions regarding a loss or an anticipated loss. Sometimes the wrong things are said and the grieving pet parent is made to feel that he or she must explain or defend the depth of feelings for the pet. Other times, well-intentioned people may try to replace the pet for the grieving guardian. It is important to remember that the bond shared is unique and cannot be replaced.

Society doesn't readily accept pet loss as significant. A client who needs time off from work to grieve may say, "I've experienced a recent loss in my family," and leave it at that. Also, it is important for the grieving client to connect with other grieving pet parents (e.g., pet loss support group or friends who have lost pets). The validation, understanding, and support given can be invaluable to a grieving client. To date, many avenues of support are available to pet parents. A pet parent can type in the words, "pet loss," on an Internet search engine and be steered to a variety of sites providing support. There are even sites available that provide support for specific types of loss (see Chapter 13 for available resources).

Clients have shared that they are afraid to cry and let out their emotions for fear of succumbing to the pain and not being able to stop. This is a normal fear. Some clients hesitate to honestly explore the depth of their emotions and the pain a loss brings. These raw emotions can and often do seem like a bottomless well of despair from which one may never climb out. Some clients hesitate to share their true feelings for fear of falling into such a deep well. However, tears are therapeutic and the release of emotion can help the person to move through the grieving process. One pet parent at the pet loss support group shared that he was often told, growing up, that boys don't cry. He adhered to this most of his adult life. After his cat died, he lay on the floor and wailed, releasing his deep pain. After a period of time he was able to calm himself and reported that he actually felt a bit better for having allowed himself this expression.

Having support and allowing oneself permission to grieve can assist significantly in moving through the process of grief, especially with an anticipated loss. We recommend that clients find or be referred to a pet loss support group as soon as serious illness has been diagnosed. Clients who receive support in the early stages of grief tend to move through the grieving process with more ease, less angst and vulnerability. In conjunction to the support group (see Chapter 11), some clients will benefit by being referred to a licensed hypnotherapist who is skilled at working on grief and loss issues (e.g., a psychologist or psychiatrist). Working through loss while in a deep, hypnotic, relaxed state can effectively and safely assist clients who are hesitant to explore their emotions (see Chapter 11). Hypnosis can be particularly beneficial to clients who may have experienced a traumatic loss or whose grief is compounded by other losses.

Anticipated Loss

Prior to the actual loss of a pet, some pet parents will begin moving through the grief process as a beloved pet ages or when a terminal diagnosis has been made. Therapists can help these clients prepare for the inevitable loss by educating them about the normal responses they may encounter.

Therapists will see the same stages of grief prior to the physical loss of the pet. For example, the client may become tearful at first or deny the diagnosis. He or she may express anger with those associated with the pet's care (e.g., the veterinarian or groomer) and attempt to involve the therapist in the denial of the diagnosis or in condemnation of some aspect of the care administered to the pet.

It is important for the therapist to recognize all of these responses as normal "grief behaviors" akin to the grief that accompanies the actual physical loss of a pet. In these instances, however, clients sometimes attempt to engage a therapist in plans or schemes that are both ill-founded and ill-advised. They may turn to the therapist for validation of their anger, denial, and fear. The therapist needs to gently assist these clients in reviewing and accepting the facts. It is at this point that a pet loss support group can be helpful.

In a support group, pet parents will meet other pet parents who are experiencing or anticipating the loss of a pet. Shared grief can help a client face the reality of a pet's fate and, at the same time, validate the grief being experienced (see Chapter 10).

Acknowledging the Loss

Bereaved pet parents often feel embarrassed by their grief at the loss of a pet since this type of loss often is an unrecognized one in our society. Clients need to know it is perfectly normal to grieve such a loss. In our society, death often is dealt with through denial, so it is vital to validate a client's loss.

As stated earlier, the loss of a pet often is viewed by others as insignificant. It is minimized and trivialized by people who deny to themselves and to others that a deep bond can be shared with animals. Acknowledging the client's feelings lets him or her know that the loss is real and significant. Referral to a pet loss support group further validates the client's feelings by allowing him or her to meet with other pet parents who have experienced a bond with a pet.

At a pet loss support group pet parents will learn about healing rituals and healthy coping methods, and will receive love and support from other pet parents. One client, Louis, talked about a wake he held for his dog, Andy. After an unexpected and sudden illness Andy had been euthanized at home by his veterinarian. Louis placed Andy's body on his favorite blanket underneath the Christmas tree. He had put several ice packs under the blanket on which Andy's body had been placed. Keeping the body cool helped to prevent deterioration for a few days, enough time to allow Louis to say good-bye to Andy and the life they had enjoyed together.

Louis shared that this time together was a gift because he was able to fully express the feelings he had for Andy. He invited close friends who had also loved Andy to come view the body and say their final goodbyes (similar to a wake that is often held for a person). Louis felt supported and cared for by his friends. He told the group members that he was glad he took this time, as it helped him come to terms with the finality of his loss. A few days later, when he was ready to bury Andy's body, his friends joined him in a final ceremony under a tree in the back yard.

Sharing rituals, grief, and feelings for a pet is a positive and therapeutic way to help others while working through a loss.

Therapists can use a variety of techniques and skills to help their clients through the loss of a pet. Attending, effective listening, reflection, and validation are essential when working with clients experiencing a crisis. Although it is helpful, therapists do not need to have shared a bond with an animal to be effective in helping clients through this type of loss.

Attending

Therapists have the ability to make it easy or difficult for their clients to express their feelings. The way they sit, stand, speak, or look at a client can inhibit or enhance communication. Therapists need to be aware of their body language and overt reactions to the information that the client is providing. It is important for bereaved clients to seek out counselors who are educated about pet loss. It is also important for therapists to educate themselves about pet loss. Having experienced a pet loss does not make a therapist fully aware of the many aspects to this type of loss. There are many ways in which a loss can occur. Also, there are many different types of bonds pet parents can share with their pets.

Pet parents often try to navigate through a loss by doing what feels right to them. As stated earlier, bereaved clients may apply death rituals similar to those used for the loss of humans. It is important to be "open" to listening to the client's needs and ideas regarding loss. Therapists and veterinarians should be open to how the client would like to honor their pet's death.

Therapists can demonstrate to their clients that they are ready and available to listen to them by keeping their legs and arms uncrossed and maintaining comfortable eye contact. In doing so they are sending the message that they are interested in what the client has to say.

It is easier to pay close attention to some clients than to others. The loss of a pet can bring up unresolved feelings for the therapist as well. It wasn't that long ago that children were discouraged from grieving the loss of their pets. Oftentimes, parents may have seemed detached from the loss or unwilling to discuss it with a child. Some clients have shared stories from their childhood of being served what they deemed as their pet rabbit or chicken for dinner. Their loss was never acknowledged because the parents, although allowing their child to play with the animal and thus form a relationship, viewed it as livestock. Therapists should be aware that some of their own buttons may be pushed, or long-forgotten memories exposed, during a counseling session. Whether a therapist has had a similar experience or not, it is important to respond with empathy. Therapists should be aware of transference issues and address them accordingly, perhaps with a peer.

Therapists who have recently experienced a loss, or who are anticipating a loss, may find that attending to a client is difficult. I remember leading a group only a week after I euthanized my dog. I found it very difficult to listen to a bereaved pet parent share his pet's euthanasia. Talking to a therapist about my concerns helped me to continue to meet the needs of the people in my pet loss support group. There is no better method of creating empathy than to be humbled by personal experience. However, it is important to remember that grief is personal and can manifest in a variety of ways. Just because you are now a charter member of the "pet-loss-experienced club," doesn't mean that you have had the exact experience or share the same feelings as those who also have gone through a loss. Clients may need to be reminded that while many aspects of pet loss are common, some grief responses are unique. The feelings and desires of each bereaved client are to be respected.

Effective Listening

Listening effectively means giving a client your undivided attention. Therapists should avoid distractions while the client is with them and allow spaces during the session for the client to cry, demonstrate anger, ramble on, or just sit quietly. If a therapist cannot relate to a client's feelings for a pet, he or she should try to equate them to feelings for her own children, friends, or partner. It is important to ask the client to describe the relationship he or she shared with the pet. If the client says that the pet was just like a child to him, the therapist can understand the level of crisis the client is feeling by equating the grief to the loss of a child.

Therapists should demonstrate that they are trying to understand what the pet parent is expressing by responding at appropriate intervals to his or her comments. Avoid using clichés or saying that you know exactly how the client feels. You don't. Instead, try saying, "What I hear you saying is ..." As stated, allow the client to tell you what the loss means to him or her. Ask, "How can I help you? What things have you done in the past that have supported you through a difficult time?" By asking specific questions, the therapist will be able to identify what the client needs from him or her and enable the pet parent to begin to take care of him- or herself.

"Carol" was devastated after choosing euthanasia for her ill bird, her companion of 11 years. She had centered much of her life around her bird, limiting her social life and friends. Her associates at work were sympathetic but not supportive about her loss. Carol sought out the help of a therapist to work through her loss. She shared the fact that she felt a void in her life and did not know what to do.

The therapist helped Carol to see that, because she had devoted so much time and love to her bird, it felt as though her life would be lonely and empty without him. The therapist said, "Would it be helpful for you to consider that, while a door has closed on your bird's life, one might be opening in yours?"

The emptiness Carol felt was acknowledged. She also understood that she could create a new life for herself, one filled with friends and social activities that she previously had denied herself in caring for her bird (Pettit, 1994, pp. 149–150).

Reflection and Reframing

Reflection happens when the therapist accurately summarizes the client's expressed emotions. The reflection lets the client know that he or she is being understood by the therapist. Good therapists can reframe the experience of loss and hopelessness into one of hope and possibility. The validation of the loss and the acknowledgment of the depth of grief felt is one of the first significant steps in being able to work through the loss. Reflection and reframing are therapeutic tools that allow the client to feel that his or her pain and anguish are understood and validated by the therapist.

In the case of Carol and her bird, the therapist reframed the loss into a triumph of how her love and devotion to her bird had added years to the life of her pet.

Validating the Loss

Therapists should have a thorough understanding of the relationship pet parents shared with their pets. In validating their loss, therapists will discover that pets can fulfill many needs for people. Therapists should be alert for key comments, such as, "Goldie was like our child," "Rex was my best friend," or "I will never feel safe in my home with Bandit gone." A pet may have served as a child to some, a best friend to others, and even a bridge to the past. A pet may have accompanied its guardian from college to career, to marriage, and on through other important life stages. It may have been a source of comfort during a stressful time such as a divorce, the loss of a loved one, a move, or a change in jobs.

Therapists shouldn't assume that all clients consider their pets to be their children. Clients will share bonds with pets that we cannot even begin to imagine. Pet parents need to tell the therapist exactly what the loss means to them. Validation of the loss happens when the therapist accurately summarizes what the loss means to the client, based on the client's own statements.

In Chapter 1, we mentioned a woman whose baby had died of SIDS. This young woman, whose name was Leah, acquired a puppy to help her through her loss. The puppy was something to cuddle, something that would need her. Though it was by no means a replacement for the child she had lost, the puppy helped her through the experience. When the dog died several years later, Leah grieved not only for the loss of her dog but for the loss of her child as well.

A helpful response for Leah would be, "Losing your dog reminds you of the loss of your child. It must be a very painful time for you."

Andrew, the Vietnam veteran whose cat, Tabby, was the first thing he learned to love again when he came home from the war, chose euthanasia for Tabby when the cat became very ill.

A helpful response for Andrew might be, "It's difficult for me to imagine what Vietnam was like, but I do know that this cat was very special to you. She has given you a gift that no one else could give you."

Staci, whose dog died of cancer, remarked that his death was more difficult for her than the recent loss of her mother (who also died of cancer), to whom she had been close.

You might say to Staci, "Your dog was a significant member of your family. The unconditional love you received is a gift that people are not always able to give to one another."

As a therapist you have your own style and language that comes from the heart. The basic premise of validation is to convey to the client the core significance of his or her loss (Pettit, 1994, p. 152).

Achieving Closure

Pet parents may take comfort in considering ways to honor their pets. A pet parent may decide to donate to a charity for animals, buy a headstone with an epitaph for the pet's grave, create a shrine of framed photos and precious items, or write a poem about the pet. It is important that clients feel free to honor their pets in much the same way they would honor any other deceased friend or family member (Pettit, 1994, p. 152).

Through the years we have learned of many creative and unusual ways pet parents have chosen to memorialize their pets. One gentleman built a tomb on his property for his beloved dog. A woman created a website that honored the life she and her cat had shared. Others have created scrapbooks, made altars, created garden stepping stones with a cat's paw prints embedded into them. Another client donated funding to an animal welfare organization in honor of her deceased rabbit. The possibilities are endless and each one is filled with love.

Conclusion

The feelings and stages of loss a pet parent experiences when a beloved pet dies are similar to most other types of loss. The differences, however, may lie in the fact that humans can share relationships with animals they may not share with other people, and that pets give people something many humans cannot—unconditional love. Understanding the types of relationships pet parents share with their pets is the first step in helping them through a loss.

Because the loss of a pet is not always viewed as significant—or is viewed in society as less than the loss of a human family member or friend—the therapist's job is to acknowledge the depth of feeling a client has for his or her pet. This will validate the client's pain and give him or her the permission needed to work through the loss. Feelings that are not validated often go unresolved.

Educating pet parents about the grief process will help them to understand their feelings and view them as normal. Letting them know they are not alone in their grief can help them to adjust to life without their pets. Assisting them in discovering ways in which to memorialize the pet can put them in touch with the good times they shared.

3

THE EUTHANASIA DECISION

One of the most difficult decisions people who share their lives with animals will have to make is the one to authorize euthanasia. Euthanasia literally means "good death," or "mercy killing." Large animals, such as horses, grow up with children and the bond is carried into adulthood for 25 years or more.

One of the most difficult decisions a pet parent must face is whether to euthanize a pet. It is important to remember that this may be the first time a guardian has ever faced making a decision regarding the cessation of life. Euthanasia is not readily offered in human medicine. It has, however, been offered for many years in veterinary medicine as an option for terminating an animal's life. Pet parents who are placed in the position of making a life-or-death choice often refer to their plight as having to "play God." They are faced with a moral and ethical dilemma at a time when they are wrought with emotion. This choice may be as difficult as if the decision were being made for a human family member. In addition, this may be the first time a therapist has been faced with helping a client make a life-or-death decision. Therapists will need to help clients work through their feelings not only regarding the inevitable loss of their pets, but also about the practice of euthanasia. Providing the pet parent with information about euthanasia, what it is, how it is performed, and why it is an option, will help the client.

"I killed my pet!" one woman cried out at the beginning of a pet loss support group session. The woman's admission was followed by tears. After a few minutes she shared the fact that she had just authorized euthanasia for her elderly sick dog. She had said goodbye to her dog and left him with her veterinarian less than an hour before group. During the group, she was consoled by others who had recently euthanized their pets. The therapist worked with the client to reframe the experience (a technique we discuss in Chapter 8, "Behavioral Manifestations of Grief and Loss"). She was educated about the euthanasia procedure and how it is performed. We explored the decision-making process that led to her authorizing her dog to be euthanized. After a couple of sessions, the client was able to view the experience from that of "killing her pet" to giving permission to aid her pet's death process through euthanasia. This helped her move out of a fearful guilt-ridden angry place and view her role as an empowered, enlightened, and positive facilitator with the courage to offer her pet a comfortable alternative to the pain and suffering he was facing.

The "Good" Death

The term *euthanasia* literally means "good death" or "mercy killing." When a pet is terminally ill or suffering, the veterinarian offers euthanasia as a means of releasing the pet from the pain or debilitating illness. However, pain and suffering are not the only reasons a pet parent may have to face the decision to euthanize a pet. Some pet parents may be forced, or may voluntarily choose to have their pet euthanized if it has harmed other animals, people, or property.

When considering plans of care for an aging, disabled or terminally ill pet, pet parents must often explore the issue of euthanasia. Whether a self-suggestion or one made by a friend or veterinarian, pet parents seriously consider life without their pets, and the grieving process is set in motion. As with any critical decision, there are mixed emotions. Ending the suffering of a pet in pain is a positive outcome of euthanasia. Terminating the relationship shared with a cherished pet is a negative one. When euthanasia is considered because the pet has harmed someone, the feelings are compounded and the emotions mixed. On one hand, the pet parent may know that he or she is doing the right thing by choosing to euthanize the pet. On the other hand, she or he remembers how loving and loyal the pet has been and may feel as if he or she is betraying the pet's trust. Clients must work through *all* of their feelings before arriving at a decision to choose euthanasia.

Jennifer and Roland. Jennifer, a caring, intelligent, 25-year-old woman attended a pet loss support group after her veterinarian had euthanized Roland, her shepherd/lab mix companion of five years. She explained to the group that she had to choose euthanasia for Roland because of his aggressive behavior toward others.

Jennifer had adopted the dog when he was 6 months old. She hired a trainer to work with her and Roland. She said that the trainer had warned Jennifer about the dog's possessive tendencies toward her. Jennifer said that she had believed that, if Roland was well trained, he would never act out or become aggressive toward others. The trainer said that Roland might end up becoming a well-trained but still aggressive dog. Jennifer decided to give Roland a chance anyway. She worked diligently to help Roland to become a very obedient dog. However, as he matured, so did his aggressive tendencies. Jennifer couldn't leave Roland in anyone's care. She also had to take him for walks and play fetch with him far away from other people and pets. Her life had changed dramatically. She felt isolated and removed from friends and fun events.

One day, when she was playing fetch with Roland in what she thought was a deserted wooded area, a child came running out of nowhere with her father not far behind. To Jennifer's horror, Roland wouldn't come when she called him. He ran up to the child and bit her.

Jennifer decided to consult her veterinarian about euthanasia. While she said that she knew in her heart that she had made the right decision, she also knew that Roland loved her deeply, trusted her, and would give his life for her. She felt in some ways that she had betrayed his trust and found this troubling. Jennifer was tearful and had difficulty sleeping and concentrating.

The therapist worked with Jennifer by acknowledging the depth of her pain, her love for Roland, and the very difficult decision she had made. The therapist helped her to see that her decision was made out of concern for others and the inability to protect Roland from harming them. Roland loved the outdoors and didn't like being contained inside. His favorite activities were swimming in a creek, running through the woods, and playing fetch with a tennis ball. A decision to isolate Roland at home would have left them both unhappy.

After several group sessions Jennifer was able to honor the bond they had shared and the many wonderful aspects of Roland's personality. She also viewed her decision as an unselfish and responsible one. She stated that Roland was born with this tendency and that ultimately she had done what her trainer warned her she might have to do—choose euthanasia—but she was glad that she had given Roland a chance. The counselor reminded her of the fact that she had given Roland a chance to have a life, one that would have been cut short at the shelter from which he had been adopted.

Jennifer embraced the therapist's words and decided how to say her final goodbyes to Roland. At the next counseling session, she told the group that she had decided to place Roland's ashes in the places they had loved to visit, places where he had been able to roam free. In her mind, she was able to picture Roland running free and playing without her having to worry about his causing harm to another person.

In euthanasia cases, where terminal illness rather than behavioral problems are involved, clients may look to the pet to offer an indicator that they are ready to die. Because pets cannot articulate their feelings verbally, clients may go to great lengths to make certain that this decision is one the pet wants too.

It is not uncommon for clients to seek the advice of a psychic to confirm that the timing of euthanasia is right for their pet. Some people believe that psychics can communicate with their pets and ask them if they are ready to die. The pet parent may find this comforting and a way to bear the burden of having to make a life-or-death decision. It places the psychic as a go-between and may assist the pet parent by feeling that the animal has a voice in the decision-making process.

This is not to imply that therapists whose clients are having difficulty making a euthanasia decision should refer those clients to an animal psychic, but rather to note that some clients believe in this practice and derive comfort from it. Some clients may report praying about the decision and receiving comfort and guidance through the prayer process. Therapists should support their clients in deriving support and comfort from healthy and positive practices that have supported them in the past during times of crisis. The majority of clients will arrive at a decision based primarily on their personal feelings and their veterinarian's advice.

Clients who do not work through their feelings before making the decision often are plagued by regrets and become stuck in the grieving process. Support for clients facing a decision about euthanasia is crucial in their adjustment to life without their pets. A veterinarian can tell a client that the decision he or she made is an appropriate one, but a client who clings to doubt will experience problems adjusting to life without the pet.

Clients often are confronted with the decision while feeling frustrated, frightened, and fatigued. They may be afraid of facing the future without their pet, fatigued from providing nursing care to a sick animal, and frustrated by failed efforts. This is particularly true of clients who have to decide between authorizing extensive and costly medical treatment or choosing euthanasia. Because pet medical insurance is limited and costly, many clients do not purchase it for their pets. Medical costs can skyrocket when the pet has an accident or is faced with a terminal illness. Often clients must authorize euthanasia for their pets rather than risk their families' financial security. In this situation, guilt may be intense, especially if other family members are aware that the pet might have lived if only the pet parent had authorized the costly treatment (see Chapter 5).

Elaine and Melon. The example of Elaine and her cat Melon illustrates the extremes to which clients may go to make certain they are choosing the right time to have a euthanasia performed.

Dr. Kranston, Elaine's veterinarian, approached the subject of euthanasia when Elaine's cat, Melon, was no longer responding to cancer treatment. The cancer had spread throughout Melon's body, and the cat was becoming less interested in food and more lethargic. But Elaine saw signs from Melon that she interpreted as a will to live. Melon purred when Elaine stroked her. She drank water and slept next to Elaine on her bed. Sometimes she even held her head up high enough to watch a bird perched on the feeder outside Elaine's bedroom window. Elaine didn't want Melon to suffer, but she didn't want to take away one minute of the life that belonged to Melon by choosing euthanasia too soon.

When Elaine brought Melon in to see the veterinarian two weeks after they had discussed euthanasia, the doctor told Elaine that Melon's deteriorating condition made her certain that the time had come for euthanasia. Melon had lost three more pounds and didn't have any fat on her body. She was very weak. Dr. Kranston gave Melon fluids and encouraged Elaine to consider euthanizing her soon.

Elaine went home and talked to Melon. Melon purred as usual and watched the birds. In desperation, Elaine contacted a psychic who said she was able to talk to pets and ask them questions. The psychic came to Elaine's home and mentally conferred with Melon, then told Elaine that Melon was ready to die and that Elaine was holding her back. Elaine believed the psychic and took Melon to the clinic. That afternoon she held Melon and said her final goodbyes as Dr. Kranston administered the injection.

The "Right" Time

Clients may ask the therapist or veterinarian how they will know when it is time to make the decision for euthanasia. For some clients, having to make the decision to end a pet's suffering is the least stressful of all. When a pet is gravely ill and the chance of its recovery is minimal, the decision may be an obvious one. Unfortunately, this is not true in the vast majority of terminal cases. Animals have a way of rallying just when it looks as though death is imminent.

For clients faced with caring for a terminally ill pet, a therapist may liken the experience to a roller coaster ride. The pet may seem gravely ill and near death for several days. The client makes an appointment for euthanasia, only to find the pet has gotten up, walked across the room, and eaten its dinner while he or she was on the phone. When the pet rallies, the parent thinks, "I was wrong this time." With guidance and reassurance from the veterinarian, the client may take comfort in knowing that he or she is doing the right thing. It is important for veterinarians and counselors to inform clients that there is no single exact, right moment for euthanasia. They can liken it to a window of opportunity.

Even with the reassurance of the veterinarian, clients sometimes experience a fear of taking the pet's life too soon. They may decide to forego the euthanasia that day and take the pet home. They wait until the pet relapses, then makes another appointment for the euthanasia. During this period the veterinarian and counselor should honor the clients' wishes and gently remind them, once again, of the fact that there is a window of opportunity to perform the euthanasia. If the pet is not suffering, the veterinarian may offer the client another day or two with the pet—sometimes providing pain medication or other means of comfort. However, the veterinarian should remind clients that he or she supports them in their decision to euthanize the pet and that euthanasia is offered to prevent pain and suffering.

Therapists and veterinarians should remind clients that it is not uncommon for a pet to rally once more just seconds before the injection. The pet suddenly sits up on the table and licks the parent's hand. This can be confusing for a client, who at this point often feels the need to justify the euthanasia appointment. "You should have seen him this morning. He was so sick, he was barely moving," he or she says. The pet parent then must decide whether to terminate the euthanasia or go through with the procedure.

The client may feel frustrated and inadequate. Clients may share with the veterinarian or therapist the fact that he or she wants to get off the roller coaster. Clients may feel guilty admitting these feelings because they are choosing not just to end the pet's suffering but to end their own suffering as well in having to endure the ups and downs of caring for a terminally ill pet. The therapist or veterinarian should inform the client that these feelings are normal, not bad or selfish. They are part of the process of living with a terminally ill pet and arriving at the decision to euthanize.

It is important that the clients providing ongoing care for terminally ill pets be directed to take good care of themselves too. Clients may be reminded that their ability to care for their pets depends upon their own health and well being. Many times, clients are quick to put their pet's needs first and their own last. There needs to be balance. Clients need to be informed of resources available at their veterinary office, mental health facility, and other animal and human welfare organizations.

When Clients Wait too Long to Authorize Euthanasia

One client who attended our pet loss support group said that he felt he had waited too long to make the decision to euthanize his dog, and believed his decision caused his pet unnecessary pain and suffering. Out of that experience, he made a vow. He asked a close family friend to be an advocate for his other dog when she became ill. The family friend didn't see the dog on a daily basis. He wasn't caught up in the ongoing daily care of the dog. He didn't see every little wag of the tail, drink of water, or bite of food as something encouraging, as the pet parent did. He was able to see the big picture of the dog's condition, both the progress and the deterioration. The client said that his friend's advice, along with the veterinarian's expertise, significantly assisted him in making a timely decision for euthanasia with his second dog.

Once the clients have made the choice for euthanasia, they may struggle with the timing of the procedure. Once again, the clients need to recognize that *there is no one correct or exact moment in time to have a pet euthanized.* The best time to schedule euthanasia is when the client can be accompanied by a close friend who knows the pet and shares the client's sensitivity toward animals. To preserve client–patient boundaries, therapists should not accompany the client to the euthanasia, but should be available to meet with the client just before or after the procedure. In the event that the client does not have someone to accompany him or her to the procedure, the veterinarian or clinic staff may support the client during the euthanasia.

Therapists and veterinarians can empower clients in the decision-making process by reminding them of the close relationship they share with their pets. Even though animals cannot speak, clients who share a bond with their pets often intuitively know when they are happy, depressed, or in pain, in much the same way a parent can "read" a pre-verbal child. Some clients report that they knew for certain when their pets were giving up and ready to die. Others report that when told, "You will know when it is time for euthanization," they really did not pick up any definite signals and remained unsure. Encouraging clients to stay close to their pets and be aware of changes in their behavior and physical condition will assist them in arriving at this important decision. However, other issues need to be factored into the decision-making process and clients should be given additional information regarding authorization of euthanasia.

In deciding on a time to euthanize a pet, clients need to know that it is perfectly all right to consider not only the pet's needs, but their own needs and those of their families as well. If the veterinarian is recommending euthanasia when a holiday, birthday, or anniversary is approaching, the client may decide to have the procedure done immediately or wait until the event has passed. The association of the upcoming event with the pet's death may be a painful reminder for years to come. If the family is moving or the client is changing jobs, the euthanasia should be scheduled around these events, if possible.

Sometimes clients feel fatigued by providing around-the-clock care for a terminally ill pet. They may also feel financially burdened and overextended, but might feel uncomfortable sharing this information with their veterinarian. They may believe it is their duty to provide for their pet physically, emotionally, and financially in order to extend the pet's life to the last possible moment. Veterinarians and therapists should address "quality of life" issues with their clients. This encourages consideration of the situation from the pet's perspective and helps to clarify parameters regarding end-of-life decisions for their terminally ill pets.

Planning for a "good death" experience takes into consideration not only the pet's needs but the survivors' needs as well. The case of John and Alicia demonstrates the powerful need to take all family members' feelings into consideration when choosing euthanasia, and the effect it can have on a relationship when this is not done.

John, Alicia, and Abbey. John and Alicia had been married five years. They had a two-year-old daughter, Abby, and an 85-pound Rhodesian ridgeback dog named Sarah. The dog was 18 years old, and had been obtained by Alicia prior to her marriage when the dog was 6 years old.

John came to love Sarah and accepted her as part of their family when he and Alicia married. But, as the dog aged, it became clear that Alicia and John had formulated divergent solutions to the problems of aging.

Sarah became intermittently incapable of bearing weight on her hind legs. John often had to carry her outside to urinate and defecate. In addition, she became confused after dark. Because of her increasing confusion, Sarah stayed in John and Alicia's bedroom at night. The couple's daughter Abby frequently awakened at night for breastfeeding. Both John and Alicia were sleep deprived, and their fatigue and increasing frustration were affecting their relationship negatively.

After getting up with the dog every night for two years, John became resentful. In his opinion, Sarah had lived a full 18 years and the time had come to consider euthanasia. But Alicia didn't see it that way at all. She thought that Sarah was still able to enjoy life. She also had seen a bond developing between her daughter and Sarah that she was hesitant to break.

When Alicia arrived at the pet loss support group, she was exhausted, disillusioned, angry, and sad. She talked about her willingness to see Sarah through any and all phases of nursing care, regardless of what effort needed to be made. Alicia viewed Sarah as elderly—not terminally ill. She sought all avenues of health care to alleviate Sarah's arthritic condition, including homeopathic care.

John believed that Sarah's time on earth had come to a natural end point. He wanted to have Sarah euthanized. Alicia pledged herself to nursing Sarah until she died a natural death at home. John and Alicia's relationship was strained to the point of divorce.

As Sarah became progressively worse, John and Alicia's lives became more strained. When it came time for their yearly family vacation, John wanted to spend it in a place that didn't allow animals. Alicia refused to leave Sarah. She was afraid that Sarah might die while they were gone and that she wouldn't get to say goodbye. They compromised on a vacation in a rented recreational vehicle (RV). The vacation took a disastrous turn: Sarah had diarrhea in the RV. The family returned home, John and Alicia barely speaking to each other.

In group, Alicia described the importance of her relationship with Sarah. She said she had a deep attachment to the dog and considered her just as important as any other family member.

The group's pet loss therapist outlined goals for John and Alicia to work on in the group:

- Defining parameters for euthanasia
- Resolving her anger toward her husband for his willingness to have euthanasia performed now
- Resolving her own frustration at not being able to "cure" Sarah by any means available
- Resolving her sadness about what she perceived to be the imminent death of her beloved friend and companion

The grieving process had begun for Alicia when her husband and her veterinarian brought up the subject of euthanasia for Sarah. Alicia had to face the fact that, sooner than she was ready to accept, the life she shared with Sarah would end. It was important for Alicia to feel that she was not being pushed by her husband into making a premature decision to end Sarah's life.

Alicia also needed to look at what the stress of nursing Sarah was doing to her family. She needed to take into consideration not only Sarah's needs but her own, as well as those of her husband and her daughter. With the support of the group counselor, Alicia was able to deal with these issues. After accepting the inevitable fact that Sarah was going to die soon, Alicia, together with her husband, authorized Sarah's euthanasia. They asked the veterinarian to euthanize Sarah at home. Alicia was able to say goodbye in a way she wanted. She shared with the group that she was able to view the decision to euthanize Sarah as a final gift to prevent further suffering. Alicia and her husband were able to continue moving through the process of grieving united in this process.

Natural Death versus Euthanasia

Most pet parents hope for a natural death for their pets. They may wish the pet to die peacefully in its sleep. When pain and suffering become issues, a natural death can turn into an agonizing one. The client is faced with the choice of whether to euthanize. The case study of Paul and Joanne depicts a client's dilemma in having to choose between a natural death and one induced by injection.

Paul, Joanne, and Jake. Paul had told his wife Joanne that when he died he wanted to be cremated along with his dog, Jake. He wanted their ashes sprinkled into the ocean from the Golden Gate Bridge. When Paul was on his deathbed, Joanne said that she would take Jake and have him euthanized so she could fulfill Paul's last wish. Paul was appalled. He told Joanne that she would do no such thing and made her promise that she would keep his remains until Jake died a natural death. Joanne made this promise.

Twelve years later, when Joanne brought Jake to the veterinarian for his annual examination, the vet brought up the subject of euthanasia. He told Joanne that Jake was in poor health: his kidneys were failing, he was deaf and blind, and he had lost control of his bladder. Joanne told Dr. Keach about the promise she had made to her husband that Jake would die a natural death.

She admitted to the doctor that caring for Jake was becoming a burden. She found the work exhausting and frustrating. Having to provide so much care for Jake limited her social life. She was afraid to leave him alone, fearing he might hurt himself. She told the doctor how she had padded her home with foam so Jake wouldn't hurt himself if he bumped into the furniture. She had put rugs on the floor to catch the urine so she could wash them daily. Joanne said that she did this willingly because Jake was the last link she had to her husband.

As Jake's conditioned worsened, the doctor explained to Joanne that Jake might soon be suffering. He said that euthanasia was a means of ending this suffering and that, without it, Jake would eventually endure a natural but painful death. Joanne was distraught and confused. She didn't want Jake to suffer, yet she was concerned that if she chose to euthanize Jake "before his time," she would be breaking a deathbed promise to her husband.

In the end, with the support of a therapist, her veterinarian, and the pet loss support group, Joanne was able to resolve her feelings and choose an appropriate time to euthanize Jake. She came to the realization that Paul would not have wanted Jake to suffer and was able to resolve the issue of euthanasia versus natural death. She chose euthanasia without guilt or regrets.

When the box with Jake's remains was returned to Joanne, she carried out her husband's final wish. She scattered Jake's and Paul's ashes together over the side of the Golden Gate Bridge.

When family members disagree, a solution for the best possible resolution should be the goal of a therapeutic intervention. Ideally, while considering the human family members' needs and beliefs, the pet's welfare should be a priority, but sometimes family members have differing opinions regarding the authorization of euthanasia. One member may be an advocate for euthanasia and the other member may be an advocate for a natural death. When this happens, the feelings about euthanasia are often based upon personal experiences or religious beliefs.

Arnie, Mia, and Jack. In a recent pet loss support group session, a man and his adult daughter attended the group. The man, Arnie, had an elderly dog, Jack, who was very ill with stomach cancer. Arnie's daughter, Mia, also shared a deep bond with Jack. Mia, who had experienced several natural deaths in which her cats had died in her arms, made it known to the group that she did not believe in euthanasia. She reported to the group that her earlier experiences were both peaceful and without trauma to the pet. She also said that she felt it wasn't her right to "play God," and that she would never make that decision. The group leader acknowledged and validated her stance regarding euthanasia.

Arnie was tearful, quiet, and listened intently when other group members addressed the topic of euthanasia versus natural death. One member shared her experience and deep regret of waiting too long to authorize euthanasia for her pet. When Arnie was asked to share his feelings about euthanasia he told the group that Jack was on heavy doses of pain medications. He thought that Jack was comfortable, but that his quality of life seemed to be significantly curtailed. He reported that Jack ate little and slept a lot. He was concerned that if the pain became worse, Jack would suffer. He shared the fact that he had once had a dog that had been euthanized and that the experience went well. He also shared that he didn't want to "play God" though, and didn't want to rob Jack of one day less than he was meant to experience on this earth.

The group leader acknowledged and validated his concerns. Many of the group members addressed the topic of "playing God." Some shared their feelings about being placed in the position. The group leader discussed the fact that the decision to euthanize a pet is often a collective decision made with the pet parents, other family members, and the veterinarian. The daughter stated that she wanted support for her father but didn't want him to euthanize Jack. She was both resistant and defensive about her stance.

The group addressed the fact that Jack might endure an agonizing death and some discussion about it followed. Some members shared painful memories of having waited too long and witnessed what their pets endured in the last moments of their lives. Others acknowledged that dog might just die in his sleep. They encouraged Mia and Arnie to work closely with the veterinarian and not to rule out euthanasia as an option if it was in the best interest of the dog.

Jack and Mia both seemed to consider much of what was being said to them. At their departure, Mia thanked the group and asked for literature on the grieving process. Although, the outcome regarding Jack's death process was never learned, Arnie and Mia were provided support, information, and validation about the loss of a pet. The group provided them both with more information and things to consider about euthanasia versus natural death.

When Clients and Animals Have the Same Disease

Because euthanasia is legally available only to animals in this country, a client's struggle in choosing it for his or her pet can be complicated if the pet has the same or a similar illness as the client or a family member. For example, a client who was suffering from lung cancer had a dog with the same disease. He was well educated on the options available to him in fighting the disease and chose a similar course of treatment for his dog. As the disease progressed in the dog, the veterinarian recommended euthanasia. The client not only had to deal with the imminent loss of his dog but also had to face his own mortality. He said that he was grateful euthanasia was available for his dog, but he was angry that it was not an option available to him if he did not go into remission.

It is not uncommon for clients to have the same diseases as their pets or to know someone who has experienced the same illness. Such clients need a lot of support in handling the loss of their pets while facing their own physical demise or that of someone close to them. A client may wonder why his or her parent, child, or best friend must be placed on life support, or why other extreme measures are used to sustain human life while the pet's veterinarian is advocating euthanasia because the pet is enduring the same painful symptoms and terminal diagnosis.

A therapist should allow the client to openly discuss the differences in the philosophies of medical treatment of humans and animals. Sometimes clients are angry that a drug for treating an illness is available for their pets but not approved for use in human medicine. Sometimes people survive life-threatening illnesses and their pets do not. This can cause clients to revisit their own demise and may question why they lived and their pet was not spared.

Tamara and Pal. A client we recently counseled in the pet loss support group, Tamara, was a three-time cancer survivor. Tamara stated that several years ago her physicians had given her just six months to live. She beat the odds and was presently living cancer free. A few years ago she adopted a small dog that soon became the center of her world, and as she described, "the love of her life." The dog, Pal, was her constant companion. He was also the runt of the litter and born with a life-threatening brain tumor. Strong willed, he had an amazing spirit. She took him to her veterinarian, who explained that Pal had a short life expectancy, a few months at the most. Tamara said that she was an odds beater and believed that Pal might be one too. She authorized treatment for her companion. To the veterinarian's amazement, Pal survived the treatment and was enjoying life with Tamara. However, when Pal was three years old, he became very ill and died suddenly. Tamara decided to attend the pet loss support group to work through her grief. During her sessions she shared the loss of several people in her life with whom she had been close. She also shared how she had experienced the loss of her mother and her unborn child on the same day. Tamara stated that while the grief of those losses was intense and very difficult to get through, the loss of Pal was even worse.

We discussed her having to face her immortality and her hopes for Pal's ability to beat the odds. Now that Pal was gone, the stark realization of Tamara's own demise was being faced once again. In addition, the loss of Pal was compounded by the fact that she had experienced several deeply felt losses throughout her lifetime. By Tamara's own admission, Pal was a gentle soul, a sweet, loving being, who was a composite of all of the people she had loved and lost in her life. When she said goodbye to Pal, she was saying goodbye again to everyone who reminded her of Pal's gentle soul.

Tamara was referred to a psychiatrist who was trained in hypnotherapy. During her session, she was made to feel safe and cared for. Under hypnosis, she was able to say her final goodbyes (in her mind) to Pal and all of the people she had loved and lost. She said she envisioned handing over Pal's spirit to God and asking that she feel at peace and be able to heal. The doctor then asked Tamara if there was anything else unresolved from the other losses she had experienced. She thought about it and said no. While still in a hypnotic trance she decided to say goodbye again to her mother, her baby, and her fiancé.

Tamara shared with the pet loss support group that she found the hypnosis session to be helpful in allowing her to safely say goodbye and no longer cling to her resistance of not wanting to "let go" of Pal. She was now free to move toward recovery.

Convenience and Behavioral Problem Euthanasia

The term *convenience euthanasia* is misleading. It implies that the client wants to terminate the life of a pet simply because he or she no longer wants to take responsibility for the animal. However, clients may choose to euthanize a physically healthy pet for a variety of reasons.

Sometimes the pet is destructive to itself, its guardian, other animals, or property, as we discussed earlier in this chapter. An elderly pet parent moving into a nursing home that doesn't allow pets may fear that the pet would be unhappy with new guardians, or perhaps a new adoptive pet parent cannot be found. In the following case studies you will see a variety of reasons people choose convenience and behavioral euthanasia. Often a client who requests that a perfectly healthy pet be euthanized does share a bond with the pet, but feels obligated to terminate its life rather than relinquish it to a shelter where it may end up dying alone.

Not all clients who seek euthanasia are happy with the decision. When clients seek support in making this decision, it is important for the therapist and veterinarian to remember that their clients when may be confused and upset. They may be unable to think clearly and rationally and may require a great deal of ongoing support while working through issues and arriving at an acceptable solution.

In cases in which the client has to move or becomes incapable of caring for his or her pet, sometimes all that is needed is a brainstorming session with a supportive person to find an alternative to euthanasia. Other times, it will become obvious to the client that there are no alternatives and the only responsible option is to relinquish the pet to a humane shelter. Some shelters or rescue organizations have a "no kill" policy and will make every attempt to find a new home for the pet. Other shelters are filled to capacity. If a new home cannot be found in a certain period of time, the shelter euthanizes the animal. I have worked with elderly parents who said that it would be traumatic for their elderly pet to be relinquished to a shelter. They view euthanasia as a means to not put their beloved pet through that process. This is an ethical and moral dilemma for veterinarians and is usually decided on an individual basis with the client. This is definitely one of the most difficult aspects for the veterinarian and pet parent in the consideration of euthanasia.

Renee, Paul, and Bandit. Bandit was a German shepherd acquired by Renee and Paul when he was eight weeks old. His name was given to him because of his quirky behavior. He enjoyed "stealing" his guardians' possessions. Among his favorite targets were shoes, belts, and jewelry. What was cute in a puppy became troublesome as he matured, however. Not only did Bandit enjoy taking things, he ate them, too. As the dog grew, so did his appetite. Renee found it increasingly difficult to keep Bandit away from her possessions. She and Paul decided to keep the dog in the back yard, where he'd be less likely to get into trouble. Bandit discovered an appetite for rocks. By the time he was ywo years old, he had endured six surgeries to remove foreign objects that would not pass through his body. One of the last items he ate was a diamond and ruby necklace belonging to Renee.

Renee and Paul consulted their veterinarian, who told them there wasn't any way to stop Bandit's behavior. The only solution was to keep him away from anything he might be tempted to chew. They tried several ways of treating his behavior, including building a kennel for him. Every time they took Bandit out to play, he immediately found something to swallow. With all avenues exhausted, Renee and Paul made the difficult decision to euthanize Bandit.

Marion and Ranger. Marion's dog, Ranger, was her "whole life," as she described the relationship of 11 years. Marion's husband had died five years earlier. Her two children were adults and lived far from her. Marion had retired from her job as a secretary. She had a few close friends, but mostly she enjoyed the companionship she had with Ranger. Ranger also reminded Marion of happier times she had spent with her husband. The dog was a link to her past. Memories of vacations and daily routines with the three of them made her smile.

As Ranger aged, he became increasingly irritable. He began to snap at Marion when she tried to pick him up. Sometimes he barked for no apparent reason. Fearing he was ill, Marion took him to the veterinarian for an examination. Dr. Carlton said that Ranger had arthritis and dementia. Marion was sympathetic to Ranger's condition, since she, too, was getting on in years. The vet prescribed medication for Ranger's arthritic condition and dementia. Still, Ranger snapped at Marion, so she stopped picking him up. One day, when she bent down to offer him food, Ranger bit her. As the months passed, Ranger began to snap and bite more. Twice, Marion was hospitalized for severe bite wounds and the nervousness that resulted from being attacked by Ranger.

Dr. Carlton approached Marion about euthanizing Ranger. Marion didn't understand why Ranger was behaving the way he did. She hoped it was temporary, and that he would get better.

Dr. Carlton referred Marion to a therapist who was trained in pet loss, with whom she found support and compassion. She was able to talk about what Ranger meant to her. The therapist helped Marion consider life without Ranger, helping her see that Ranger could severely injure her and that he was no longer able to control his behavior. Marion chose euthanasia for Ranger. For a few more months after Ranger died, Marion continued to see the therapist, who helped make the transition into a new chapter of her life.

Planning Ahead for Euthanasia

How euthanasia is handled can either help or hinder the client's grieving process. It is important for clients to be informed about their options when saying goodbye to cherished pets. Most veterinarians and clinics will inform clients about their options and office policies regarding euthanasia procedures. Others, unfortunately, do not.

Veterinarians and therapists are in a position to help their clients think ahead about how they will handle the procedure, what that day will be like for them and for their pets, and additional choices they may want to make regarding the procedure. Encourage your clients to discuss their wishes with their veterinarian ahead of time. If the veterinarian is unwilling to follow those wishes or is not supportive, the client may need to choose another veterinarian to perform the euthanasia.

Here are a few considerations about which the veterinarian and therapist might approach a client:

- Does the client want to be present for the euthanasia? If so, he or she should be prepared for what he or she might witness during the procedure. Clients should ask their veterinarians to explain the process to them beforehand.
- The client may want to have a friend or family member attend the euthanasia. Often it is a good idea to have a support person present to drive a tearful or distraught client home afterward.
- Many clients have detailed and elaborate wishes for how the final moments of their pets' lives should be. A client may want to have the euthanasia performed in the pet's favorite resting spot at home, perhaps with a ceremony that includes friends and family members. One of our clients had her cat euthanized near the pond in her back yard, which was the cat's favorite spot. After the procedure, the client took the cat's body and sprinkled holy water on it. Rituals can be therapeutic for clients, helping them acknowledge the loss, say goodbye, and honor the life they shared with the pet.

- Clients also must consider burial options. As clients begin to accept the inevitability of a pet's demise, therapist and animal health care professionals should bring up the subjects of burial, rituals, ceremonies, and ways to honor the pet. Many veterinary clinics offer a variety of options for saying goodbye to a pet.

- If the client is to take the pet's body home for burial, he or she needs to consider how the body will be transported. Most clinics will place the deceased pet in a plastic body bag.

- If the client has questions about the pet's illness or death, a postmortem examination should be considered to clear up any misunderstandings and answer any questions.

- The client may want to ask the veterinarian if a private room will be available where he or she can spend time alone with the pet before or after the procedure.

- Clients should ask the veterinarian about the best time of day for the euthanasia (if it is being performed at the veterinarian's office) or if there is a special room for clients whose pets are being euthanized. Clients often feel angry or rushed if they are asked to leave an exam room to make way for the next scheduled appointment.

- Some clients may want to pay for services beforehand or receive a bill in the mail later, rather than facing the bill right after the procedure. Other clients may not want a bill sent to their home. Ask the client what he or she prefers. The client should never be asked to settle the bill right after the loss. It takes away from solemnity of the event and also imposes on the clients at a time when they are most distraught.

- If children are to be included in the procedure, please see Chapter 5, "Pet Loss and Children," for other considerations and answers to any questions clients might have.

- Clients can be helped to feel empowered by encouraging them to state their desires for their pets' final moments of life. One of our clients became disturbed during the procedure, and afterward did not believe that his pet really was dead. The veterinarian resolved this by offering the stethoscope to the client and allowing him to listen for a heartbeat himself. The client then was satisfied and able to leave the clinic. If there had not been open communication between the client and veterinarian, that client might have gone home still wondering if his pet was really dead.

- Clients should be encouraged to make decisions prior to the loss, thus exerting some control over the process. Negative feelings, unanswered questions, anger toward the veterinarian or staff, and unfulfilled wishes can have lasting effects on a bereaved pet parent.

Understanding the Procedure

Small-Animal Euthanasia

It is important and necessary for mental health professionals to know what happens during the euthanasia procedure. Whether the therapist has had personal experience with the loss of a pet or not, it is best to know the different methods used and what happens to the animal when the procedure is performed. Sometimes clients may have ideas about euthanasia that are not based in fact.

One woman who attended our pet loss support group said she was too embarrassed to ask her veterinarian what euthanasia was. She didn't want to appear ignorant. A friend had told her that the animal was placed in a decompression chamber until its lungs collapsed. Although this is a plausible means of euthanasia, it is not one that is widely, if ever nowadays, practiced. Most often, a client's fears will be eased if the methods and details of the euthanasia procedure are explained by the veterinarian.

Clients may feel flustered or upset when discussing the death of a pet with the veterinarian. Help the clients by encouraging them to communicate with the veterinarian both prior to and during the procedure. One way to make the process easier is to suggest that, prior to the euthanasia, they write down any questions they may have regarding the procedure, the pet's medical condition, the postmortem examination and burial options.

According to Mark Ross (2006), DVM, although the actual procedure varies among veterinarians, most small animals are given an intravenous injection of a concentrated dose of sodium pentobarbital. This produces unconsciousness within seconds. Breathing and heart function cease as a result of the profound cardiovascular depression caused by the injection of the drug. Dogs and cats are given an injection into a vein. The veterinarian may also choose to insert a catheter prior to the actual injection of the euthanasia. When a vein cannot be located, the injection may be given directly into the abdomen or heart. In order to calm an anxious pet, an oral sedative may be given prior to euthanasia.

Clients who know what to expect and who are prepared prior to the procedure can make an informed choice about whether to be present. Those who decide to be present for the procedure may suddenly decide to leave the room. Most of the time, clients decide to leave when they have not been fully prepared prior to the procedure. Clients who decide not to be present may regret their decision afterward and feel they've cheated themselves out of a final goodbye or have abandoned the pet to die alone. While the client's decision to stay or to go should be respected, clients should be encouraged to think about these issues ahead of time. If the client does not want to be present, veterinary staff will care for the pet throughout the euthanasia process.

Clients who do not want to be present at the euthanasia may want to have some time alone with the pet to say goodbye beforehand, or time to say goodbye after the procedure is performed. Veterinarians and therapists should encourage their clients to consider their options carefully and think through all the "what ifs" and "if onlys."

Charlotte and Princeton. Charlotte, a woman in her mid-60s, attended the euthanasia of Princeton, her dog of 20 years. At the moment of Princeton's death, Charlotte began to relive the deaths of her daughter, husband, and mother. She described what she had witnessed with each family member. She repeated the events as if she were describing a movie she was seeing in her head.

Charlotte said she was surprised by how quick and painless Princeton's death seemed. She wished that the deaths of her other family members had been as peaceful. Several months later, Charlotte was able to view the euthanasia procedure as a final gift to Princeton. Princeton had died quickly, with dignity, and without suffering. This view helped Charlotte accept the loss, and she was able to feel she had done the right thing not only for Princeton but for herself as well.

Large-Animal Euthanasia

Large companion animals such as horses and llamas are euthanized at large animal hospitals or outdoors. An intravenous catheter is placed and the animal is given a sedative before the solution to end its life is administered. Veterinarians may try to lower the animal to the ground by attaching it to a rope ahead of time. Sometimes the animal simply drops to the ground. This can be disturbing for a client to witness. You should encourage the client to discuss the procedure ahead of time with the animal's veterinarian.

Although infrequent, with both large- and small-animal euthanasia there is always the chance that things will not go smoothly. In the absence of an intravenous catheter, it may take several attempts to find a vein. There may be agonal breathing, loss of bladder control, reflexive muscle contractions, and vocalizations. Clients should be prepared for these possibilities before making a final decision about being present for the euthanasia procedure.

Gloria and Dusty. Gloria, a 42-year-old school teacher, had owned her horse, Dusty, since receiving him as a gift on her 10th birthday. Gloria and Dusty had grown up together. She had made the painful decision to euthanize Dusty two days before her 42nd birthday. She thought it was poignant that she had received Dusty on her birthday and said her final goodbye to him near her birthday 32 years later.

Gloria had difficulty adjusting to life without her companion. She had trouble concentrating on any one task. She sought help from a therapist trained in the grief and loss of companion animals. Gloria said she felt depressed. Her appetite had diminished and she was having trouble sleeping. The therapist reassured her that these were normal responses to loss that would dissipate in the weeks to come.

Gloria attempted to continue teaching her first-grade class. One day, she broke down in class and cried. The children wanted to know what was wrong. She told them she was sad because her horse had died. She said the children were supportive and accepting of her loss.

Soon after, Gloria learned that a fellow teacher had been given time off to grieve the death of his brother. She told the school administration how she was feeling over the loss of Dusty and asked for time off as well. The administration refused to acknowledge the loss of a companion animal as justification for time off. Gloria was hurt and angry, not only because she had to continue working when she was grieving but also because her loss was unrecognized and not validated.

The therapist referred Gloria to a support group for people who had experienced the loss of companion animals. At the group, Gloria met another person who had recently lost a horse. They shared photos, memories, and feelings. What helped Gloria in dealing with her anger was the validation she received from other people who understood her loss. It gave her the strength and courage she needed to confront her daily life. The group also provided her with hope that one day she would be able to remember Dusty without tears and pain.

When she was feeling stronger, she approached the school board with information on the bonds people share with companion animals. She encouraged them to rethink their grief policy.

Hospice Care

The term *animal hospice care* is used to describe the aiding of a pet's death process. It assists in providing the pet parent by allowing more time to say goodbye. It also allows the pet to live life to the fullest while minimizing any pain and possible suffering. The practice of hospice care for animals that is provided by veterinarians is not new, although there is a growing trend in the use of the term. However, the majority of the veterinary community has incorporated an animal hospice care into their veterinary practices and hospitals for many years. Veterinarians offer death process support as a means to give the client and animal more time together. Pain management is offered to the patient and emotional support provided to the client during the end-of-life phase of treatment. This practice allows clients to not feel rushed into a decision for euthanasia, and provides them with time to say goodbye and consider death and burial options. Many veterinarians will make house calls to their patients' homes and are willing to perform at-home euthanasia. Clients are referred to a pet loss support group as they go through the process of caring for a terminally ill pet.

Some new organizations offer hospice care for animals. They may not encourage the practice of euthanasia and rely on increasing pain medication support in an attempt to relieve pain and suffering. It is important to make certain that clients fully understand the choices available to their pet once it has been deemed terminally ill.

The vast majority of the veterinary community supports the practice of euthanasia as the most humane procedure for relieving an animal's suffering. Clients should ask their veterinarians about the types of support their practice offers their terminally ill patients.

Pet Parent Support Groups for Ill Pets

Another new trend in veterinary medicine is to provide specific types of support groups for clients of terminally ill pets. One such group that has been discussed is that has been recently brought to our attention is working with clients whose pets have been diagnosed with cancer. A support group geared to a specific type of illness or disease is best run in a specialty practice where veterinarians treat patients with this illness. The group assists clients in not only working through their feelings of having their pets diagnosed with the disease, but also allows them to share and discuss information on various cancer treatments and care for the pet. If the pet becomes terminal, they may then be referred to the pet loss support group (see Chapter 11).

Conclusion

While there are many reasons for a client to consider euthanasia, including pain and suffering, deteriorating physical and mental condition, behavior problems, and convenience, each case should be viewed as unique. The decision to euthanize a companion animal is one of the most difficult a client will face in his or her lifetime. Clients who receive support prior to the procedure tend to have less difficulty working through the grieving process. They are also better informed in making the decision about whether to authorize euthanasia, and when, where and how they would like to say their final goodbye. They seem to experience less guilt, regret, and anger regarding their pets' death.

If children are to be a part of the euthanasia process, special considerations and education need to be provided (see Chapter 5).

When clients are given support in working through all of their feelings from the beginning—when they first consider euthanasia—until after the death of a pet, they will be able to make a healthy adjustment to the loss. Support may be in the form of working individually with a therapist, joining a support group, or inquiring about animal hospice care.

Communication is very important when working with clients. Clients need to fully understand the euthanasia process. Therapists should encourage clients to work closely with their veterinarians. They should be open to discussing parameters regarding the euthanasia decision. Clients should also discuss their own needs regarding caring for a terminally ill pet and what they might need in the way of saying goodbye. These needs should be combined with those of the animals to arrive at the best possible time to perform euthanasia. This will assist clients in working through their losses and in making a healthier adjustment to life without their pets.

4

SPECIAL TYPES OF PET LOSS

There are many ways in which the bond with a pet is broken. Pets run away, are lost, stolen, missing, killed, die suddenly, or may be the victims of both manmade and natural disasters.

Many pet losses occur because the animal is euthanized, but it is important to remember that there are other types of loss a pet parent can experience. Each type of loss poses a unique challenge in seeking resolution for the client. Manmade and natural disasters are just two of the special types of losses we've discussed throughout this book (see Chapter 10, "Pet Loss Due to Natural Disaster and Personal Tragedy" for a comprehensive look into this special type of loss). A pet loss also occurs when the pet runs away, is stolen, is given away, is killed suddenly (e.g., is hit by a car), is killed by someone else, dies unexpectedly (e.g., choking on a chew toy or strangling in a tangled leash), or is lost in a custody battle. Pet parents who are divorcing may wage as fierce a battle for a beloved pet as they would for a child. A pet parent who has fought to keep the pet will grieve the loss in much the same way someone grieves the loss of a spouse, friend, or child. Clients whose pets are killed or stolen may experience the same rage and feelings of lack of control as parents whose children are abducted or murdered.

Missing Pets

Perhaps one of the most devastating losses pet parents can endure is the missing pet. Many of the Hurricane Katrina victims became missing pets. Pet parents are left to wonder what happened to their charges, and in many cases the fate of the pet is never discovered. When pet parents of missing pets cling to the hope of their pets' eventual return, resolution of grief is unattainable.

One client in our group compared her loss to that of the mother of a missing child. She responded to her situation in much the same way, and felt her grief intensely. The fury such a client feels toward the unknown person who abducted the pet, or who found the pet and failed to search for its owner, can be as intense as that of a parent whose child is missing.

A client may experience intense guilt over having left a pet unattended or neglecting to fasten a gate or door. For these individuals, it is nearly impossible to obtain closure on the event. Days and weeks pass without any information on the welfare and whereabouts of the pet. This kind of loss does not always heal with time. In fact, with time, the guilt may intensify rather than dissipate. The client may need help in working through feelings of guilt, shame, anger, and sorrow.

The job of the therapist is to help the client invent an ending to the story with which he or she can live. This process may include role play, journaling, healing rituals, participating in goodbye ceremonies, writing a letter to the pet, creating a story, or joining an animal advocacy group in honor of the missing pet. Some clients have found comfort in volunteering at animal shelters. These clients are able to help other pets in the belief that someone is providing kindness and care for their pets. The therapist should support and encourage these activities that help the client gain closure under difficult circumstances.

Alice and Pierre. Alice, a woman of comfortable means, brought her toy poodle, Pierre, home from the groomer. While she was carrying grocery bags from her car to the kitchen, Pierre barked once and disappeared behind the house. Pierre had always been obedient to heel and had never left his mistress's side before. This time he not only left the property, he disappeared without a trace.

Alice searched everywhere for him. She took out advertisements, went from door to door, and drove endless miles calling for him. As time went by, she became obsessed with Pierre's disappearance, and her frantic and desperate search cost her hundreds of dollars—and, eventually, her marriage. Her intense feelings of guilt were persistent and unassuageable.

Finally, Alice engaged the services of a psychic for missing children who was able to construct in some detail the events leading to the disappearance and probable demise of Pierre. With the psychic's assistance, Alice was able to lay her guilt and self-blame to rest and attain closure. Extreme measures were required to finalize the loss for this client. Most clients can achieve significant closure in the healing environment of a pet loss support group (Pettit, 1994, pp. 170–171).

Families with missing pets are vulnerable to the same kinds of problems as families with missing children. Unresolved guilt and sorrow can lead to marital discord, depression, a decrease in job performance, and estrangement in relationships that once were rewarding. Combined with the numerous challenges disaster victims face, the ability to move through the process of loss becomes complicated and may hinder the grief process. Families who have survived a disaster must take care of their immediate needs. This includes obtaining water, food, shelter, and medical care. Once these pressing needs are taken care of, the process of rebuilding their lives begins. Trying to navigate through insurance claims, finding work, building new homes and lives, getting their children back into school, and finding their pets can be a daunting task. Because pets cannot speak, identification tags get lost, and finding a lost pet can be nearly impossible. Hope at being reunited eventually gives way to grief and despair. When this happens, therapists need to assist their clients in working toward resolution.

When Hope Fades and Reunification is Unlikely

Soon after the Hurricane Katrina disaster, the media featured stories of pet reunification with their guardians. Sadly, however, there were very few reunification stories. The majority of pets died and some still are missing.

Pet parent Shirley Rush found a creative way to express her grief by writing a story she titled *Tiffany the Elegant Cat*. In the story, Rush imagined where her cat might have gone, including Yosemite and all the other places they had visited together. She envisioned Tiffany sending her flowers with a note about her travels. A neighbor destroyed her illusion by speculating that the foxes that lived in back of the property had probably killed Tiffany. So, at the end of the story, Rush answers a knock at her door, and discovers a fox who presents her with a bouquet of flowers from Tiffany.

Most clients of missing pets have heard stories of animals being stolen and sold to research laboratories. Such clients may report nightmares about their pets' being tortured and express fears for the safety of other pets and family members. They may express strong feeling of guilt and failure. You may hear sentences beginning with, "If only I had …," "If only I had not …," and "I wish I had …." These are expressions of guilt and culpability.

In situations like these, a client may have made a mistake or been negligent in a way that set the stage for the pet's disappearance. The mistake must be validated, and the circumstances surrounding it acknowledged and evaluated. The therapist's role is to help the client recognize the "humanness" of the error and to see that, even though the action produced a negative result, it was not his or her intent to harm the pet. The client is on the road to resolution when he or she is able to accept the fact that the pet is gone, that the pet is not likely to return, and that the mistake was a human one. At group, pet parents are frequently reminded that "caring pet parents do not begin their day by considering what bad choices they might make today on behalf of their pets." While pet parents often aspire to possess the same loving, caring, forgiving qualities pets bestow upon them, it's important to remember that people are only human and their best decisions may still result in bad outcomes. We remind clients that their pets, who have always displayed unconditional love and acceptance toward them, would want them to forgive themselves if their best decisions did not produce the desired outcomes.

To assist clients in attaining closure, the therapist might encourage them to hold a memorial service for their pet or to write a letter of apology or a poem to the pet. Clients may want to donate their time or money to a favorite animal cause in honor of their pet. These actions can help bring closure to a situation that otherwise seems never-ending.

When Pet Parents Are Reunited with Their Pets

Sometimes pets do return. Karen's cat returned home after being gone for 25 months. He had disappeared the day Karen was to have taken him to be neutered. She didn't even recognize the cat at first because of his mangy condition. Upon his return, Karen took him to her veterinarian's office. The veterinarian encouraged Karen to neuter the cat, explaining that neutering might make him less likely to roam. The day before the scheduled surgery, the cat disappeared again. Karen blamed herself. She was certain that the cat had heard her make the appointment and left again because he didn't want to be neutered. She held out hope for two years that the cat would return, but he never did. Karen finally resolved her grief by deciding that the cat was happier roaming than being contained in her home.

Stories of pet parents being reunited with their pets that were abandoned during Hurricane Katrina circle the globe. It's wonderful when a match is made and the pet is reunited and its human family members are together again. However, while stories such as these make the news, there are thousands more in which a happy ending, or an ending at all, (the pet's fate known) doesn't occur.

It is important to remember that, while clients of missing pets share the same issues and some of the same feelings about the loss, they may resolve them in different ways. Some clients will be able to attain closure in a timely manner. Others will need support for much longer. This is especially true if the client feels to blame for the loss. Many hurricane victims were forced to leave their pets behind. They may have left food and what water they had, hoping that the pet would be rescued soon, only to discover that the pet is missing or dead. Family members of a missing pet will benefit from attending a pet loss support group that can provide a safe environment in which to share feelings of resentment, hurt, anger, and sadness (see Chapter 5 on how to assist children through a loss).

Placing a Pet for Adoption

Making the decision to place a pet for adoption can be difficult, especially if there is dissension among family members. It is best if all parties involved can discuss the pros and cons of adoption and its impact on individual family members. Pets are placed for adoption for a variety of reasons, including these:

- Allergies to the pet
- Housing restrictions due to a recent or anticipated move
- Animal behavior problems
- Problems in the way children in the family behave toward the pet
- Behavioral problems between a new pet and an older pet
- A divorce, death, or birth in the family
- A drop in income
- A failure to bond with the pet
- Pressure from neighbors or law enforcement (e.g., for animals who bark excessively or get loose)
- Moving out of the country or to another state
- A job that requires frequent travel
- A child leaving home to attend college and parents refusing to take care of the pet
- The pet parent's terminal illness or disability

Veterinary allergist Edward Baker noted (Baker, 1988, p. 101) that separation due to adoption can be even more traumatic for a client than the death of a pet. Death resulting from injury, disease, or old age can be explained, mourned, and ritualized. Separation from a healthy pet is difficult to understand and rationalize, especially for children.

In a study by Dr. Baker (1988, p. 102), 55% of allergists polled said they had observed guilt, psychological trauma, and other emotional reactions in pet parents following the forced separation from their pets. He noted that other family members often harbored feelings of resentment toward the person who caused the separation from the pet.

Rosemary and Arlo. Rosemary was forced to return the kitten she had adopted from the Humane Society for her two elementary school children. Her husband demanded that the cat be gone by the time he returned home from work that same day. While she discussed her plight with the therapist, her two children lovingly stroked the kitten. Rosemary felt certain that the children hadn't bonded with the kitten they had named Arlo, since they had only had him for a few days. She told the therapist that she was sure the children would enjoy having a bowl of fish just as well.

It soon became apparent, however, that despite what Rosemary was saying, she and the children *were* attached to the kitten. Rosemary expressed feelings of guilt about having adopted the kitten in the first place, while she was working hard to deny everyone's feelings. The therapist listened, then gently pointed out how Rosemary's children were lovingly interacting with the kitten at that very moment. The therapist said that she sensed Rosemary had sought her assistance because she and the children needed support in severing the bond they had formed with Arlo (see Chapter 5).

The therapist encouraged Rosemary to include her children in the process of finding a new home for Arlo. When the therapist met with Rosemary the following week, Rosemary told her that a neighbor had agreed to give the kitten a home, and that the children would be able to visit it on a daily basis.

Sometimes clients adopt pets for enjoyment, then find that the relationship isn't what they had expected. Sometimes a person is given a pet as gift when he or she is not prepared for the responsibility of pet guardianship. Clients may have trouble bonding with a pet if it was adopted as a replacement for one that died. It's not uncommon for a grieving client to name a new pet after a deceased one in the hope that the pet will have the same personality. When the pet parent fails to bond with the pet, he or she gives it up for adoption.

Jonathan. For the second time, Jonathan's dog got out of its kennel and killed his chickens. Jonathan was so angry he drove the dog to the Humane Society and relinquished it. When his anger had subsided, he regretted his actions. He had robbed his family of the right to say goodbye to the dog and he now had to live with their anger and sorrow. Jonathan needed support in accepting his decision and in apologizing to his family for the hurt he had caused them.

Bonnie and Felice. Bonnie and Felice were adopted from the pound when they were puppies. They are now seven and nine years old. They were kept outdoors, with a warm house to share and an acre of land where they could dig for gophers, chase cats, and bark at rabbits. They grew used to a flock of range chickens, giving half-hearted chase to the odd rooster that came too close to a food dish or a cherished bone.

Suddenly, and without explanation, the pair began to pursue the flock of chickens. Over a period of five months the dogs killed a dozen chickens, including some hatchlings. When the mother hen and chicks were placed behind chicken wire, the dogs burrowed underneath so the chicks could squeeze out and into their waiting jaws. Their behaviors did not cease even in the presence of their owners. Finally, Bonnie and Felice were confined to a kennel in the yard. Though the kennel was spacious, the dogs were used to roaming far and wide. They were miserable in their new environment. Repeated trials out of the kennel were disappointing to the owners and fatal to several more of the flock.

The family reluctantly decided that the pair would have to be split up. The one chosen to stay would become an indoor dog. A search was conducted to find a home for Bonnie, a large chocolate Labrador retriever. Felice, part Australian shepherd, was chosen as the indoor dog.

The clients had two sons, ages six and 15, who were quite upset at the decision to give Bonnie away while keeping Felice. Both boys said they wanted to keep the dogs together. The parents responded by taking the boys to counseling to help them understand why the decision was in the best interest of the animals.

The therapist acknowledged the boys' anger at not being included in the decision to put Bonnie up for adoption. He gave the family an opportunity to discuss their feelings and come to terms with the decision that was made. The parents apologized for not having included the boys in the decision-making process. They also explained to the boys that, as the dogs aged, they would be happier and safer indoors. Their home was too small to include two indoor dogs. In addition, the dogs' veterinarian had advised separating them because it was likely that one of the dogs was the aggressor in the chicken killing.

The therapist encouraged the parents to allow the children time to say goodbye to Bonnie and to include them in finding a new home for her. The oldest son had a friend whose family was willing to provide a home for the dog. This meant the boys would have visitation rights.

This situation worked out well for the family and the pets, but that is not always the case. Some pets entering new homes are unable to make the transition smoothly and are returned to the original owners or relinquished to an animal shelter. A therapist should prepare the pet parents for the possibility of the pet's failure to adapt to his or her new environment. Contingency plans may be developed for this scenario. Most pet parents who are planning to adopt out a pet do so sadly and with reluctance. They feel a sense of failure in their inability to provide the proper environment for their pet. They also feel a sense of loss at breaking the bonds they have shared with that pet. Although they know their pet is not dead or dying, the feelings they experience are similar to those they would have if the pet was dead.

When a pet poses a danger to itself or to others, a pet parent may be unable to place it for adoption, and be forced to choose euthanasia. In such cases, feelings of anger, guilt, and failure will combine to interfere with resolution of the loss.

One client had to euthanize her dog after it bit her three times. She was hospitalized after two of the attacks. In such cases, successful adoption is unlikely and attempts are ill-advised. The pet parents are left to wonder what they might have done to encourage or "bring out" bad or bizarre behavior in their pets. Such a situation often can be resolved if the client embarks on a healthy, positive relationship with another companion animal.

HIV-Positive Status and AIDS

Persons who are HIV+ often are encouraged to get rid of their pets because of the risk of zoonosis, the transfer of a disease from animal to human. Although the risk of transmission is small, most physicians advise on the side of caution and encourage a patient to find a new home for the pet. This can be devastating for a pet parent who views the relationship with the pet as a reason for living.

In fact, by following some simple precautions, most HIV+ pet parents can safely care for their pets. For example, the risk of toxoplasmosis infection—spread from cats to humans—can be significantly reduced by having someone else change the litter box (Ross, 1995, p. 39) or by using gloves and a mask to do so. There also are service organizations that exist to preserve the bond between HIV+ pet parents and their pets. These organizations provide volunteers to help a pet parent care for a pet, help with expenses, even provide veterinary care. Then, when the person becomes too ill to care for the pet or dies, the organization finds a suitable home for the pet.

Unfortunately, it still is common for people with AIDS to lose their jobs, financial security, friends, family, companions, health, and self esteem to the disease. Pets often are the primary source of emotional support for people with the AIDS virus.

Jack. Jack wanted to die. He was bedridden with swollen legs, sores in his mouth, cramping, severe pain, and listlessness. As the result of his losing battle with the AIDS virus, he was placed on an IV. Over the course of two years he had lost his health, his life partner, his career, his financial security, and several of his friends to the disease. The one thing he still had was his pets. They kept a vigil by his bedside during the bleakest of times. His two cats purred and lay next to his body. His dog sat by the bed, his head resting near Jack's hand. Jack drew strength from his pets each time he reached out and touched them. He described the relationship with his pets as one of emotional support and unconditional love.

Jack worried about what would happen to his pets when he became too sick to care for them. He also wanted to make arrangements for homes for them after his death.

The medication he needed was expensive. His state disability had run out. He was too sick to work and refused to accept food stamps, saying he didn't want to use resources other people truly needed. Jack was fortunate because his family and friends provided for him. Still, it was difficult to come up with money for pet food and veterinary care for his brood.

Jack was placed in touch with an organization that understood the importance of the bonds between AIDS victims and their pets. When Jack became too ill to care for his pets, someone from the organization came to his home and took care of the animals. When money was scarce and his dog needed veterinary care, the organization found a veterinarian who donated his services.

When Jack died, the organization placed his pets in good homes. Because the organization understood the importance of the bond he shared with his pets, Jack was able to continue to receive support, love, and affection from his animals during his final moments.

Clients Who Have the Same Illness as Their Pets

Sometimes clients experience the same illness as their pets, most often cancer. Clients who have gone through the diagnosis and treatment of cancer—either themselves or with close family members—are forced to relive the process when their pet becomes ill. They may experience anxiety and grief at having to cope all over again. The reverse also happens: A client who has watched a pet die from cancer is faced with the same prognosis for him- or herself.

In her book *Animal as Teachers and Healers* (1996), Susan Chernak McElroy wrote about losing her dog to cancer and then being faced with it herself. She included her testimony to the unique gifts her dog bestowed upon her as well as testimonies from other pet owners.

Clients may discuss the lessons they learned from watching their pets endure difficult treatments. One terminally ill client whose dog had died in his arms said eloquently, "As I watched Sparky die, I was overcome by the quiet and peaceful way he left me. He taught me how to die with dignity."

Losing Custody

Pet parents who are divorcing often face the same issues that divorcing parents of children face. Some pet owners amicably decide who is to receive primary or sole custody of the pet; others fight it out in court. Some are able to share custody of a pet.

In a divorce, a pet may become the focus of anger and resentment or it can remind a client of happier times shared with a spouse. Some clients genuinely love and want the pet, while others use the issue of custody to get back at their spouses. Some clients, in an ultimate act of cruelty, even euthanize or abandon the pets as a way to get back at a partner seeking a divorce (Baker, 1988, p. 102).

The parent who has primary custody of the children in a family ideally should keep any pets with whom the children share a bond. If the parents share custody of the children they should also share custody of the pet, allowing the pet to accompany the children from home to home. It is important for children experiencing divorce to have as many bonds and routines as possible left intact. If the pet is a source of support and comfort to the children, then separation from it imposes yet another trauma upon them (see Chapter 5, Pet Loss and Children).

Sometimes, however, children of divorcing parents will express a desire for the *noncustodial* parent to have custody of the pet because they worry the parent will be lonely without them. In this case, it may be better for the noncustodial parent to keep the pet so that the children feel the parent isn't alone when they are not there. Whatever is decided, it should be in the best interest of both the children and animal family members.

Shelby and Jelly. Shelby, the seven-year-old daughter of a recently divorced couple, was the second-youngest of four children. Her mother had primary custody of the children. Shelby stayed with her father one night during the middle of the week and every other weekend. Although she had her siblings to keep her company when she visited her father in his new surroundings, she had difficulty falling asleep at his house.

One night when she was to stay at her father's house Shelby asked her mother and father if she could take her cat, Jelly, with her. Both parents agreed. That night Shelby had no trouble falling asleep because Jelly slept with her in her new bed. Shelby's parents discovered that taking Jelly with her helped reduce Shelby's anxiety in new surroundings.

Therapists may choose to handle the issue of pet custody in the same way they would child custody. The pet's needs should be considered in much the same way a child's needs are considered. All family members should express their feelings about the pet, and each should have his or her feelings validated. The role of a therapist is to allow each family member to honestly express his or her feelings, even though the outcome may not seem fair to all parties. Special care must be taken to help small children see the need for compromises even when it means they cannot have their pet with them all the time.

Joe, Kate, and Krystal. Joe and Kate, a young couple married five years, both had full-time careers. They were childless and viewed Krystal, their white poodle, as their child. Joe and Kate lavished affection and attention on Krystal. On her second birthday, Karen bought the dog a brass dog bed complete with canopy top and satin comforter. Joe and Kate took Krystal with them on vacations and for evening walks in the park.

When Joe and Kate decided to divorce they fought bitterly over custody of Krystal. When Kate moved out of the house, she took Krystal to live with her at her parents' house. Joe was furious to find that Kate had removed Krystal from their home without his knowledge. Kate's and Joe's attorneys tried to work with the couple to arrive at a custody agreement. At one point in the negotiations, Joe said that if he wasn't allowed joint custody of Krystal, he would have the dog euthanized. He felt that if he was to be denied a relationship with Krystal, Kate should not be allowed to have one either. Kate was extremely upset and warned Krystal's veterinarian of Joe's threat.

After several months of negotiations, Kate and Joe finally agreed to joint custody of Krystal on alternate weeks. Joe signed an agreement that Krystal would not be euthanized without Kate's consent and that they would continue to see the same veterinarian.

Joe and Kate's story illustrates that custody disputes over a pet can be filled with as much emotion as custody disputes over a child. Joe and Kate fought for the right to be her primary caretaker out of their need to be with her. This case illustrates how one partner may use the custody issue to hurt the other.

Pets Who Are Killed Or Purposely Injured

A loss that poses a particularly difficult challenge to therapists occurs when pets are killed. Sometimes they die at the hands of children who are cruel to them or are not supervised properly during play. One young child tried to give her rabbit a "bath" and left it to drown in a bucket of water. Another client watched as a teenager purposely ran over her cat as it was crossing the road.

A client who has experienced the intentional killing of a pet has to cope not only with the physical loss, but also with the feelings of rage at the situation or perpetrator. A client who allows a dog to run freely, only to see it shot by a rancher who discovers the dog on his property, will experience regret, self-blame, and anger. One client who was resistant to euthanizing her dog discovered it had been shot by a family member who wanted to alleviate its suffering. She blamed herself for the tragic end to her pet's life and was haunted by guilt for a long time. Years later, when she authorized her veterinarian to perform euthanasia on another dog, her guilt resurfaced with renewed intensity. She discussed the fact that she thought she might have waited too long—as she did with her previous dog. She needed to work through both losses and realistically view her role in the previous instance, and the role of others who had robbed her of her chance to say goodbye. Clients need to make sense of these situations, work through the accompanying emotions, and find ways to cope with these uncomfortable feelings.

Clients who lose their pets in this way are at risk of experiencing a great sense of anger at society itself. Even if the perpetrators are discovered and brought to justice, clients of murdered pets may be awarded only damages to compensate the cost of the pet; they may not be compensated for the emotional cost. According to the law, pets are property; the law does not view them as family members. Loving bonds shared between the animal and the pet parent are not taken into consideration in a court of law. Clients may find this a further affront to the emotional and psychological trauma they have already endured.

One couple who attended our pet loss support group tearfully walked away from a courtroom having won a judgment for $250, the cost of "replacing" their dog. They thought that the judgment should not have been an awarding of replacement costs but one in which the court addressed the emotional aspect of the loss and the bond they had shared with their dog.

Dealing with Rage

Clients who feel victimized by the loss of a pet may feel absolute rage and even plot revenge. These clients need special assistance in working through their feelings. In such cases, the role of the therapist is one of careful intervention in a one-on-one or support group setting. As with any crisis, effectively working through the loss can create an opportunity for growth for the victims. Clients need to take control of those parts of their lives where they feel they have lost control and learn to accept the parts they cannot control.

Therapists can best help victimized pet parents by allowing them to fully express their feelings of failure, rage, helplessness, and isolation. Because animals typically are seen as adjuncts to human existence, our society doesn't always view the loss of a pet with much compassion. Therapists should explore their own feelings about relationships with pets before attempting to assist their clients. If a therapist is having trouble empathizing with the depth of anger being expressed by a bereaved client, it will help to consider how the therapist would feel if it were his or her human child, best friend, or spouse who had been murdered. Understanding the relationship the clients share with their pets is the first step in assisting them with the loss.

When therapists are working with clients whose pets have been brutally beaten, purposely injured, or killed, they should help the clients review decisions made before, during, and after the incident. This will assist in combating the distorted, retrospective perceptions that lead to self-blame and guilt. Clients need to remember that any decisions they made were based on their knowledge and perceptions *at the time*. Therapists must reassure these clients that they did the best they could in the given situation (Herek & Berrill, 1992).

Sometimes a client whose pet is hit by a car will vehemently insist that a neighbor who always hated the animal was responsible. This may be true; however, deep down such a client may feel guilty because he or she didn't put the cat in the house before leaving for work or knew the dog could dig out of its kennel and get loose. It is important that therapists allow the clients to vent anger and frustration, even if it is unfounded. Once the anger begins to subside, therapists can help the clients work through other feelings about the loss, including self-blame and regret.

Cheryl and Chief. The first time Cheryl, a married 24-year-old mother, came to the pet loss support group, she sat quietly while others talked. Finally, the therapist asked Cheryl what had brought her to group. Her face hardened and through clenched teeth she said, "My dog was murdered by my neighbor a week ago." She went on to tell the story of how Chief had died.

Cheryl had raised Chief since he was a puppy. The six-year-old pit bull was trained and stayed in her fenced backyard. Chief was constantly being annoyed by a neighbor's two dogs that roamed the streets and barked at other animals. Although complaints had been filed by other neighbors, the people who kept the dogs refused to obey the leash laws and often allowed their dogs to roam freely.

One evening when the dogs were loose, they charged at Cheryl's fence. One of the German shepherds tore a plank from the fence and ran into the back yard, followed closely by the second dog. A vicious fight ensued. The guardians of the two dogs arrived and tried unsuccessfully to separate the fighting dogs. Then one grabbed a rope and strangled Chief to death. Cheryl arrived home from work to discover Chief's lifeless body in her back yard, and her husband and brother screaming at the neighbor who had killed him. Cheryl was in shock. She couldn't speak or cry. Later, when the shock wore off, she was overcome with rage toward the neighbor.

Although her husband and three-year-old son were able to grieve for Chief, Cheryl was not. She was consumed by pent-up hatred, and she reported harboring murderous feelings toward her neighbor. She attended group several times but remained stuck in her anger, unable to give way to the tears that would initiate the healing process.

The group urged Cheryl to file a police report, which she did. Reporting the incident to a law enforcement agency relieved some of the stress of carrying the burden alone. In addition, she was encouraged to give vent to the tears she longed to shed and to seek the services of a private therapist. By taking definitive action, group members urged, Cheryl would be released from the paralysis that had consumed her since the incident and would finally be able to reach the sadness that lay deep within her. Cheryl accepted a referral to a private therapist and did not return to group.

Before she left, however, the group leader questioned Cheryl privately about her homicidal ideation. She did not have a plan to commit murder, but admitted that, at times, she wished her neighbor dead. She entertained fantasies of retribution, but she knew she would not act upon them.

Nonetheless, the private therapist would need to intervene quickly in this situation to defuse the anger and move Cheryl into her sadness, where forgiveness, perhaps in honor of Chief, might be realized. As her anger dissipated, Cheryl might be able to engage in conversation with the neighbors involved in Chief's death, after which some closure might be achieved.

The Crisis Response

Sometimes a loss or injury occurs despite a client's attempts to prevent the loss of a pet. In this situation the client needs to be reminded that the seriousness of the event brought forth a "crisis response" in the client, and that this response was the best one he or she could generate under the circumstances. Victims of natural disasters often "what if" and "if only" the roles they played in the loss of their pets. It's important to assist clients in seeing the situation as it really was and that they, in all likelihood, made the best decision possible at the time. One example might be of a mother who had a young child and a beloved dog. The family, stranded in the attic of their flooded home for days, is now being rescued. However, the rescue volunteers state that the dog may not come too. The mother then has to make a decision between staying with their dog in living conditions that include running out of food and water and being subjected to disease, or leaving the dog and saving her child.

When working with a client who has had to make a similar choice, it's important to remember that the mother may have loved the dog as deeply as she loves her child. She may feel guilt at leaving the dog behind, anger at having to make a decision like this in the first place, the absence of a rescue plan that included animals, deep sadness at the loss or unknown fate of their dog, and anxiety in rethinking her choices now that she is in a safer place.

A therapist might help the client to work through each one of her feelings, keeping in mind that the choices she made then were without the hindsight she has now.

Julie and Harrison. Julie was awakened by the sound of crying very early one morning. She got out of bed and looked out the window to see if it was her cat. She couldn't see anything, so she climbed back into bed. The crying grew louder. Concerned that it might be her cat, Harrison, Julie got dressed and went outside. She saw two big dogs growling at something underneath her car, which was parked in the driveway. Julie told the dogs to get away. They wouldn't move. She decided to take a hose to them. The dogs backed away slowly and then turned and ran down the street. Julie got down on her hands and knees and was shocked to see Harrison lying on his side. His breathing was agonal when she gathered him up in her arms and brought him into the house. She covered him with a blanket, grabbed her keys, and rushed to the car to take him to the veterinarian. When she arrived at the veterinary hospital, Harrison had stopped breathing. Tearful and frantic, she ran with him in her arms into the hospital. The veterinarian tried unsuccessfully to resuscitate him for several minutes. Julie was devastated and blamed herself for Harrison's death. The veterinarian surmised that Harrison most likely was frightened to death by the two big dogs.

When Julie arrived at the pet loss support group, she was tearful and guilt-ridden. She told the group leader she was certain that if she had gotten the dogs away from Harrison sooner he might still be alive. She also thought that she should have attempted CPR on Harrison while driving to the hospital. The group leader reminded Julie that she didn't know Harrison was under the car until after the dogs had left. He also reminded her that when she was driving to the hospital she was facing a crisis and made the decision that felt like the right thing to do, deciding to take him directly to the veterinarian and not stop to perform CPR. He helped her see that her response to the crisis situation was the best one she could generate under the circumstances.

After several group counseling sessions, Julie was able to forgive herself. One night, she shared with the group how she had knelt by Harrison's gravesite in her back yard and asked him for forgiveness.

She told him how she hadn't known he was in trouble and that she regretted not responding sooner to his cries. She had accepted the loss of her cat and now was learning to live without him.

Housing Restrictions

Sometimes a client must find a new home for a pet because of housing restrictions. Often when an elderly person must enter a residential care facility or an apartment closer to family who will care for him or her, pets are not allowed. One client angrily shared that while she was petting the cat that lived in the nursing home she just entered, she reminisced to one of the staff members about her own cat that she was forced to give up because the nursing home didn't allow clients to bring in their own pets. The staff member reminded her that she would soon forget her cat because now she had a new one with which to interact.

Other times a family must move from a house to an apartment because of a divorce or job loss, or sell a home they owned and move to a rental unit. Many landlords do not allow pets.

If clients are unable to find suitable housing that allows pets, they may seek euthanasia of the pet instead of adoption. Pet parents often express fear that the pet with whom they have bonded will not bond with anyone else. The pet may be elderly, like the client, and difficult to place in a home. This places the client in an emotional struggle with feelings of guilt, sorrow, and anxiety over the future of the pet.

Therapists can help these clients assess their options and carefully examine their feelings about their choices. Sometimes, by brainstorming options, clients may discover opportunities they hadn't considered. If a client has chosen euthanasia or relinquished a pet to an animal shelter, a review of the choices he or she was given at the time will help him or her work through lingering feelings of guilt and regret.

Elise, Greg, and Moocher. When an earthquake destroyed the foundation of the home Elise and Greg shared with their cat, Moocher, they were forced to move from the condemned building. The couple, both of whom were disabled and used wheelchairs with an attached respirator, were unable to find immediate suitable housing that would meet their needs and allowed cats.

Seeing no other options, Elise and Greg moved with Moocher to the home of Elise's parents. Her father was allergic to cats and her mother disliked them. She told Elise and Greg they could not keep the cat in the house. Elise was afraid to let Moocher outside because he was declawed. Because they lived on a fixed income, Elise and Greg couldn't afford to board Moocher; they needed their money for a security deposit on any suitable housing they could find. Moocher was 12 years old and had spent all of those years with Elise and Greg. They didn't want to place him into another home and believed the chance of finding suitable placement was slim. They also loved Moocher as if he were a child and couldn't imagine life without him.

Greg made an appointment with a local veterinarian for Moocher's euthanasia, but the veterinarian refused. She said that Moocher was in good health and would likely live for another few years. Greg became angry with the veterinarian, then tearfully broke down and told her why he was requesting euthanasia. The veterinarian offered to house Moocher free of charge for six months while Elise and Greg looked for housing. She invited them to visit Moocher any time.

Unfortunately, not all situations have such generous solutions. Therapists may have to work with clients who have no such options available. They need to help these clients see that their decisions—whatever they may be—were made with the knowledge and choices available at the time. Therapists also may have to work with a client to find a solution with which he or she can live more comfortably. The therapist who can view the pet as a full-fledged family member is best able to serve clients like Greg and Elise.

Wendy and Toby. Wendy had graduated from high school and was packing for college when her mother asked what she planned to do with her dog, Toby. Wendy replied that she had assumed her parents would keep the dog she had owned since she was 12. Her mother reminded Wendy that it was she who had wanted the yellow Labrador retriever, and that she had promised to always care for Toby. Wendy reminded her mother that dogs were not permitted in the dorm, and asked what she expected Wendy to do. Her mother suggested that Wendy find Toby a suitable home, because she and her husband planned to travel a great deal and wouldn't be able to care for Toby.

Wendy was furious. She felt her parents were betraying her and abandoning Toby. She was unhappy to be leaving Toby, but she had imagined they would be able to spend holidays and summer vacations together after she left for college. Wendy's mother didn't want the responsibility of caring for the dog. She was sad that her youngest child was leaving home, but she also was looking forward to doing some of the things she had always dreamed of, including traveling with her husband.

The family decided to seek counseling. Wendy was allowed to express all of her feelings, and Wendy's mother did the same. The counselor helped them to see that both of them had valid feelings and to understand each others' issues, desires, and needs regarding Toby. Eventually, the family decided to give Toby to some friends who lived on a ranch. Wendy would be free to visit the dog during holidays and summers. Her parents offered to provide financial care for Toby, paying for veterinary bills and food.

Having sought the advice of a therapist who was trained in issues of pet attachment and loss, Wendy and her parents were able to work out a solution in which all parties benefited. Toby was no longer viewed as an expendable nuisance. His status as a family member was proclaimed by Wendy, validated by the therapist, and ultimately supported by the parents.

Conclusion

It is important for a therapist to be familiar with the wide variety of pet losses that their clients' experience. Pets run away or are stolen, killed, placed for adoption, lost in custody battles, fall prey to natural and manmade disasters, or become victims of accidental death. Regardless of the circumstances surrounding the loss, the therapist must question the client closely to ascertain the meaning of the loss and the specific emotions the client attaches to it. For example, clients who are ill or dying often are reminded of their own mortality when a bond with a pet is broken.

In cases of accidental death, the therapist must realistically define the client's role in the pet's death. If clients perceive that they are in some way responsible for the death, the focus of therapy initially is to alleviate the guilt with which they are struggling.

The therapist must allow the client to present symptoms on his or her own terms. Once the client describes the parameters of his or her loss, the therapist can assemble tools for facilitating the healing process, tailoring the interventions to meet the client's specific needs. Initially, therapy may be focused on crisis intervention, but later the therapist must help the client deal with the guilt, sorrow, loneliness, and self-esteem issues that surface during the process of grief resolution.

5

CHILDREN AND PET LOSS

Barrett plays with his geckos. Children often develop bonds with pets that may be similar to the bonds they share with other siblings. They may choose to bond with traditional pets or more exotic ones. Oftentimes, a pet loss is the first loss a child experiences. Acknowledging and grieving the loss of a pet helps to lay a healthy foundation for future losses, ones that include other people, moves, loss of jobs, or loss of health.

I stood by our 12-year-old daughter, Savannah, as she held our beloved Jenny, an 11-year-old English cocker, and "sister" to Savannah, as my husband, a veterinarian, euthanized our family dog. I watched as Savannah hugged, stroked, and finally kissed Jenny as the life passed out of her furry body. Savannah gently laid Jenny's head down and then folded herself into my arms for comfort. What a brave and strong young girl, I thought.

My husband didn't want Savannah to hold Jenny. His feelings came out of a natural concern to shield her from that part of the death process. I reminded him of how we work with families in preparing them and their children for the euthanasia process, and of the fact that Savannah was determined to be there for Jenny. She was also well prepared for what she would experience and mature enough to understand the process, some of the criteria we use with families in determining whether it is in the best interest of their children to witness and participate in the euthanasia of their pets.

Our family's participation in the euthanasia of Jenny was a fitting farewell to a loyal companion from the girl who loved her. It was also one in which my daughter felt good about how she chose to say her final goodbyes. Savannah wanted to be with Jenny right up to the end. Later that day she told her father that she wanted to be a veterinarian. She was taught that euthanasia is a gift that ends pain and suffering. Jenny was in pain and we were not going to allow her to suffer. She had an inoperable tumor that was making it difficult for her to breathe; she was senile and severely arthritic.

Children actually know more about the cycle of life than we might give them credit for understanding. Even very young children continually participate in the cycles of birth and death:

> Children grow up witnessing change in nature. They learn that there is a natural rhythm and flow to life. They watch the leaves grow on the trees, see them go from green to red to brown and then fall from the branches. They watch as the barren land becomes covered with snow. They feel the temperature change and then witness the process of rebirth and death every year that they are alive. With change comes anticipation, sometimes with dread and sometimes with joy for the good things that it brings (such as butterflies or snowflakes). Children of any age can feel the discomfort of the bitter cold on their bodies and the pelting rain against their cheeks. As they grow older they often learn that even the worst of thunderstorms brings rainbows afterward. Before children can even articulate the changes they witness around them, they have come to accept them as part of the cycle of life. From this knowledge children can build on a foundation, of the cycle of life, that includes the birth of people and animals and the death of both as well. (Ross, 2005, pg. 1).

Because a pet typically lives only one-fifth as long as a person, it is realistic to expect that its death will be the first loss a child encounters. Our society tends to remove children from experiences of death and dying. Sometimes parents and caregivers do this to "protect" the child from a difficult experience. In past generations, death was viewed as a part of life and was present in the home environment. Grandparents often died at home among family and friends. Because most elderly people die in nursing homes and hospitals today, children are separated from this process.

Relationships Children Share with Their Pets

The grief children feel at the loss of a pet will depend upon how they view their relationship with the pet. Understanding the relationship they share with pets is the first step in helping them through a loss.

A pet may be a best friend to a child; an only child may even view the pet as they would a human sibling. The pet may serve as a confidante and source of support for a child going through a transition (e.g., a recent move or divorce). A sick child may view the pet as a source of comfort and protection. A pet will play with a child when other children cannot or will not. This is especially true for disabled and withdrawn children.

One adult pet parent related that she had back surgery when she was 12 years old and had to spend several months in a body cast. Because she was confined to bed for part of her recovery, her friends soon grew bored visiting her. Her sister gave her a kitten during this time. "That kitten kept my spirits up during a really tough time. If it wasn't for that kitten, I don't know what I would've done." The cat lived with her for many years and they shared a close bond.

A child's relationship with a pet may be strained and limited due to a separation or divorce. A child who saw his or her pet daily may get to see it only on the weekends because of the change in living arrangements. Children may have little or no say about a pet's fate. Some children may be denied the opportunity to say goodbye to their pets. When working with children, therapists should encourage them to express all of their feelings about the loss.

Aline Kidd, professor of psychology at Mills College, interviewed more than 300 children ages three to 13 who owned pets (Gentry, 1987). Kidd concluded that children between the ages of three and five years thought that their pets could talk and play games with them. At age seven, children could distinguish behaviors between specific types of animals. Kidd also discovered that many children stayed close to their pets as they grew older, while some distanced themselves from their pets as well as from family members during adolescence (Gentry, 1987).

In the many years we have worked with children in the pet loss support group, we are continually reminded of the important roles animals hold in the lives of children. Whenever people come to the group seeking support for a current loss, inevitably we visit the first pet losses encountered as children. Some are remembered fondly, others have unresolved issues they need to work through.

Pet Loss: A Family Experience

The therapist can help parents and children see that grief is not shameful. Sharing tears as well as laughter is healthy and normal. Children learn that it is healthy to express such emotions when they witness the grieving of someone they love and respect. Such sharing of grief gives children permission to face their own feelings when experiencing a loss.

However, children should never have to take care of a grieving parent. Adults should share their feelings about the loss without expecting the child to comfort them in a parental capacity. Sometimes when a parent is attached to a pet and the child is not, the parent may become angry with the child for not displaying any feelings about the loss. Other times, parents hide their own emotions out of fear of upsetting a young child or seeming ridiculous or inappropriate to an older one. Openly demonstrating feelings for a loss teaches children of all ages that this is appropriate, healthy, and normal behavior when someone or something we love dies.

Therapists can assist parents by encouraging them to talk to their children about what the pet and the loss or impending loss means to them. This will help children to understand why it is painful for the parents and others when it doesn't seem so painful to them. Ultimately, this teaches the child to respect others' feelings, especially when the feelings are not shared by the child (Quackenbush & Graveline, 1985, p. 48).

Promoting Healthy Communication within the Family

Open and honest communication helps a child build a secure foundation for facing future losses. When a loss occurs, concerns about mortality, fear, and abandonment arise. These issues need to be addressed and not minimized. Parents must be taught that sharing feelings in a family validates the child's right to have those feelings. Such openness teaches children that grief doesn't have to be hidden or endured alone. Shared grief can be a catalyst in promoting a healthy family unit.

When divorce threatens to collapse the family structure, sharing the grief can bind the family together and help establish a new structure in which the children realize they are still deeply cared for and loved. They also realize that there is still a family structure in place even though it has taken on a different form. The same is true when a pet loss occurs. Death changes the way a family functions. Openly sharing feelings promotes closeness among family members. Children need to express feelings of isolation, abandonment, anger, fear, and sorrow. Adults need to know that showing respect for and validating children's feelings enables children to develop a sense of self-confidence leading to increased self-esteem.

Therapists can help children by teaching them that death is final, real, and irrevocable. Therapists working with adult caregivers should help them understand that using euphemisms and pretense when discussing death with a child can actually hinder the child's ability to work through an emotionally felt loss. Children also need to be taught that death is part of the cycle of life. This concept can be taught in an ongoing and basic way. For example, as stated earlier, death education can be explored when observing nature. Children can be shown life cycles of insects and animals, and encouraged to observe the changes in the seasons. They can be told that when living plants die they return to the earth and become part of it. In becoming part of the earth again, the dead plant helps new plants to grow.

A child who shares a relationship with a companion animal may be exposed to other aspects of loss as well. When an animal has been stolen, runs away, or is placed for adoption, it can be traumatic for children in ways many adults may not consider. Children may fear for their own safety if a pet is stolen. They may wonder if someone might steal them. If a pet runs away, children may think that *they* did something wrong and that the pet doesn't love them anymore. If the pet is placed for adoption, very young children may fear that their parents will give them away as well. It is important to establish open communication between parents and their children so that children are free to voice any concerns and fears they may have.

Lying about the fate of the pet may be well-intended, but it is unfair because it excludes children from the decision-making process. It takes away their right to say goodbye and ignores their need to do so. Though it may be tempting for parents to avoid discussing the issues surrounding the loss of a pet, it is not in a child's best interest to do so. Often parents will ask the veterinarian to lie to the child about the pet's fate. Some well-intentioned parents make up elaborate stories to explain the loss of a pet. As children mature, they often question these stories and discover that they were lied to. They may feel angry and betrayed by the persons they trusted the most.

Creating a Safe Environment for Communication

Children need a safe, secure environment in which to ask questions, receive answers, and express feelings. Children should be allowed to work through their grief even if it is painful for a parent to watch. Choosing to "protect" the children from this process does more harm than good, as that teaches them that displaying their feelings is wrong. If children are not allowed to work through their loss, it may never be resolved.

An important aspect of providing pet loss support to families is creating a child-friendly environment. Children are willing to share their feelings when they feel they are with someone who understands them. One way to create a safe environment is to display pictures of animals in the office. Providing stuffed animals for children to hold can help alleviate their anxieties and gives them the message that pets are valued by the therapist. Some therapists keep a pet cat, fish, or bird in their offices. Therapists may even display photos of their own pets. Creating an environment in which children view pets as valued helps to promote effective communication between child and therapist.

Dr. Boris Levinson, a child psychiatrist, studied the effects of having an animal present during counseling sessions with children. He found that the presence of a dog in the counseling setting worked as a social "icebreaker." Children who were reserved about talking to a psychiatrist would readily interact with the dog and feel less threatened about revealing their concerns to a stranger (Lagoni et al., 1994, p. 16).

Sometimes the therapist's pet can be an object of transference for a child's feelings. The child feels free to express his or her feelings through the pet. A three-year-old girl sat by the fishbowl in a therapist's office sadly watching the fish. When the therapist asked her what was wrong, she replied, "I'm sad because the fish are so sad. Their mom's mad at them."

How Children Assimilate Loss

Openness and honesty encourage children to ask questions about death and loss. Sometimes children will ask their questions immediately, but it is not uncommon for questions to surface for several years as children mature and their levels of awareness increase.

Some mental health experts believe that children are not mature enough to work through a deeply felt loss until they are adolescents. Children are likely to express their sadness on and off over many years, and in indirect ways. This is normal, and children should be encouraged and supported in continuing to express their feelings about a loss, even if it has been years since the pet died or went missing.

As children mature, their knowledge expands. They need to integrate what they learn about death with the rest of their knowledge about the world. Although it can be painful for parents to have the loss brought up repeatedly, it is important for them to remember that children need long periods of time to work through a loss. A useful analogy is to compare the process of guiding children through grief with building play structures from blocks: If a sturdy foundation is laid, the blocks will become a tower that does not easily topple.

Never presume to know exactly what the relationship is between a child and a companion animal. A teenage girl who had been an only child described the feelings she had for her dog after it was euthanized. She summed up the depth of her loss in four words: "She was my sister." She grieved for the loss of her dog as intensely as she would have a human sister. The girl went on to express feelings of regret at not having spent more time with her dog, saying that she had assumed her dog would always be there for her.

Sometimes parents are surprised at the intensity of a child's grief. They may comment to the therapist that the child didn't seem as interested in the pet when it was alive as he or she does now that it has died. Children may go through periods of distancing themselves from pets, as they do with other family members when they are seeking their own identity. Parents shouldn't assume that the child didn't care deeply for the pet even while experiencing a period of autonomy. Most importantly, a parent should never make a child feel guilty because he or she didn't seem to care about the pet prior to the loss. Children need to have support for the feelings they are experiencing at the moment.

A Pet Is a Family Responsibility

Sometimes parents tell children that if they don't take good care of a pet, it will be given away. This can be disastrous for the child. Parents often fail to realize that children can and do develop relationships with their pets that are as intense as those with siblings. Therapists may need to help parents be sensitive to the relationship children share with their pets.

One eight-year-old boy drew a picture of his pet hamster. His parents were divorced and his hamster lived with his mother. The child alternated living between his parent's homes. After a stay with his father, the boy went to stay at his mother's. When he arrived, he found his hamster dead. The mother told him the hamster had died because he didn't take care of it. Apparently, he had forgotten to feed it before he left. The boy said that he felt very bad that he had "killed" his hamster. The lesson the mother was teaching the child—about caring for living things or they will die—was not fully thought out. It was difficult for the child to provide for the pet when he was staying at his father's home. It also is developmentally unrealistic to expect an eight-year-old child to be solely responsible for a pet. The lesson only served to fill the child with feelings of loss, regret, and self-blame.

Children whose parents give a pet away because they believe the children were not taking enough responsibility for the pet's care will need particular understanding in fully working through any feelings of guilt associated with the loss of the pet. Parents should be encouraged to explain to a child that the pet needed to have a home where it could be cared for on a regular basis. Children should be allowed and encouraged to say goodbye to their pets. If possible, they should be able to visit their pet in its new home. Deciding to adopt and care for a pet should be a family decision. I cannot stress this fact enough: all family members should share in the responsibility for the pet's care. Children whose pets are not well cared for should not be blamed for the pets' demise or be shamed in any way. When adopting a pet, children can be told what is expected of them regarding its care and expectations should be age appropriate (see Ross, pg. 26).

Cognitive Age and Effects of Loss

Children of any age need to know four things about death:

1. They need a definition of death.
2. They need to know what caused the death.
3. They need to understand what feelings are associated with loss.
4. They need a philosophical frame in which to place the information (Arkow, 1987, p. 45).

When helping a child cope with pet loss, therapists should ask the parents about their spiritual or religious beliefs. This will help them support and respect the family's views about death, dying, and the hereafter, even if they do not share those beliefs.

In his book *Talking About Death: A Dialogue Between Parent and Child*, Earl Grollman (1990) warned parents against expressing any religious convictions they don't actually hold. Children will detect the inconsistency and deception in a tale about heavenly happiness when they see their parents struggling with feelings of hopelessness, finality, and despair. Painting too beautiful a picture of the hereafter can even entice a child to want to join the pet in heaven. Telling children that God took Mittens because he was special and good can frighten them; they may fear that if they are too good, God might decide to take them too. Grollman encouraged parents to share only honestly felt religious convictions that they are willing explain to their children.

Caregivers Do's and Don'ts

Do say the following:

- I'm sorry.
- I cannot imagine how difficult this must be for you.
- How are you feeling?
- I don't know what to say (if this is the case).
- I'd like to hear about your feelings.
- I care about you.
- We have a lot of memories together regarding (pet). Do you remember when …?
- Tell me about your pet.

Do not say the following:

- At least you have other pets.
- You can get another pet to replace the one you lost.
- God needed your pet more than you did.
- Your pet is in a better place.
- It is God's will.
- I know just how you feel.
- It was just a pet.
- Don't cry.
- You should …
- You shouldn't …
- You have to be strong.
- Big boys (or girls) don't cry and carry on.

Know that there is nothing you can say to make it "all better" for the child. It is not the job of a parent or therapist to "fix it" or make it right again for the child. While it is painful to watch a child grieve, the most beneficial thing that can be done is to support the child through the loss by being there for him or her (see Ross, p. 12).

How much can children understand about an emotionally felt loss, and what should they be told about it? A child's level of cognitive development directly correlates with the effects of loss the child experiences. Based loosely on Piaget's stages of development, the following outline illustrates what grief reactions can be expected from children of varying ages.

Birth to Age 2. Studies have shown that even infants can experience stress, resulting in feelings of isolation and abandonment. Infants can sense when there is discord in their environment. They may react by crying, clinging, being hard to console, withdrawing, sleeping too much or too little, and regressing to previous behaviors. Children of this age can be reassured through touch, hugs, holding, and rocking. Speaking to them with a soothing voice also helps reduce their stress. It is important to maintain an infant's or toddler's routine as much as possible during times of stress and loss.

Ages 2 to 5. A young child's ability to understand and use information about what is happening in the immediate surroundings should not be underestimated. Children should be told what has happened to their pet and why.

As the child matures, pet loss will be linked to imaginary play. Preschoolers may hold a funeral service. They may think of the pet as alive in some other place, such as heaven. They may believe that when a pet dies it is only asleep and will one day awaken. They may ask how the pet will be able to return to them after being buried in the ground. Too often their belief that the pet is only sleeping is reinforced by the common euphemism for euthanasia: "put to sleep." A child may bury a dead animal, then dig it up a few days later to see what is happening to it. Children this age need help in understanding the finality of a pet's death. They need to be told that the pet is not sleeping and won't be able to return home.

The most severe symptoms of distress appear in children who are not informed about their pet's fate. Symptomatic behaviors in a child this age include hitting, biting, kicking, disobeying, regression to previous behaviors (e.g., sucking a thumb, refusing to use the toilet, increased need for transitional objects), temper tantrums, withdrawal, masturbation, and separation anxiety. The child may have nightmares or psychosomatic symptoms (e.g., stomachaches, preoccupation with small hurts). The child may or may not display immediate signs of grief.

Children this age need encouragement to work through their feelings through dramatic play, drawing, or talking about them. They should be encouraged to ask questions and receive honest answers. They may need reassurance that their parents are not leaving them and are available to give them support.

Ages 6 to 11. When children are 6 years old and older, they are able to view death as the final stage of life. Children may believe that death is something that happens only to others or see it as a punishment for having done something bad. They may rationalize that the pet died because it was bad, or because the child was bad, or because the child's angry thoughts killed it.

Because children this age are egocentric, they are most at risk for blaming themselves for a pet's death. A child may surmise that the pet's death is a direct result of something the child did or did not do. Some children believe that wishing for a pet to die (when they were angry at it) caused it to die. Children need to be reassured that feelings cannot cause a pet's demise. The concept that death is part of the life cycle and that it happens to every living thing can be grasped at this age.

Children this age may show signs of grief sporadically. They may feel angry with the pet for dying and say that they never wanted it and are glad it is gone. These children need encouragement in working through their feelings. They may find it therapeutic to write a letter to the pet, draw pictures, or use some other form of self-expression. Children should be encouraged to express all their feelings about the loss. School and interactions with peers can be positive factors during a loss. Children can share their sadness with others. Activity at school can be a positive distraction for the child, much like an adult's job.

Children this age may express their fears through depression, aggression, dependency, phobias, compulsive eating, feelings of rejection, denial, and anxiety.

Ages 12 to 17. Children in this age group may ask questions about what would happen to them if their parents were to die. These children need to be reassured that plans have been made in case this were to happen. They also need to be told that the vast majority of people live for a long time. The loss of a pet may remind children of a previous loss they experienced that they may not have worked through. They may ask questions about the previous loss. Some of these questions may require philosophical answers. Children this age also may ask about disposal of the pet's body. Truthful information will help to lessen the child's anxiety about the loss. The child is the best guide in letting others know how much information he or she needs.

As children enter their teen years, they begin their search for the meaning of life. They want to know how to cope with loss. Children need encouragement to share their feelings openly. A child who has endured other losses—such as a move, changing schools, the loss of friendships, or divorce—may have viewed the pet as a source of comfort throughout childhood. When the bond between the child and pet is broken, the child may not know how to handle difficult situations without the pet.

Depressive symptoms in children this age can include thoughts of suicide. They need to have their feelings validated and to learn ways to cope with loss. Interactions with peers who have experienced a similar loss may be helpful. Children this age are able to empathize genuinely with and support one another.

Over 18. If an adult had a healthy experience with loss as a child, he or she will possess the cognitive and emotional abilities to understand death and loss throughout his or her life. Adults continue to look for meaning in life and death. Healthy adults have the ability to reason, to seek help when needed, and to handle difficult situations.

Young adults may have to leave their pets with their parents or find suitable homes for them when moving to another location. Saying goodbye to a beloved pet can be difficult. Many young adults describe leaving a pet as closing a chapter on their childhood. Therapists can help young adults recognize that they may be grieving not only the loss of their pet but the loss of their childhood, as well (Ross, 1987, p. 37).

Children Who Have Lost a Parent

For many reasons, children who have been through a divorce or the death of a parent may be more vulnerable to the loss of a pet. A pet that was part of a child's life prior to the divorce or death can remind the child of happier times spent with both parents. The pet may have been a source of companionship for a child whose parents were at odds with one another. In a study of 114 college students, 50 from intact families and 35 who had lost a parent through death or divorce, it was discovered that, in general, children who had lost a parent were more apt to attempt suicide. A frightening statistic when "[a]lmost half of all marriages will fail eventually, and almost 45% of all children will see their parents permanently split" (Sipchen, 1997).

A family pet may have to be abandoned because of a change in finances after a divorce or death of a parent. Studies show that most families take a 30% drop in their standard of living when the custodial parent is the mother. The custodial parent may have to move from a house to an apartment where pets are not allowed (Hodges, 1991, p. 63).

Losing both the parent and the pet with which a child has shared a close relationship can compound the loss and make it even harder for the child to resolve his or her grief. Mental health professionals must be sensitive to a child's situation and provide as much support as possible to help the child work through both losses.

Recognizing Hidden Grief

Chosen Hidden Grief and Unaware Hidden Grief

Children do not always show immediate grief. They may internalize their feelings and express them through acts of aggression—verbal or physical. They may say they never liked the pet anyway. They may feel angry at the pet for abandoning them. In an effort to minimize a child's pain, an adult may underplay the significance of a pet's death. If adults treat the loss as insignificant, children may fear that if something were to happen to them, their parents would not care.

There are two kinds of hidden grief parents and therapists should be aware of in children. The first is a chosen hidden grief that involves grief feelings the child chooses not to share with the parent or therapist. Children may take on the role of protecting their parents when the family is experiencing a loss. Another type of hidden grief is one in which the child is unaware of the deeper feelings arising from the loss and lacks the understanding about how to integrate them into the process of grieving.

The following case example demonstrates how one family and therapist dealt with a child's unaware hidden grief and fears resulting from a pet's euthanasia:

Emily and Harvey. According to her mother, nine-year-old Emily's best friend was her cat, Harvey, who disappeared one day. He was discovered hiding under the front porch of their house several days later. He was injured. The veterinarian who examined Harvey gave a poor prognosis for recovery. The only treatment available would be extensive and costly. The family discussed the options and included Emily in the discussion. Emily's mother said that she could not afford the costly treatment. She was concerned that even if she could find a way to pay for it, Harvey would experience a great deal of misery with little hope of recovery. Emily said that she wanted Harvey to live. Her mother explained to her how Harvey would suffer if they chose to treat him. In the end, Emily and her mother opted to euthanize Harvey.

Emily was permitted to say her final goodbyes to Harvey at the veterinarian's office. A few weeks after Harvey's death, Emily would cry intermittently. She had difficulty concentrating in school and chose to remain at home instead of playing with her friends. Emily's mother sought the help of a therapist when her daughter's appetite diminished and her sleep was disturbed.

Emily finally shared with the therapist her fear that if she became seriously injured or ill her mother would not be able to afford treatment for her. Emily's fears were resolved when her mother reassured Emily that she was her first priority. Emily's mother said that she would always make certain she could adequately provide for her. She also reminded Emily that she had loved Harvey too. She told Emily that although financial considerations were a factor in making the decision, a more important factor was the suffering Harvey would have endured if they had not chosen euthanasia.

Emily was able to accept this new information and resumed her normal activities. She and her mother found ways to memorialize Harvey: Emily named a favorite stuffed animal after him, and she and her mother created a collage from their favorite photos of Harvey. They held a ceremony at Harvey's gravesite.

Emily's relationship with Harvey was one of a "best friend." In understanding how children are affected by pet loss we need to have specific information on the level of importance and meaning the pet represented in the child's life. Emily's mother was able to fill in the emotional gaps that Harvey's death left for Emily. She became Emily's friend and confidante by validating the importance and significance of her loss. She demonstrated the depth of her feelings for Emily by acknowledging the loss and finding ways in which she could assist Emily in coping with it.

More importantly, once the therapist informed the mother of Emily's fears, her mother communicated effectively with Emily, thus quieting them (Pettit, 1994, p. 160–161).

Children and Euthanasia

In the case of euthanasia, it has been suggested that children receive the same information as other family members about the euthanasia process. Children should be included in any family discussions on the subject, and should be allowed to decide for themselves how they would prefer to handle the pet's death. They should be given the options of being present, saying goodbye beforehand, or saying goodbye after the procedure. One of the most important aspects of the process is for parents to talk about their own feelings with the child and to encourage the child to express his or her feelings (Quackenbush and Graveline, 1985, p. 52).

If a pet is terminally ill, children can be prepared for the impending loss over a course of days, weeks, or months, depending on the pet's condition. Allowing children to begin the grieving process before the pet dies is healthy. It gives them control over how they want to say goodbye and allows them time to make plans for their goodbyes and to say or do anything they feel they need to before the pet is gone. Finally, it gives them the opportunity to work through some of their feelings and be part of the decision-making process.

Choosing the Right Words

It is important to use the correct terminology when working with children. It is confusing for a child to hear that the pet has been "put to sleep." The medical term *euthanized* should be used. If they are told that a pet has been "put to sleep," children may resist falling asleep themselves for fear of not waking, or they may be afraid to bury a "sleeping" pet.

The euthanasia procedure should be explained to children in terms that are age-appropriate. A child could be told that the pet will be put to death with an injection of a powerful medication administered only by veterinarians. Stress that this is not the same type of injection children receive from their pediatricians. It is given *only* to animals.

Parents often ask if children should attend the euthanasia of a pet. Some professionals say absolutely not, citing adverse emotional effects on the children. Others argue that permitting children to experience and express grief in a supportive setting can establish a healthy foundation upon which to build for future losses.

When addressing this issue, parents and therapists must take into consideration the child's past experiences with loss, his or her cognitive level of understanding and awareness, family dynamics, and his or her support systems. The parents' and veterinarians' willingness to support the child through a procedure must be addressed as well.

Stevenson suggested that children often are spared the "guilt" of having to decide on euthanasia for a pet by being excluded from the decision-making process by well-intentioned adults. Taking them out of the decision-making process, however, only serves to reinforce their feelings of guilt about not being able to help their pet (Stevenson, 1988, p. 75).

Fudin and Cohen (1988, p. 84) have stated that children mature enough to assist with the care of a sick or elderly pet should be allowed to hear a detailed description of the euthanasia procedure and be given a choice about attending the euthanasia. Children who are mature enough to care for a pet are mature enough to provide care and comfort until the moment of the euthanasia procedure.

The following case study demonstrates how two children and their parents witnessed the euthanasia of their dog:

Tim, Joyce, Brandon, Katie, and Peanut. Tim and Joyce had two children—Brandon, age eight, and Katie, age six—and a 17-year-old dog named Peanut. Peanut had been a member of the family since he was a puppy, and the family shared a common love for him. The dog was dying of complications related to old age. He could no longer stand and he had problems with bladder control. Tim and Joyce had talked with the children ahead of time and, along with the veterinarian, had compassionately explained what the euthanasia procedure would involve.

Brandon and Katie were given the choice of attending the euthanasia procedure, saying goodbye to Peanut beforehand, or coming into the room after the procedure to say their final goodbyes. Both children chose to be present.

The entire family went to the veterinary clinic with Peanut. The veterinarian told the family he thought they were doing the best thing for Peanut in allowing him to have a peaceful death. He then asked the family if they were ready for him to give Peanut the injection. They all nodded yes.

The family gently stroked Peanut while the veterinarian administered the injection. Peanut slowly wagged his tail against the table. In a matter of seconds, Peanut's body became still. The veterinarian listened to the dog's heart. Everyone in the room was silent. When the veterinarian said that Peanut was dead, Katie began to cry. Joyce held her close as she wept. Brandon was silent and looked from one person to another questioningly. Tim told Brandon that Peanut was gone now and that he was relieved of the pain he had felt. Brandon pressed his face against his mother's skirt and silently sobbed. Tim's eyes filled with tears. The children slowly moved from their mom and went to pet Peanut's body.

Brandon spent a lot of time staring into Peanut's open eyes. He asked, "If he's dead, how come his eyes are open? Can he see us?" The veterinarian explained that animals usually died with their eyes open, and that Peanut couldn't see or hear them anymore. Tim and Joyce chose this time to explain their beliefs to the children. They told Brandon and Katie that Peanut's spirit had been set free—that the part that had housed his spirit was Peanut's body, and that was all that was left of him here. Joyce told the children they could keep Peanut's memory alive by remembering all the times they had shared with Peanut. Joyce and Tim then shared a story about the time they first adopted Peanut as a puppy.

Drawing from a children's story called *The Tenth Good Thing About Barney* by Judith Viorst (1971), Joyce and Tim asked the children to remember ten good things about Peanut. Brandon said that Peanut was a good friend. He urged his mom to tell some good things. Joyce said Peanut never bit anyone. She recalled how he loved to run in an open field near their house. Katie said he was nice and Tim agreed.

The family was ready to leave when Brandon suddenly asked if they had done the right thing for Peanut in authorizing the euthanasia. Tim and Joyce were surprised by the question. Both parents and the veterinarian reassured Brandon that it was not only the right thing to do, but a loving, unselfish act. Katie gave Peanut one last hug goodbye and the family left.

Two weeks later, Tim and Joyce reported that the children had accepted Peanut's death and did not seem to be experiencing any adverse effects from having been present at the procedure. This can be attributed to the parents' having made the children aware of Peanut's deteriorating condition before he was euthanized. This is very important in preparing children for the loss of a pet.

The children were included in the process by participating in the decision of euthanasia, being allowed to voice their concerns and fears, and being given options in how they would like to say goodbye to Peanut. They also were in a setting in which the veterinarian was supportive and helpful. Most significant was the support, openness, and honesty Tim and Joyce gave to their children. They took time to encourage Brandon and Katie to ask questions and to share their grief, giving them information in terms they could understand.

It is important to remember that, although being present for the euthanasia was right for this family, it is not right for everyone (Ross, 1987). The following case study demonstrates what happens when a child is not adequately prepared for a pet's euthanasia:

Mike. Mike's mother dragged her son into the room where his pet was to be euthanized. The three-year-old was not prepared to witness the animal's death, nor was he given a choice about attending.

As the veterinarian started to administer the injection, the boy began to scream. The euthanasia was stopped and the child was removed from the room. He was inconsolable, and his mother could not be present for the pet's euthanasia because she had to calm her son. It was later discovered that Mike had a fear of needles and would scream when he went to the pediatrician's office. Witnessing the euthanasia of his pet was a traumatic, rather than a helpful and educational experience in this child's life.

Burial

After the death of a pet, families are given different options in disposal of the pet's body. Pet parents may choose to bury their pets at home (depending on city ordinances), place them in pet cemeteries, or opt for cremation. Larger animals, such as horses and cattle, are given to rendering services. Children may benefit from helping their parents decide what to do with the pet's body. A child may request to see a deceased pet right before it is placed in a grave. Other children want to know what cremation or rendering services are. Children should have these choices explained to them in age-appropriate language.

Explaining death to young children can be likened to explaining sexuality to them. The same rule follows: the younger the child, the simpler the explanation. The more lengthy or wordy the explanation, the more confusing it is for the child. Children should be told honestly what will occur or has occurred. In the case of rendering, the child can be told the positive aspect of this type of service. An adult can say, "We can't visit Bentley's grave because there isn't one. A horse's body is rendered. Bentley's body has been made into other products that people and animals use. Giving his body to this service has helped to continue the life cycle."

If a pet's body has decomposed or is traumatically deformed and the parent does not want the child to view it before placing it in a grave, the parent needs to be honest with the child and say, "I'd prefer that we do not open Pete's body bag. Pete's body is not in good condition. I'd rather remember him the way he was."

Saying Goodbye

Given the opportunity, children of any age will come up with creative and meaningful ways to say goodbye to their pets. In my work with children I have been invited to many pet funerals. These have ranged from simple ceremonies to elaborate undertakings with music, flowers, a casket, photos, and food. Often special words and prayers are said over pets. Children have written beautiful poems expressing their feelings over the loss and the love they have felt for their pets. Some children have written letters, complete with photos of the child and pet, to be included in the body bag for cremation. Others have created collages, scrapbooks, and photo albums of their pets. Some have felt the need to cuddle and keep their pets' toys, blanket, or collar.

Children should be encouraged to say goodbye in a way that feels right to them. Their decisions and choices around this should be respected.

Choosing To Adopt Another Pet

Children should be allowed to express their feelings about when and if they want another pet. Children may be ready to accept and love another pet when they can remember the pet they lost without experiencing a great deal of sadness. Adopting a new pet should be a family decision. It should not happen until everyone in the family feels ready and willing to accept the responsibility of another pet. Children who are forced to adopt a pet too soon are at risk for rejecting the pet. They may believe that the loss was not meaningful and that everyone (including them) can be replaced. The term "replacing" the pet should not be used. Pets, like people, cannot be replaced. Children need to know that they can choose to love again but the pet that died or is missing was a unique being and there will never be another one like it again.

A nine-year-old girl wrote a poem about the loss of her cat:

Once You Were With Me

Once you were with me
No sorrow that I spot

Once you were with me,
Then you were not.

I wish you could see
The pain that I've got

I cry all day
I cry all night

I can see you play
I can see you fight

Once you were with me
Then you were not.

by Angie, dedicated to Billy, 1988

Jessica, age eight (2004) wrote about the death of her hamster:

I had a hamster named Oreo. I played with her a lot and I haled her a lot. She was really cute, and really fun to play with. She would bite me a lot. Then one day she didn't move at all. I was so afraid because when I called her name she didn't even move. When I reached to grab (her) she was hard. She was dead. I started to cry, in fact, my whole family started to cry.

Even though Oreo was dead, I still dream about her. Every night, and I have a little hamster, Beany-Baby, and I pretend its Oreo, and I play with her every day, and sometimes whenever I think of her I cry. I really loved her and I'm rally sad and mad that she's gone. (Ross, 2005, p. 161). ·

Pets teach children about birth and death, loving and grief. It is interesting to note Jessica's impressions upon discovering Oreo. She was afraid, she felt his body, and it was hard. She also states that even though she has another hamster to love and play with she still has feelings of grief. Most notable is her comment, "I pretend its Oreo," and then the following comment, "I really loved her and I'm really sad and mad that she's gone."

Jessica is learning that we grieve the animals that we loved and who have died—even if we have another pet to love.

Children and Therapy

One of the most challenging but equally rewarding groups of bereaved pet guardians to work with is children. Children want and need to understand the feelings that envelop them when the loss of a beloved companion animal takes place. Often, the grief experience can be so overwhelming for a family that sometimes children are overlooked. Furthermore, children are not always able to articulate their feelings coherently. Talk therapy may work for older children, but in the majority of cases, children benefit from play therapy.

Play Therapy

Some therapists believe that children are able to resolve many of their own fears, worries, and questions about life through play. Play is a child's work. It is necessary for the child's social, physical, and psychological maturation. Play therapy is an opportunity for a child to work through a grief experience and the accompanying feelings. Ultimately, this can help children alleviate their fears and anxieties.

When a pet has served as a source of comfort and security for a child, learning to live without the pet can be an extremely difficult transition. Children can acquire new coping mechanisms through play therapy.

The goals of play therapy should be to increase awareness, recognition, and acceptance of the child's feelings and to provide an opportunity for the child to creatively deal with his or her distress. Through play therapy, children can be shown alternative ways of looking at the world and coping with problems. They can learn how to cope during an emotionally difficult period. If play therapy is successful, children will be able to identify and understand the variety of emotions that may surface as they progress through grief (Hodges, 1991, pp. 301, 316).

Storytelling

Some children, however, resist play therapy. With these children, you can use storytelling, books, and games to help them in their grief work. One game we use for children who are experiencing the anger stage of the grieving process is *The Angry Monster Machine* (Center for Applied Psychology, 1992). It encourages interaction and discussion between child and therapist, working as a catalyst for the child to reveal the issues and conflicts that underlie his or her anger. The game teaches children that angry feelings often are appropriate and shows them acceptable ways of expressing and coping with angry feelings while working toward a healthy resolution.

There are several books for children about feelings associated with animals and death. In many of these books, children make up stories about the pictures they see or are encouraged to tell stories about their own pets or friends' pets that have died. This activity allows them to mix fantasy and reality, and helps them to arrive at a belief system about the loss that is comfortable for them.

Kyle. Six-year-old Kyle's father and mother frequently argued over the loss of their nine-year-old Irish setter. Apparently in response to these arguments, Kyle often cried and refused to play with his friends. He also told his parents how much he loved them and tried to hug them when they were in the middle of an argument.

Kyle's parents became concerned when his teacher noted this type of behavior at school. The parents decided to consult a therapist who worked with children. Kyle was told that he was going to see a "worry doctor," someone who helps with worries.

The therapist asked Kyle to look at a book of photos titled *Feelings Inside You & Outloud Too*, by Barbara Kay Polland. She told Kyle he could choose any photo and make up a story about it.

Kyle chose a picture of a man walking down the front steps of a house. A little boy sat in the window with a sad expression on his face, watching the man. Kyle said the man was the boy's father, and that the father was mad and was leaving his son because their dog had died.

The therapist determined that Kyle thought his parents were angry with him and might leave because of the loss of their dog. Kyle's parents reassured him that they were not going to leave him, that they were not angry with him, and that they didn't blame him for the death of their dog. They apologized for arguing in front of him and told him that, despite their angry and sad feelings over the dog's death, they still loved each other and were committed to working through the loss as a family. The family then worked together on acceptable solutions for managing the anger stage of the grieving process.

Art Therapy

Working with art supplies often helps children work through their feelings. Children who have a difficult time articulating their feelings might express themselves freely when focusing on imaginary play, storytelling, or artistry rather than focusing directly on the pet loss. Free expression through artistic endeavors often provides insight as well as a release of pent-up feelings. This kind of therapy often is successful because it allows for "safe" forms of expression. While Art Therapy is best done with a specially trained art therapist, parents can gain insight when viewing a child's art project. Ask the child to explain the art piece. Encourage children to openly share what they have made. One child drew a picture of her cat, Butterfinger, sitting next to a road. The child explained to me that her cat had been killed on the road.

Working with Adolescents

When working with adolescents, it is important to remember that they frequently demonstrate fierce loyalty to friends and social groups in an effort to establish their emerging adult identity. The adolescent period is an emotionally intense and often difficult time in a child's life. According to psychiatrist Erik Erikson's theory of psychosocial development, a crisis often is faced at each stage of development during maturation. The way the person resolves the crisis significantly affects how the next stage of development is approached by that person (Schell & Hall, 1983, p. 13). The crisis the adolescent faces can be intensified by feelings of loss and grief. In addition, the grief response can be intensified by hormonal changes experienced by the adolescent. The following case study depicts how an adolescent's loyalty is challenged by the suggestions of others that the object of her love and affection can be replaced and the intense response this challenge elicits:

Jennifer and Buttons. Jennifer's best friend was her dog, Buttons. When Buttons was hit by a car and killed, 15-year-old Jennifer first denied it and then went into a deep depression. She refused social invitations and chose to stay at home watching television. She quit the track team and slept a great deal. She stopped talking to her friends on the phone. For a while she refused all food except diet soda and chocolate. After two weeks of this behavior, Jennifer's parents sought the help of a therapist.

Jennifer was angry with her parents for making her see a therapist. She told the therapist she was upset that her dog had died and that she didn't want anyone's help. The therapist asked Jennifer if she would agree to see her just three times: After three sessions, Jennifer could decide if she wanted to continue to see the therapist. Jennifer agreed to this arrangement.

The therapist helped Jennifer to see that her feelings were normal. Losing Buttons was Jennifer's first experience with death. She felt isolated in her grief. Her family and friends had expected Jennifer to get over it. They encouraged her to get another dog, and this made her angry. She also wondered if she was abnormal for having such intense feelings for Buttons. The therapist assured Jennifer that her feelings were appropriate, pointing out that no one would be encouraging her to adopt a new best friend if the friend who had died had been human.

Jennifer decided to continue seeing the therapist after the initial three sessions. Her feelings were validated in therapy. She completed her grief work and learned valuable coping skills for working through future losses.

A therapeutic tool that has been proven effective in assisting children through a traumatic loss is eye movement desensitization and reprocessing *(EMDR)*. With young children, EMDR might be combined with play. Other times, the therapist may use EMDR in conjunction with hypnotherapy. Whichever therapeutic modality is chosen, the therapist gently guides the child to pinpointing a problem emotion or event that becomes the target of treatment. For example, one 11-year-old child accidentally left his bunny in its cage in direct sunlight. He later discovered his pet's lifeless body and empty water bottle. He realized that he had caused his rabbit's death when he saw his mother's look of shock and horror, and heard her surprised comment that he shouldn't have left his bunny in the sun. After a couple of months, although this traumatic event was in his past, the child could not think about the event without experiencing the emotions associated with the loss. He still had feelings of guilt, anger, and sadness. He began to think of himself as "a bad person." He became moody and withdrawn. His mother took him to see a therapist who used EMDR therapy. After two sessions with the therapists he was able to recall the event without experiencing the intense emotions associated with it. His mother reported, one month later, that he slowly gained his confidence and began to be more outgoing.

Conclusion

The unconditional love a pet offers is something a child doesn't always receive from other people. The relationships children share with their pets and the bonds they form must be acknowledged.

Minimizing or diminishing the child's feelings over the loss or impending loss of a pet can cause the loss to go unresolved for many years. Avoidance, outright lies, and trivializing the significance of the loss all can have a devastating effect on children.

On the other hand, the loss of a pet can lay a foundation on which children can build for the rest of their lives. Children can develop healthy coping skills when they are allowed to say goodbye to their pets and participate in the decision-making process. Animals teach children about both the beginning of life and the ending. They provide children with affection, love, and consistency. They also allow them to begin to build a healthy foundation for grieving when the pets die. It is the sensitive caregiver and therapist who will assist children in taking this information and integrating into their lives the ability to love, trust, let go, and love again. This cycle of love and loss will be replayed throughout their lives.

Acknowledging and validating a child's feelings over the loss gives the child permission to grieve openly and to ask questions. In helping children cope with issues of separation, parents and professionals can provide a solid foundation for coping with life, which is a process of endings and new beginnings.

There are numerous therapeutic techniques to assist children through loss. Special care should be given when working with children who have experienced the traumatic loss of their pets. Honesty, openness, and encouraging communication can significantly assist a child through a pet loss and help to establish a healthy foundation for future losses. Please refer to *Pet Loss and Children, Establishing a Healthy Foundation* (Ross, 2005) for a description of comprehensive, thorough, and most recent therapeutic techniques in helping children to cope with loss.

6

PET LOSS AND THE ELDERLY

Trudy and Bebe share a close bond. Since Trudy's husband Bob died, Bebe is her constant companion. Pets help us to feel connected to happier times and past experiences. They also provide us with something to care for outside of ourselves.

In the aftermath of Hurricane Katrina, television viewers watched as an elderly woman, stranded at her flooded home, held a gun to her temple and threatened to pull the trigger if officials did not allow her to evacuate with her only family members, her pets. She had lost her home, her possessions, but wasn't about to lose her family.

For an older person, the loss of a constant companion and best friend can have devastating effects from which it may be difficult to recover. The process of aging, for anyone, involves a series of losses. With age, one's social, physical, and mental abilities frequently diminish, as may financial security and independence. Friends and family may be deceased, ill, or emotionally unavailable. Many elderly people have endured numerous losses throughout their lives. Their success at coping with loss in the past is a good predictor of their capacity to recover from the most recent loss.

An elderly person's ability to successfully work through grief often is inhibited by a diminishing support system. Elderly people may be unaware of grief support services, may not be able to afford such services, or may be too proud to seek help, historically having chosen to handle their losses in private.

Bereaved elderly pet parents are often overwhelmed by the loss of a pet that provided them with love and support through other losses in their lives. Without their animal companion, and in the absence of other family members, they may be unable to cope on their own. This can intensify feelings of despair, loneliness, and isolation. The elderly person who has lost a pet may become depressed or even lose the will to live. He or she may experience feelings of social isolation and abandonment. The current loss almost always awakens memories of past losses, compounding feelings of sorrow and loneliness (Pettit, 1994, p. 164).

Therapists should try to understand what the challenges of day-to-day living might look like for a bereaved elderly pet parent. The counseling community needs to find ways to reach out to this population and provide support services that validate the grief and loss felt when a pet dies, becomes terminally ill, or must be given away.

Relationships Elderly People Share with Their Pets

Elderly pet parents often view the relationships they share with their pets as the main reason for getting out of bed each morning. Their daily routine is likely to center around the care of the pet. Feeding, walking, and playing with the pet provide activity and exercise for a pet parent who might otherwise spend an entire day in lonely isolation. Owning a pet can invite social interactions with other people, as, for example, young and old alike may approach an elderly person walking a dog and comment on the animal's breed, personality, or behavior.

In addition, the pet may be a source of security in the home. A pet can scare away intruders, alert its elderly parent that someone is at the door, or attract his or her attention in the event of fire or catastrophe.

Finally, for older people living alone, often isolated from human interaction, a pet can be a source of tactile warmth and affection. Pets often remain loyally by their pet parent's side throughout the day and night, providing unconditional companionship and affection. When the pet dies, daily routines are altered and the simple pleasures of daily living can be seriously diminished. Therapists can best assist grieving elderly pet parents by understanding and validating the importance and the significance of the relationships they shared with the pet.

Mabel and Wesley. Mabel lived with her cat, Wesley, who was her sole companion. Her children had moved far away and her husband had died years before. Many of her friends were in nursing homes or deceased. Mabel lived in an apartment complex and was only casually acquainted with her neighbors. She volunteered at a senior center two days a week and the rest of her time was spent in the company of Wesley.

Mabel and Wesley shared daily routines. When Mabel knitted, Wesley played with the ball of yarn at her feet. When Mabel brushed her teeth, Wesley sat at the sink and batted his paw at the running water. When Mabel ate breakfast, Wesley ate his meal at her feet. When she watched television, she talked to Wesley about the characters on TV while he curled up on her lap.

When Wesley became ill, Mabel provided loving nursing care until he died in her arms. Mabel was devastated and found she couldn't stand to be in the apartment; everywhere she turned, she was reminded of Wesley. She retreated to her bedroom, where she watched TV, read, and took her meals. She avoided the kitchen and living room as much as possible. She felt empty inside and cried frequently.

Her friends at the senior center encouraged Mabel to adopt a new cat, but she did not do so, fearing that the animal would outlive her. She also knew that the bond she had shared with Wesley would not be replaced, and was reluctant to invest her emotions in another animal that could not measure up to Wesley. For those reasons, she vowed never to have another pet. Wesley's death reminded Mabel of her own mortality. She began to see her life as mostly over. She told herself and others that her time on earth would be ending soon. Mabel lost her zest for life, became depressed, and eventually moved to a retirement facility.

A Link with the Past

A pet can represent a link with the past for an elderly pet parent. Often, the responsibilities for the pet were shared with a spouse who is now deceased. The loss of the pet can trigger intense memories of the loss of the spouse and can open wounds that go beyond attachment to the animal. An elderly person may remember the happy times he or she shared with the pet and spouse. It is not uncommon for the elderly to talk about special interactions or routines that the pet had shared with a deceased spouse. These memories can compound emotional pain for the person who is missing the pet and a family member at the same time.

It is not uncommon for pets to assume the role of surrogate children for people whose children have grown and moved away. Elderly persons often reminisce with their pets about their children, spouses, and other people who are now gone. People may tire of hearing the ramblings of an elderly person, but a pet always listens.

Health Benefits

Physical problems are common among the elderly: In fact, more than 85% of elderly people report one or more physical impairments (Arkow, 1987, p. 216). Pets can serve as distractions from worries and concerns and provide a sense of security for elderly individuals living alone. They are sources of exercise, amusement, and tactile stimulation, and can open doors to social interaction as well.

The Institutionalized Elderly and Visiting Pets

Today there are many therapeutic programs to help institutionalized elderly people maintain relationships with animals without actually having one in the home. Programs established through humane societies and other animal care organizations send volunteers with specially trained animals for visits with the elderly. Although they are by no means a replacement for the pets the elderly residents have lost, they do provide residents with an opportunity for conversations, tactile and sensory stimulation, and a way to connect with others.

Elderly people benefit from reminiscing about past pets and previous losses. Pets may serve as "touchstones" in the lives of the elderly, from which they shape their view of the world, themselves, and their beliefs. Animal visitors to geriatric residential care settings can help residents recall pleasant events and personal experiences from the past (Savishinsky, 1988, pp. 143–144).

Housing Restrictions

When an elderly person moves to a retirement facility, he or she may not be allowed to bring along a beloved pet. Or, if the pet is allowed to move in with the resident and then dies, often a replacement pet cannot be acquired. Not only does the elderly person grieve the loss of a cherished pet, he or she must also adjust to the idea of never being a pet parent again.

With this in mind, the therapist needs to pay close attention to the grief that an elderly person feels when giving up a pet. Faced with the choice of finding a new home for a pet or authorizing euthanasia for it, the pet parent may experience a deep sense of inadequacy and a loss of self-esteem. It is often difficult to find homes for older pets. Pet parents may fear their pets will not bond with new parents and will be unhappy. When this is the case, the elderly person is faced with relinquishing the pet to the humane society or county animal shelter or requesting the pet's euthanasia (see Chapter 3).

David, Yvonne, and Suzi. David and Yvonne, both in their late 60s, came to a pet loss support group when their 15-year-old springer spaniel, Suzi, had to be euthanized because of complications due to old age. At the time of her death, Suzi needed assistance getting to her feet, exhibited a staggering gait, had vision and hearing deficits, and suffered weight loss due to decreased appetite. The couple's son and daughter had moved away from home several years before and were busy with families of their own. David and Yvonne wept openly as they spoke of the unconditional love and loyalty Suzi had shown them since puppyhood. They agreed that their love for Suzi was in some ways greater than their love for their human children, who were spoiled and demanding, often disagreeable and uncompromising, and neglected them on holidays.

Before retirement, David had been a construction foreman, directing the work of 20 to 30 men. Now, he was retired but earned extra money managing the retirement condo complex in which they lived. He kept things "up and running" and reported requests for repair services to the parents. Yvonne, a nurse, still worked part time at a local nursing home, but she was close to retirement. Both were looking forward to extensive motor home travel in the years ahead. They already had crisscrossed the United States and much of Canada, with Suzi along for the ride.

When the condo complex had changed owners some years before, they had been informed that they could keep Suzi, but after her death they would not be permitted to adopt another pet. The complex would become pet-free by attrition. At the time, this rule, though troublesome, didn't have great implications for David and Yvonne, because Suzi was young and would see them into "their old age." Now that she was gone, the future stretched before them, devoid of the joy and comfort her presence had brought.

David said he wished it was he who had died rather than Suzi, and he wished he and Yvonne could join her so they could be a family again. Before Suzi's euthanasia, David had purchased a beautiful coffin in which she was buried in their yard. The burial ceremony and prayers they said for Suzi did little to reduce the anguish and bitterness this couple (especially David) felt over their loss. His inability to rescue Suzi from death left him feeling frustrated and impotent. These were new feelings with which he had to cope as he struggled for resolution of his grief.

After attending group for four months, David and Yvonne began to remember the good times they had shared with Suzi and their sorrow dissipated. In the support group they learned more about the significance of pets in people's lives. They decided they wanted to bond with another pet.

Although they had initially stated they would never want another pet, they longed for one now. David petitioned the retirement complex parents for permission to acquire a new pet. He solicited support from other residents who felt the same. Ultimately, David persuaded the owners to modify the rules and permit all residents to have one pet. Six months later, David and Yvonne returned to group with their new six-month-old springer spaniel. They were making plans for future travel and looking forward to life again.

Lifestyle Changes Caused by the Loss of a Pet

Losing a pet can mean a drastic change in lifestyle for an elderly person. A pet may have assisted the person in remaining independent. Pets can take on the role of therapy assistance dogs, intuitively becoming the eyes and ears for an elderly pet parent as his or her capacity to see and hear diminishes with age. Pets also can retrieve items for their elderly pet parents and help them negotiate curbs, stairs, and crosswalk signals. An elderly pet parent may not fully appreciate the many ways a pet has been of assistance until the pet is gone.

Visits to the veterinarian, groomer, feed store, and parks will end with the pet's death, and bring to a halt the socialization opportunities that the pet provided for the pet parent. The pet's absence may leave a void in the elderly person's daily routine that may go unfulfilled for the rest of his or her life.

Providing a dependent animal with good care and affection does much to bolster the self-esteem of an elderly person. Sometimes the pet represents a kind of "you and me against the world" feeling. Elderly pet parents can lose their self confidence and independence when a pet dies. Bereaved pet parents may choose not to participate in the same activities they did when a pet was alive. They may fear they can't do the things they once did because they no longer have their pets with them for moral support. This was the fear of one elderly pet parent who attended our pet loss support group.

Henry and Brittany. Henry, a 75-year-old retired physician, had been divorced from his wife for 10 years and lived independently in a retirement community. Henry had friends in the retirement community and was involved in activities there during the day. He had two grown children, one who lived near him and one who lived in another state. He arrived at the pet loss support group six weeks after his dog, Brittany, had died in his arms.

Henry and Brittany had been a team. Henry said that with Brittany by his side, he felt as if he could accomplish anything. He acquired the dog when she was three years old from a good friend. He viewed their relationship as unique. He felt certain that no other person shared as strong a bond with another pet as the one he had shared with Brittany. He said Brittany had chosen him, because, when he was getting into his car to leave his friend's house, Brittany had jumped into the vehicle and wouldn't get out. His friend had told him he could keep her, as Brittany had clearly chosen him to be her pet parent.

At home, Brittany had followed Henry wherever he went. When they went for walks, she always stayed by his side. Henry said that her behavior might have annoyed some people, but he enjoyed it. When Brittany was five years old, Henry adopted another dog, Linus, as a playmate for her. He said that another reason he had adopted Linus was so that in the event of Brittany's death, he wouldn't be without a pet.

Brittany and Henry had lived together for 10 years before she was diagnosed with cancer. The dog endured surgery and chemotherapy treatments. When she achieved remission, Henry said that he realized he had few photographs of her. He purchased a camera and discovered that he enjoyed photographing Brittany so much that he began a new hobby—traveling with Brittany and Linus in an RV to photograph many different places.

Henry didn't know what to do with the hundreds of photographs he had taken of the dog. The hobby he had enjoyed was over. It would never be the same again, he said. The group leader acknowledged that it would never be the same, but encouraged Henry not to make any hasty decisions about the photographs of Brittany or about giving up his hobby forever.

Asked to describe their relationship, Henry said that his bond with Brittany was like that of grandfather and granddaughter. His two grown children were childless. He considered Brittany his grand-child. He also said that the unconditional love she had given him was the purest form of love he had ever experienced.

Henry said he had grave doubts that he would survive the loss because his reason for living was gone. When asked if he was con-templating suicide, he said no, but he felt he might become afflicted with a disease that would ultimately kill him as a result of the loss. He cited numerous studies documenting that patients who had suffered a deeply felt loss were more likely to become terminally ill.

Henry returned to the support group the next week. The other group members asked how he was getting along with Linus. Henry replied that Linus had made several attempts to become closer to him. While Brittany was alive, Linus had been very independent. Now Linus seemed to take over many of the roles Brittany had played. He followed Henry everywhere and sat by him. Henry enjoyed this some-what, but felt that in developing a closer relationship with Linus, he was betraying the bond he had shared with Brittany. One of the group members, while validating the fact that the relationship he had shared with Brittany was unique and special, pointed out that it was okay to love more than one dog.

Henry said he felt old, and that he would never be able to have a relationship again in his life like the one he had shared with Brit-tany. He thought he didn't have many years left. He reported that he believed he would never recover from the loss of Brittany. A well-meaning friend had given him a copy of a story about joining our pets in heaven after we die. The group leader asked him again if he was considering suicide. He said no, but that he was hoping he would become terminally ill.

Another group member asked him if he had considered how his children would feel if he were to suddenly die and reminded him that their grief would equal or surpass that which he was currently experi-encing. His eyes opened wide as he realized this possibility.

At the next meeting, Henry said that his daughter had telephoned him recently and told him she had cried all the way to work thinking about what he had said about wanting to become terminally ill and what life would be like without her father. She told him that she loved him. Henry said they had never talked that openly before. He realized just how much his daughter cared about him, and that he didn't want to cause her pain. That was a turning point for Henry.

Henry's pain subsided over several months. During this time he bonded with Linus and the two of them commenced their travels in the RV.

Helping Elderly Clients through Their Grief

Most elderly pet parents have had many experiences with grief and loss. They may have seen animals euthanized in their younger years, and these experiences may not have been good ones, because in years past, many animals were drowned, shot, or died painful lingering deaths. Elderly pet parents may not realize that today euthanasia is performed in a humane way, by injection. In addition to the way pets were killed when they were children, their grief experiences may not have been validated.

A pet's death can provide an opportunity for elderly persons to discuss their fears about their own mortality. Providing care for a terminally ill pet may prompt pet parents to create a living will so as not burden their families or themselves with prolonged care and suffering.

An elderly person seeking support from a therapist may not be forthcoming about the recent loss of a pet. The person may be embarrassed at the depth of his or her grief and feel that the therapist (especially if he or she is younger) cannot possibly understand the value of the relationship with the pet. The elderly may experience increased anxiety, physical or emotional problems, displaced fears, or questions about mortality. An initial visit should include questions about health, physical symptoms (real or imagined), and any pets that have died, are living at home, or have recently been relinquished for adoption. The therapist should ask about the person's ability to care for any animals in the home, and determine whether any recent problems have arisen with regard to the pet's health or care.

For an elderly pet parent whose self-esteem may already be compromised by a dwindling support system and personal health problems, a show of concern and respect for the vulnerabilities that accompany aging and pet loss is deserved and will meet with appreciation.

Elderly people may be on a limited fixed income due to retirement. They may have had to take finances into consideration when facing decisions regarding extensive treatment versus euthanasia for a pet. They may feel guilty for not being able to allocate the funds necessary to pay for a pet's treatment. Pets whose parents cannot afford to pay for medical treatment often are euthanized to prevent suffering. The following case study depicts one couple's decision to authorize euthanasia for their pet because they could not afford additional treatment.

Mr. and Mrs. Bennett and Bethany. Mr. and Mrs. Bennett brought their 12-year-old miniature poodle, Bethany, in for her yearly examination. While examining Bethany's teeth, Dr. Stedman discovered that the dog had severe periodontal disease and several root infections. Dr. Stedman advised teeth cleaning and removal of the infected teeth and a course of antibiotics for the infection.

Bethany was placed under routine anesthesia for the procedure. During the procedure, Bethany's mandible broke. Dr. Stedman had advised the Bennetts that this could happen. He told them it wasn't an uncommon consequence for a small dog with infected teeth and periodontal disease. The Bennetts explained to Dr. Stedman that they lived on a fixed income, and that they could afford the dental procedure but might not be able to pay for additional procedures.

Dr. Stedman offered to donate his services in repairing the jaw, but he would have to refer Bethany to a veterinary dental specialist to remove the remaining teeth. After discussing it, the Bennetts decided they could not pay for a veterinary dental specialist and the cost of additional procedures. Tearfully, they authorized euthanasia for Bethany.

Dr. Stedman talked with the Bennetts after the procedure. He felt bad that the complication, although not unforeseen, had arisen. He acknowledged the Bennetts' love for Bethany and said that he understood their reasons for making the decision to euthanize her.

The Bennetts were forced to make a difficult choice because of their financial situation. Because of the support they received from their veterinarian, they came to terms with their decision and eventually bonded with another pet.

When assisting elderly pet parents who have been the victims of a natural or man-made disaster, special care should be taken in helping them to navigate their way through the many losses they may have endured. The loss of a pet, along with the loss of a home, belongings, and cherished mementos of past life experiences can be devastating to an elderly person. The pet may have been the last significant living being in their life. It is important to help them to find hope and meaning again.

Being separated from a pet that may still be living can be confusing and frustrating as they try to find their beloved companion animal. Appropriate steps should be taken to help the elderly person reunite with his or her pet if at all possible. Making appropriate referrals to a pet loss support group or other pet loss services can help to provide support for elderly people at a time when they are most vulnerable.

Conclusion

The bond shared with a pet can hold significant value for an elderly person. The pet can provide a reason for living, give social and tactile stimuli, and even function as a physical extension of the pet parent, operating as his or her eyes, ears, or legs. Pets afford elderly pet parents a sense of security and companionship that often cannot be found in their human relationships. Pets also can be links to the past, reminding an elderly person of times shared with family and friends who are now gone.

When a pet dies or becomes ill, elderly pet parents may come face-to-face with their own mortality. They may have to accept life without another pet because they live in a facility in which pets are not allowed, they don't have the financial ability to care for a pet, or they fear a new pet would outlive them.

Because a pet may be the focus of an elderly person's entire day, it is important that a therapist carefully assess the bereaved person's emotional status. When a loss is experienced, the therapist will need to provide support and instill hope that the elderly individual will find new meaning and purpose in life, in the absence of a treasured pet.

It is particularly important when working with elderly disaster victims that information about a missing or deceased pet be gathered upon the initial intake form or meeting. Elderly clients need sup-port in working through a loss or help in finding their missing pets. Appropriate referrals should be provided and follow-up care should be done to ensure that the elderly pet parent has pet loss support.

$$7$$

DECIDING TO LOVE A NEW PET

Sammy and Billy share laughter and playtime with their little dog Shirley. Shirley is often treated as a sibling. She came into their lives after they experienced the loss of their big dog Charlie.

> We love the things we love for what they are.
>
> **—Robert Frost**

After a pet loss, many pet parents choose to adopt again. Some even decide to acquire a new pet prior to the impending loss of an elderly or terminally ill pet. Others insist they will never adopt another animal. The decision to bond with a new pet is a personal one. Even if it is obvious to medical professionals that a grieving client will benefit from adopting a new pet, they should never suggest this to him or her. The decision to bond with a new animal should be left solely to the individual experiencing the loss. In addition to their personal wishes, however, the needs of other family members, including remaining pets, must be considered as well.

Each Bond Is Unique

Most people would not even think of suggesting to a grieving widow that she should replace her deceased husband with a new one. Those we love can never be replaced. We can choose to bond again with another person, pet, place, or thing, but we can never *replace* the one lost. Yet the term *replacement* is commonly used when referring to the adoption of a new pet. This suggests that animals can be interchanged; it doesn't acknowledge that the unique bond shared with a particular pet can never be duplicated.

Many pet parents in our pet loss support group have told stories of well-intentioned friends, relatives, and acquaintances who suggest that they "go out and get another pet" to replace the lost one. This attitude usually angers the bereaved pet parents, who then feel they must explain to these well-meaning people what the pet meant to them and how much they loved the pet. The pain and loss they feel is not validated by such suggestions. In fact, suggesting replacement trivializes the pet parent's feelings.

When working with bereaved pet parents, it must first be acknowledged that the bond they shared with a pet was special, significant, and unique. They need to hear that there was only one "Molly" in the world, and that there will never be another exactly like her. Acknowledging the "uniqueness" of the loss gives the bereaved parent permission to openly grieve the loss and ultimately move toward a resolution—at which point acquisition of another pet becomes an option. When the decision is made to acquire another pet, it is important for the pet parent to realize that the bond formed with the new pet will not be exactly like the one shared with the previous pet.

Avoiding Grief by Adopting Again

If a pet parent views a lost pet as replaceable, he or she may use replacement as a way to avoid grieving. This approach usually backfires. If the grieving process for a lost pet was thwarted in some way, it is not likely that a healthy bond will readily form with a new pet.

Pet parents may become discouraged or even angry when the pet they choose doesn't live up to their expectations—expectations based upon the relationship they shared with the previous pet. Often these new pets are neglected, abandoned, relinquished to humane societies, or given away. This can result in even more grief, as pet parents feel guilty that they are unable to love the new pet. They may find that, no matter how hard they try to avoid grieving for a deceased pet, feelings of sadness, despair, anger, and depression still appear.

If a client rushes into a new relationship with another pet, expecting the new bond to be like the one that was lost, the results can be heartbreaking, as the story of Nancy, Princess, and Mason demonstrates.

Nancy, Princess, and Mason. Nancy's children had left home, she had recently gone through a divorce, and she had started a new career. With so many changes, the one constant in her life was the relationship she shared with her Scottish terrier, Princess. Nancy was lovingly and enthusiastically greeted by Princess every time she came through the door. Princess was a source of comfort and joy during some of the most difficult times in Nancy's life.

When Princess became ill and the veterinarian told Nancy that she was experiencing kidney failure, Nancy chose not to take extraordinary measures to lengthen the dog's life. She didn't want Princess to experience discomfort or pain.

Nancy was grief stricken when Princess died at home. Without a dog in the house to protect her, Nancy felt uneasy at night. She was depressed. When she came home from work in the evening, she was overwhelmed by loss and loneliness. One day a co-worker suggested she locate a breeder and adopt another Scottish terrier. Nancy was skeptical, but eager to end the loneliness and fear she felt. She chose a puppy and named him Mason. She brought Mason home, gave him food and water, and left for work.

That night, when she returned home, Mason didn't greet her at the door. She found him in the living room, where he had urinated on her sofa and chewed her slippers to shreds. Nancy was furious. She scolded Mason and told him that Princess never did anything like that.

As the weeks went by, Nancy grew tired of dealing with the demands and responsibilities of owning a puppy. She was constantly reminded of how much Mason was *not* like Princess. She decided that Mason would have to stay in the garage while she was at work.

At night, she felt even more depressed that all the little routines she and Princess had shared were not the same with Mason. He was a very active puppy. He cried for attention and enjoyed running through the house. Nancy missed Princess's demure manners and quiet presence.

Nancy's daughter came to visit and meet Mason. She was shocked to see how little affection her mother displayed for Mason. She knew her mother loved dogs and had treated Princess like her namesake. To Mason, Nancy seemed indifferent and even uncaring.

When she brought this to her mother's attention, Nancy decided her daughter was right. She hadn't bonded with Mason because she had wanted another Princess. She decided to find a new home for Mason and took time to work through the rest of her grief with a therapist.

Working with the therapist, Nancy realized that she was trying to avoid the experience of loss by finding a replacement for Princess. She had not bonded with Mason because of the unresolved feelings of grief she felt for Princess. The therapist told Nancy that once she went through the process of grieving for Princess, she would be in a more favorable position to bond with a new pet.

In *Pet Loss: A Thoughtful Guide for Adults and Children*, Nieburg and Fischer wrote, "Stifling one's emotions by investing energy and love in another pet does not eliminate grief; it merely pushes it into the background and delays its resolution. The sense of loss may take years to dissipate—or it may never disappear" (Nieburg & Fischer, 1982, p. 80).

Therapists should encourage pet parents to answer the following questions when they bring up the subject of acquiring another pet:

- Are you ready for the responsibility of a new pet?
- Do you want to have freedom from the responsibility of caring for another pet?
- Have you resolved your loss?
- Do you feel open to loving and caring for a new pet, or are you trying to avoid grieving for the one that is gone?
- Will you be able to view the new pet as a unique and special being?

- Do you feel as if you are being pressured into getting another pet by family members or friends?
- What would adopting another pet do for you?
- Are you aware that your pet may be entirely dissimilar to the one that is gone? (Nieburg and Fischer, 1982, p. 74)

A therapist may intuitively know when a grieving pet parent is ready to invite another pet into his or her home and life. Having another pet to love can be therapeutic and healing, especially for a person who lives alone and has centered much of his or her life around a pet.

A pet parent may have resolved his or her grief at the loss of a pet, but still feel apprehensive about bonding with another animal. In our practice, we have often heard people say that they couldn't stand having their hearts broken again. Elderly people, especially, often want and need the companionship of another pet but express fears of becoming ill and not being able to care for the pet or of having the pet outlive them. There are ways to gently approach the subject of a new pet; however, if resistance to the idea does not dissipate, the therapist should respect the client's decision. Care must be taken to only suggest and not force the issue. The therapist may need to help support the pet parent in his or her decision to not adopt in the face of opposition from friends and family members, who can be helped to see that the choice to adopt a new pet ultimately lies with the ones experiencing the loss.

Isabella and Mickey. Isabella was grieving the loss of her Persian cat, Mickey, who had been euthanized a week before. Mickey had been the center of Isabella's life for 16 years, ever since she had immigrated to the United States from Italy. In fact, Isabella had named the cat Mickey because he was an American cat and she thought he should have an American name (even though she preferred the name Stefano).

Isabella was accompanied to the group by her daughter Felicia. Felicia was supportive of her mother, acknowledged her heartfelt grief, and validated her loss. However, it was her position that her mother would benefit from adopting another cat right away. She worried that Isabella was lonely and needed the company of a cat.

As Isabella listened to her daughter, she became angry. She told Felicia and the group that there was only one Mickey in the world and he had died. She then burst into tears. As her crying abated, she explained how Mickey would drink milk from a spoon, curl up in her lap to watch their favorite television shows, and sit by the refrigerator when he was hungry to "tell" Isabella to feed him.

Another group member said she understood Isabella's feelings because she would never bond with another pet either. She couldn't endure such intense grief again. That's when Daniel spoke up. He said he had loved his dog Roger, but that the emptiness Roger's death created in his life was a void he wanted and needed to fill. He wasn't planning to look for another dog, but if the right one came his way, he would adopt another pet.

Shortly after Daniel's testimony, Robin joined in the discussion, telling how she had tried to get another bird right after her bird, Feathers, had died. She ended up returning the new bird to the pet shop. She explained that she had wanted another bird just like the one she had lost, and the new one wasn't at all like Feathers.

Isabella chose not to adopt another pet even though her daughter was insistent that she do so. With the support of the therapist, she was able to help her daughter realize that this was not the right time for her even to consider adoption because of her intense loyalty to Mickey and the depth of her feelings over the loss.

A new pet adopted Daniel. A cat wandered into his yard and into his house and refused to leave. When attempts to find the cat's parent failed, Daniel welcomed the cat into his life and bonded with it.

Robin chose not to adopt another bird. She resolved her grief and remained content with her decision not to be a pet parent. When last seen at the group, Robin made known her intentions to travel. This was something she had chosen not to do when she had Feathers.

There are many good reasons for a bereaved pet parent to adopt a new pet. Here is a list of healthy reasons to bond again:

- Companionship
- Affection
- Exercise and social contact
- Protection

- Physical assistance for the disabled
- A need to nurture

However, rushing to get another pet in an attempt to avoid grief is typically a mistake. Here are some unhealthy reasons to get another pet:

- To avoid feeling grief
- To resolve guilt feelings (if the loss is perceived by the client to be his/her fault)
- To appease other family members and meet their needs

The pet parent will know when it is time to bond with a pet again as he or she focuses less on the lost pet and more frequently imagines the benefits of acquiring a new friend to love.

Loyalty Conflicts

Some pet parents report that bonding with another pet would seem like an act of disloyalty toward the deceased pet. They should be told that their feelings are perfectly normal and shared by many others. By openly sharing their beliefs, emotions, and expectations about adopting a new pet, they will better position themselves to make the appropriate decision.

In their book *The Human–Animal Bond and Grief,* Lagoni et al. (1994) wrote that some pet parents take comfort in talking with their new pets about their old ones. They suggested showing the new pet a photo of the deceased pet as a means of introducing the two. When walking the new pet, the pet parent could say, "Rusty and I used to walk this same path every day." This approach may be helpful to people who are working through their disloyalty issues.

Some pet parents may feel silly or uncomfortable doing this. Give them permission to work through their feelings of disloyalty by letting them know that it is *not* silly or unusual to want to share the past with those we love and care for in the present. Remind them that it is okay to have feelings for the deceased pet while bonding with a new pet, but it is important to avoid comparisons that will place the new pet at a disadvantage. New pets need time to adjust to a new family and, as they do so, their unique traits and personalities will emerge, paving the way for bonds of love and loyalty.

Mrs. Epp, Kitty, and Sally. Mrs. Epp, an elderly widow, lived alone with her two cats, Kitty and Sally. Mrs. Epp was very close to Kitty, the older of the two, whom she had acquired while her husband was still living. Kitty slept next to her pillow, responded to her call, and even played fetch with a favorite toy. Kitty was a constant source of companionship and amusement to Mrs. Epp. When Kitty became ill, Mrs. Epp had to euthanize her.

Sally had wandered into the yard five years previously, cold and thin and sick. Mrs. Epp had offered the cat food and lodging, but had planned to turn her out in a day or two. In the end, she had lacked the heart to do so, although she did attempt to find a permanent home for Sally. Sally was quiet and shy; she kept mostly to herself and rarely interacted with Mrs. Epp or Kitty. Despite coaxing, Sally remained timid and aloof.

After Kitty's euthanasia, Mrs. Epp experienced intense loneliness and sorrow. She was angry that her beloved Kitty was gone and Sally, with whom she had no substantial relationship, remained. As the days passed, Mrs. Epp's anger grew rather than dissipated. She felt cheated of her greatest source of comfort and companionship.

About a week after Kitty's death, Mrs. Epp awoke to find Sally watching her from the foot of the bed. She was surprised and somewhat amused, since Sally had never ventured upon the bed before. As the days passed, Sally increasingly ventured closer to Mrs. Epp. One night, about two weeks later, Sally suddenly jumped into Mrs. Epp's lap as she sat watching TV in the living room. In time, Sally began to fill the void left by Kitty's death. Each week more of her personality emerged, and Mrs. Epp discovered she had a friend in Sally. Where previously Sally had existed at the periphery of the family circle, she now saw an opportunity to come closer to Mrs. Epp.

Although Mrs. Epp had determined she would not open her heart to another animal, Sally had made the decision to bond with Mrs. Epp. With Kitty gone, there was space for Sally's personality to surface. As time passed, the bond between Mrs. Epp and Sally grew stronger. Mrs. Epp reminded group members not to overlook a less favored pet when a favored one passes on.

Other Family Members' Needs

Not all family members will choose to bond with another pet, and different members have different needs that must be taken into account. Children should always be included in the decision process (see Chapter 5). Well-intentioned parents may rush to replace a deceased pet with a new one, thinking it will eliminate the grief a child is feeling. This is ill advised. Children who are given a new pet too quickly may feel their loyalty lies with the deceased pet, or they may believe that their parents did not really love the lost animal. It is not uncommon for children who shared a sibling relationship with a pet to wonder how quickly their parents would replace them if they died.

If family members have mixed opinions on adopting another pet, you should draw up a list of pros and cons with each family member. Consider everyone's views and discuss them with the entire family present.

The following suggestions should be given to clients to help assure success in bonding with a new pet:

- Remember that the decision to acquire another pet does not represent disloyalty to a deceased pet.
- Do not expect the pet to become an instant family member. Give the relationship time to develop.
- Bring the new pet home when things are calm. Holidays are not the best time to introduce new pets into the family.
- Don't expect the new pet to be like the deceased pet.
- Allow your feelings for your old pet to surface. If your new pet is doing something that reminds you of your deceased pet, allow yourself to feel and express those feelings.
- Allow other family members to adjust and bond in their own time (Nieburg and Fischer, 1982, p. 84).

Bonding with a New Pet While Anticipating a Loss

The "right time" for acquiring a new pet varies widely among individuals. Some pet parents simply cannot bear the thought of living without a pet. They need their pets for comfort, companionship, and security. People with disabilities often need to acquire a new pet if their service dog is terminally ill. For these individuals, adopting another pet before the death of their current one not only makes sense but is essential for maintaining an acceptable level of independence. The same guidelines apply to others who are anticipating the loss of a pet: They must decide if they are emotionally, physically, and financially able to care for another pet.

If other family members are involved, they should be brought into the discussion regarding the need to bring a new pet into the family before the existing one dies. Otherwise, resentment and loyalty conflicts may arise among family members. Consideration must be given as to whether a new pet in the family would cause unnecessary stress to an elderly or terminally ill pet. All these issues must be addressed before the family agrees to the adoption of another pet.

Some pet parents never experience loyalty conflicts and simply have a deep need to always have a pet. The following case study illustrates this need:

Gloria. Gloria said she couldn't live without a pet. Whenever a pet became elderly or ill, she immediately acquired another one. It wasn't uncommon for Gloria to have three or four pets at a time.

Gloria lived alone and considered her pets family members. She enjoyed the companionship, entertainment, unconditional love, and support they gave her. At one time, Gloria had had only one pet, a golden retriever named Winston. When he died, Gloria was left alone. It was the most traumatic experience with pet loss that she ever endured. Subsequent pet loss experiences were just as painful, but she found comfort in the love and affection her remaining pets provided.

Choosing a New Pet

When an individual or family is ready to bond again, what type of pet should they choose? Some will feel that getting the same breed is, in a sense, replacing the old pet. They may want to choose a different breed altogether to avoid comparisons. Others may want a new pet as much like the old one as possible. This is, of course, a personal decision that must be left to the individual or family.

Mature animals can be perfect pets for elderly people. Older pet parents often worry that they won't have the patience or energy to care for a puppy or kitten. Some fear they will die before the pet does. These are practical, thoughtful concerns. Many humane societies have programs that match elderly pet parents with older pets. These organizations often will provide a new home for the pet if the pet parent becomes unable to care for it. These programs give the elderly a chance to bond with a pet again and give mature animals a chance at adoption they normally would not have (see Chapter 6). Some people, however, do not want to adopt a pet that was raised and was trained by others. These are issues that can be explored with a program director.

Pet parents should be encouraged to research different breeds of animals before adopting. A useful resource for exploring is *The Perfect Puppy; How to Choose Your Dog by Its Behavior*, by Benjamin and Lynette Hart (1988), which describes various breeds and rates them by temperament, trainability, playfulness, destructiveness, and so on. Talking with breeders, knowledgeable staff at animal shelters, and veterinarians also can help pet parents arrive at a decision.

Conclusion

A pet parent stands the best chance of success at bonding with a new pet if he or she has grieved the loss of the previous pet; feels emotionally, financially, and physically able to bond again; and has researched and thought about what kind of pet he or she would like to have. To ensure a positive outcome for the adoption of a new pet, it is important to take into consideration all family members' needs, as well as those of an existing pet.

Respecting the needs of those who choose not to bond again and encouraging them to have friends and family members respect their decision is a must. Animals who are given to grieving pet parents by well-meaning family and friends often end up neglected, returned, or relinquished to another person or humane society.

The acquisition of a new pet should be viewed as a tribute to the love, trust, and companionship shared with the previous pet. When adopting a new animal is viewed in this light, the chances for making painful comparisons are diminished as the probability for successful bonding is enhanced.

8

Behavioral Manifestations of Grief and Loss

Some times people will experience an extreme response to the loss of a pet. This loss may be compounded by other types of losses.

Sometimes, the loss of a pet may trigger unusually intense responses in bereaved pet parents. Normal grief responses, when carried to the extreme, may manifest in maladaptive coping mechanisms and require timely effective crisis intervention in order to prevent the client's progression into self-destructive behavior. Recent U.S. disasters (9/11 and Gulf Coast floods) exposed the need for first responders to be educated about pet loss issues when debriefing victims. The sudden, and sometimes horrific manner in which pets become separated from people during disasters can cause significant trauma to individuals and families who are already struggling with the challenges of day-to-day survival. When the human-companion animal bond is broken, whether the loss is anticipated (as with lingering terminal illness), or sudden (as with accidents or disasters), people may be so traumatized that they are at risk for developing symptoms of serious mental illness. This may also be true for first responders assisting animals in a disaster. When talking with an animal rescue volunteer who worked tirelessly, two weeks after the levees broke, to save the lives of pets abandoned in homes in New Orleans, La., she said that many of the volunteers would run screaming and crying from houses. The scenes they had witnessed, of the last few hours of an animals life, were more than they could stand. Many volunteers went on to develop post traumatic stress disorder (PTSD).

In this chapter, we will present several case studies illustrating "red flags" that should alert pet parents and therapists to the need for immediate intervention. Specific interventions designed to alleviate the despair, anxiety, and guilt related to a pet's death are readily available. Remember that is not uncommon for one to grieve for an animal family member just as intensely as for a human friend or relative. The loss must be acknowledged and validated if the pet parent is to progress through the grief continuum in a timely manner. In order to achieve positive outcomes from therapy, a therapeutic partnership between pet parent and therapist must be built upon recognition of the pet as family member. When the depth of the bond between pet and pet parent is accurately defined by both therapist and client, healthy coping mechanisms can be established and reinforced.

Anger

Anger is a common response among pet parents who have lost or are anticipating losing their pets. In most cases, it is short-lived and dissipates once the pet parent has had time to assimilate all the facts related to the pet's illness or death. For example, a pet parent may initially be angry at the veterinarian because of a missed diagnosis.

When all the facts are established, it may become clear that the cause of death of the pet was due to a new disease process that did not previously present in examination of the pet.

When the anger is projected outward, it serves to protect the pet parent from the impact of his or her own rage. If the pet parent actually engaged in some form of unintentional neglect that contributed to the pet's demise, the associated anger may overwhelm his or her defenses, and the anger may be turned inward.

Those who live at the periphery of mainstream society may not have others around with whom to discuss personal feelings and so may be completely unaware that others have experienced similar feelings of anger and shame. These individuals may experience such intense feelings of self-loathing and loneliness that they entertain thoughts of suicide. A suicidal gesture is a real possibility when a client's unchecked anger progresses toward rage that, previously directed at another, is now turned upon him- or herself.

Some pet parents may be referred for counseling services directly from a veterinarian's or physician's office, from a grief or pet loss support group, by a family member, or by self-referral. A pet parent who expresses despondency over the death of a pet needs to connect with a mental health professional as soon as possible. Delay in seeking services may compound the problem for the pet parent and increase the chances that self-destructive behavior will occur. Psychiatric emergency services, staffed with trained mental health professionals, are available in most counties or large cities. These services are available 24/7 and bereaved pet parents will be kept from harming themselves or others while their needs are assessed and connections with ongoing counseling services are made.

The primary goal of intervention is to keep the pet parent safe while providing an opportunity for verbal expression of anger, fear, guilt, and sorrow. Grieving pet parents need to remember that therapists and counselors can help to alleviate the unpleasant intense emotions related to the loss if an open, honest account of events regarding the loss is presented to the therapist. In the presence of a trained, compassionate therapist, the client should feel that he or she has permission to state feelings without fearing they will be trivialized or discounted. When experiencing an emotional crisis, it is a good idea to be accompanied by a trusted friend to the first therapy session. When emotions are running high, an understanding friend can continue to tell "the story" until the client is composed enough to take over.

Typically, guilt lies at the root of the rage and anger a client is feeling. We will discuss the causes and manifestations of guilt later in this chapter. Therapists should remain alert for danger signals that might warrant an evaluation in a safer, more secure setting. Emergency mental health services can be accessed, if necessary, on an involuntary basis. Steps to securing these services for someone who is judged to be a danger to themselves or to another person are spelled out in state and local mental health laws. Be familiar with laws in your state that allow you to call for emergency psychiatric services for your client, even if you must do so against the client's wishes.

Mrs. Wilson and Sheba. Mrs. Wilson, a widow in her mid-70s, took her long-haired eight-year-old cat to be groomed at the veterinary clinic. She dropped Sheba off in the morning and was told to come back for her at closing time. Sheba always received a general anesthetic for this procedure because she would not tolerate it otherwise.

Mrs. Wilson arrived at the veterinary office promptly at closing time. She paid the bill and waited for the receptionist to return with Sheba. When the receptionist returned, she told Mrs. Wilson that the cat was still very groggy and suggested that Mrs. Wilson leave her at the clinic for the night, although there wouldn't be anyone at the clinic that evening to observe her. Mrs. Wilson decided that Sheba would be safer on her lap at home than alone at the clinic. She asked to speak with the veterinarian about Sheba's procedure, but the veterinarian was with another patient and unavailable, so Mrs. Wilson took Sheba home. She was concerned about the cat's condition and frustrated with the veterinarian for not being available.

Three hours after returning home, Sheba was wandering around the house still looking dazed and confused. Mrs. Wilson's attempts to comfort her had no effect. Ninety minutes later, Sheba darted underneath the sofa in the living room, suffered what appeared to be a mild seizure, and died.

Mrs. Wilson was stricken with grief and despair. The next day, she attempted to speak with the veterinarian, but he did not return her calls. In fact, she was unable to elicit any response of concern or explanation from anyone at the veterinary clinic. In desperation, she contacted the local humane society, which referred her to a local pet loss support group.

When Mrs. Wilson arrived at group, she was barely able to contain the rage she felt at the unexplained loss of her best friend and only remaining family member. She was alternately tearful then enraged at the veterinarian. She blamed herself for taking Sheba home, and talked of suicidal feelings with which she could barely cope.

Other group members validated Mrs. Wilson's feelings of rage and helped her to see the futility of harming herself. They encouraged her, instead, to persist in her attempts to contact the veterinarian for an explanation of the events and to write a letter to the local veterinary peer review committee.

The group meetings provided Mrs. Wilson with a source of support and understanding she was unable to find elsewhere. Writing the letter gave her a focus outside herself and allowed her to express her feelings in a more articulate, goal-directed manner. She was contacted by the peer review board, which intervened on her behalf with the veterinary clinic in question.

By taking definitive action, Mrs. Wilson was able to channel her anger into healthier activities and, in time, the anger dissipated, giving way to sadness and loneliness. Mrs. Wilson attended the group for several months. A year later, she notified the group leader that she had adopted a new kitten from the humane society that had originally referred her to the group. She was once again embracing life and the new little friend that had come to live with her.

Prolonged Despair

Persistent despair—that is, loss of all hope that things will ever be good or feel good again—is not part of the normal grief response. It requires the attention of a skilled therapist who can quickly identify where the client has gotten "stuck" and what will be most effective in moving him or her out of it quickly.

A pet parent who has a weak or absent support system may regard a pet as the only being who truly cares if he or she lives or dies. Once the pet is gone, the pet parent may feel such intense loneliness that his or her will to participate in normal activities is seriously depleted. In addition, guilt associated with the death of the pet can so damage a pet parent's self-esteem that he or she may disengage from social commitments, break off personal relationships, and even jeopardize his or her livelihood by failing to report to work.

Arlene and Bentley. Arlene had experienced the death of her eight-year-old chocolate lab, Bentley, a month prior to attending the pet loss support group. Bentley had cancer, and after exhausting treatment options over the past several months, Arlene had chosen to euthanize him at home. During group she mentioned that she was not able to sleep through the night. She would easily fall asleep and then awake three hours later and then be unable to return to sleep. Upon further questioning by the therapist, she mentioned that Bentley had been very ill for the last three months of his life. He slept in her room and would often "have an accident," soiling himself with diarrhea three hours after going to bed. Arlene would get up, clean up the mess, and bathe Bentley. This took her more than hour to do. After she finished, they would return to sleep for another four hours. Since his death, she was waking up at the same time she had needed to attend to him. She was so distraught at the painful reminder that he was no longer there that she would be unable to return to sleep.

The sleep deprivation she endured over the past few months was causing her to feel extremely fatigued during the day. She was unable to shower or get dressed until late in the afternoon. She asked the therapist if she would ever feel better again. The therapist reassured her that she would, and together, they create a plan in which to assist her in moving forward through the grief continuum.

The therapist asked Arlene if she had seen her family physician recently or had worked with another therapist in the past. She stated that she had seen a therapist three years ago when her adult daughter committed suicide. Arlene then shared the fact that the death of Bentley was bringing up feelings about the loss of her daughter. She said that she didn't know why her successful, intelligent daughter had chosen to take her life. She said that she had busied herself with the business of taking care of her daughter's affairs and attending to

Bentley, who had endured life-threatening health problems on and off since her daughter's death. Arlene said that Bentley's health care had been an ongoing project in her life and that everything came to a halt when Bentley died. Suddenly, she was taken out of caretaker mode and didn't know what to do with the free time she had. She admitted to feeling anxious, depressed, and overwhelmed by her emotions. While she did have friends who came to see her and helped her to plan a memorial for Bentley, she lived alone on some property a good distance from town.

The therapist explained to Arlene that she needed to make herself her "project" now. She congratulated her for finding the will and energy to attend the pet loss support group. She also asked her to call her physician to make an appointment for a checkup. The therapist suggested that she be screened for depression and that she contact her former therapist. The therapist and Arlene discussed the importance of taking care of her own needs, getting enough sleep and rest, eating right, and continuing to work through her losses.

The other attendees in the support group reminded Arlene that Bentley wouldn't want her to suffer and would want to see her happy. One of the other women in the group, Katherine, shared that she too had felt at a complete loss when her dog died. Arlene and Katherine bonded at the group. Both women had similar life experiences, having lost children, gone through divorces, and suffered the death of their dogs. Both women lived alone, and both were struggling to find a way through the loss of their beloved companions.

Arlene promised to contact her physician the next day. She also said that she would be returning to the pet loss support group the following week.

Substance Abuse

In both group and individual sessions you will occasionally encounter clients who have a primary or secondary problem with substance abuse (e.g., alcohol, prescription drugs, or illegal substances). Because alcohol is relatively inexpensive and readily available, it frequently is the drug of choice during a crisis. It also is the most easily detectable. The classic symptoms of odor on the breath, slurred speech, and compromised gait are the hallmarks of alcohol intoxication. Most therapists do not see individuals who are intoxicated unless an emergency situation exists, at which point contact should be brief, with firm limits set regarding future sessions and alcohol or substance use.

Grieving pet parents may be tempted to use alcohol to soften the edges of reality during periods of intense sorrow or loneliness. This may produce a short-lived feeling of euphoria, but continued consumption often leads to dysphoria accompanied by reality distortions, impaired judgment, and sleep disturbances. The loss of sleep can further reduce the ability to cope with the emotional roller coaster that embodies the grief process.

Therapists should raise the issue of substance abuse with these clients and educate them to the detrimental effects that will complicate and interfere with their recovery. Once substance or alcohol abuse has been identified as a problem, referrals to substance abuse programs such as 12-step programs would be appropriate. There are many agencies, low- or no-cost, that deal with issues of drug and alcohol dependence. One cannot effectively work through the grief continuum until substance abuse issues have been addressed.

Bill and Beatrice. Bill, a 48-year-old divorced man, came to the pet loss support group after his one-year-old kitten, Beatrice, was run over in front of his house. Bill had adopted Beatrice when he found her on the sidewalk, alone, hungry, and shivering, on a cold winter night when she was only six weeks old.

Bill revealed little of himself at group. When he spoke, he appeared distraught. He sobbed as other group members spoke, and he made infrequent and poor eye contact with the group leader and members. At the end of the meeting, he told everyone that he blamed himself for Beatrice's death. She had died, he said, because he had let her outside the night she was killed. The group leader gave Bill the phone number of the local psychiatric emergency clinic and encouraged him to attend group the following week.

Bill returned to the group, and gradually he began to trust the others enough to talk about what the loss of his kitten represented to him. He had never obtained closure on his divorce 15 years earlier; he had few friends and no support system. He tearfully reported that since his two grown children had moved away, his kitten had become the central figure in his life. She made him feel needed and loved. He blamed himself for not being able to keep his marriage and family intact. He already suffered from low self-esteem; now unresolved issues related to the divorce combined with guilt over the kitten's death.

Eight weeks later, it became apparent that Bill had a drinking problem. On one occasion he was asked to leave the group meeting because he was intoxicated. Later, when confronted by the group leader, Bill denied any problem with alcohol. "Even though I drink every day I always show up for work. Drinking is not a problem for me," he insisted.

Bill was told that he could only attend group when sober. During the following weeks, Bill was unable to stem the tide of tears that overtook him whenever he talked about Beatrice. He remembered how helpless and alone she had been on the night he rescued her from the street, and he cried every time he thought of her dying alone in the gutter by his house. He continued to blame himself for not keeping her indoors, even though Beatrice had loved to explore outdoors. He clung tenaciously to his guilt, despite the efforts of group members to dislodge it.

Bill attended group for six months, finding comfort and support in the company of other bereaved pet parents. However, Bill stayed stuck in the sorrow phase of his grief because of his alcohol consumption and his unwillingness to accept a referral for individual therapy and 12-step programs. As a middle-aged, divorced, isolated alcoholic (in denial), Bill's profile matched the clinical criteria for probability of self-harm. Individual therapy would have afforded him the opportunity to differentiate between losses, handle disappointment and sadness related to his failed marriage, and come to terms with the recent loss of the kitten that had come to represent his family.

Guilt

Guilt feelings are reported by nearly all those who have lost or are anticipating the loss of a cherished pet. Guilt also poses the greatest obstacle to the client's attainment of resolution of the loss. It is important to focus on alleviating guilt feelings as early as possible in your professional relationship with the client. Common themes that elicit intense guilt feelings include these:

- Bad timing for the euthanasia. "I waited too long. She suffered because of me." Or, "I should have waited to see if he would get better. Maybe he would have rallied."
- Failure to detect symptoms early in the course of an illness, resulting in the delay of diagnosis and treatment. Sometimes the pet parent blames the veterinarian for this.
- Lack of funds to pursue expensive heroic treatment. Pet parents often feel ashamed and angry with themselves if they cannot provide for their pets.
- Inability to be present during the euthanasia procedure. In retrospect, many pet parents experience a sense of inadequacy at not being able to provide comfort and support for their pets during their last moments of life.
- Contributing to the events leading to a fatal accident (e.g., failure to lock a gate or door; walking the dog without a leash; forgetting to put away toxic substances). The pet parent's contribution to the tragedy may be real or imagined.

Those experiencing guilt must be reminded that they did all that was within their means to assure the best care and treatment for their pets. They need to know that each decision along the way was made out of love and concern for their pet and was, therefore, the best decision that could be made at the time.

For example, pet parents who are unable to afford extensive treatment for their pets must be helped to know that they did all they could within their means to assure the best care possible. The therapist can validate their feelings of inadequacy and sadness by acknowledging that decision-making is very difficult in these situations. In reality, pet parents should harbor no guilt for failure to pursue costly tests and treatment that they cannot afford and that would compromise their ability to pay for everyday necessities for themselves or their families. In emotionally laden situations, where passions run high and a pet's life hangs in the balance, people need to pursue commonsense solutions to their pet's medical problems, making treatment choices they can afford and that promise relatively positive outcomes. The pursuit of

expensive heroic treatment modalities must be weighed against afford-
ability and the pet's prognosis both with and without treatment.

Similarly, clients who agonize over the timing of the euthanasia
need the therapist to reframe the events and decisions at the last stages
of the pet's life. Most devoted pet parents instinctively know when
their pets are suffering. Some cling to denial and false hope to delay
making the decision, but most do make the right decision at the right
time. It is typical of pet parents to second-guess their actions when
they have had time to step back and review the course of events of the
often chaotic final days of their pet's illness and physical decline.

It is of the utmost importance that therapists and clients understand that, in a time of crisis, pet parents make the best possible decisions for their sick or injured pets, often in the middle of the night and
under a great deal of emotional stress. These decisions, regardless of
the outcome, are decisions made out of love and concern for the pet's
well-being, and guilty feelings do not belong in this picture. Guilt is
the enemy of healing. Clients who accept that their decisions were the
best they could make at the time will be able to jump the hurdle of
guilt that stands between them and resolution of their loss. In therapy,
pet parents are given the opportunity to forgive themselves for making
decisions that did not turn out as hoped. It is a fact of life that good
choices sometimes lead to bad outcomes. Once pet parents recognize
and accept that their choices were made out of genuine love for their
pets, they will be able to forgive themselves and move on.

Compound Loss

Faced with the loss of a pet, a pet parent often is reminded (either
while awake or in dreams) of other losses from the past, both human
and animal. This compounded effect of past, present, and anticipated
loss can feel overwhelming to grieving pet parents who may seem
confused by the sheer power of the grief being experienced. In these
cases, they may be unaware that they are experiencing multiple losses
simultaneously. Previous losses must be taken into account when
assessing the impact of the current loss on the pet parent. Past reactions to divorce and deaths of loved ones (including pets) should be
considered. A pet parent who seems unable to progress through the

grief process may be reacting to previous losses for which closure was not effectively attained. A client may be experiencing several losses simultaneously or may unconsciously be recalling unresolved losses from years ago.

Clients may need help in identifying the past and concurrent losses that may be "contaminating" their progress in therapy. As losses accumulate over the years, they often go unacknowledged until something in the present stirs them. When a pet loss threatens or occurs, losses from the past, both resolved and unresolved, rear up and call out, "Remember me? I'm important, too. I deserve some attention. What about me?" Clients may not recognize these intrusive, unbidden memories and sensations for what they are; they may simply know they are feeling overwhelmed and unable to cope with their emotions.

In therapy, the client may sort through previous losses and identify coping mechanisms that were helpful during that stressful period. Guilt often is the source of unresolved grief. As a therapist works to eradicate the guilt associated with the current loss, he or she may apply the same techniques toward resolution of the old ones.

Clients harboring excessive guilt may exhibit intense grief responses, including these:

- Unremitting tearfulness that cannot be controlled by imposing will, after several weeks or months have passed
- Sleep pattern disruption
  - Inability to fall asleep accompanied by excessive anxiety and worry
  - Early morning awakening; inability to fall back asleep
  - Nightmares
- Appetite fluctuations
- Increase in alcohol or prescription drug use, or use of illicit substances to control symptoms noted above
- Social isolation (previously enjoyable activities no longer pursued), friendships neglected
- Decline of performance at work or school
- Rage projected outward, or the urge to kill another (homicidal); or rage project inward at oneself (suicidal)

One or more of these grief responses should alert pet parents to seek counseling as soon as possible so that a thorough assessment of symptoms can be made. When negative thoughts and emotions are allowed to continue unabated, the mental status of the grieving individual may deteriorate to the point that emergency intervention is required.

Suicidal Clients

In a recent group session of six participants, Rhonda shared that she lost an adult son to suicide in the past and that, upon the recent death of her 12-year-old dog, she had entertained thoughts of suicide. She had recently adopted and bonded with a new dog and reported feeling more emotionally secure. She was forthright with the group regarding these sensitive issues and, fortunately, had never acted upon her suicidal ideation.

Rhonda told the group that she was getting her affairs in order (she had met with an attorney to create a will), and had been formulating a plan to take sleeping pills when she began attending the group a month earlier. She explained that the support of her closest friends, who she said stayed by her side and frequently checked in with her, and attending the group helped support her through the darkest part of her grief. It was also during the first few group sessions that, although she did not mention her intent to commit suicide, the group leader discovered that she had been having difficulty sleeping and concentrating. Rhonda told the group leader at the end of the meeting that a private therapist was helpful to her after her son's death. The group leader strongly suggested that she reconnect with that therapist and inform her of this most recent significant loss. The group leader attempted to elicit a promise from her that she would contact the therapist and let her know that she had endured another loss. She also encouraged her to see her family physician for a checkup and to disclose her loss and her inability to sleep and to concentrate. The client promised. However, she admitted that she had never followed through.

Rhonda's disclosure of her suicidal ideation opened the door for other group members to share their thoughts and feelings about suicide. Many of the members shared that they too had wanted to die and "go be with their pets," in the first weeks following the death of their pets. They also declared that while they had these thoughts and feelings, they would never act upon them. One woman, Jessie, had a near-death experience when she was involved in an accident that precipitated cardiac arrest. She told the group while she "knows for certain," there is another place beyond this one, she isn't certain that she would be able to be with her pet again if she chose to take her own life.

That night, the group validated the self-destructive thoughts that one can experience when dealing with the intense grief associated with loss. They acknowledged that, although suicide may seem an option for some, there are a variety of life-affirming ways to cope with the feelings of hopelessness, helplessness, and desperation that may surface during an acute grief reaction. By inviting the topic of suicide into the discussion, group members validated the darker side of the grief response. They discussed ways in which they could be more supportive of one another and identified a variety of healthy coping mechanisms that could serve to displace thoughts of suicide. From this open discussion of challenging issues, the group gained valuable insight and the reassurance that even an intense grief response will resolve over time, and that positive outcomes can be achieved.

Therapists unskilled in suicide assessment will need to make rapid referrals to appropriate agencies or individuals to assure the safety of their clients in these cases. Sometimes a pet parent may not be forthcoming about his or her intent to self-harm, and key questions with regard to plan, means, and prior history should be asked.

Nora. In the middle of the night the answering service forwarded the call to the therapist's home. A frantic voice yelled, "Help me! Help me! My baby is dead!" The female voice on the line repeated these words, and the therapist was unable to calm the caller enough to engage her in meaningful conversation.

Finally, the therapist shouted, "Did you call 911?"

The caller answered, "The police are not going to respond to a call about a dead cat."

The therapist now spoke softly, forcing the caller to calm herself. The therapist calmly asked that the caller, Nora, state her address and then tell her story from the beginning, so that she could piece together the events leading to the death of the cat. Nora's speech seemed somewhat slurred, and the therapist asked her about recent alcohol consumption. Nora had previously participated in 12-step programs for alcohol and drug abuse, but did not currently have a program sponsor.

Nora went on to say that she could not imagine life without her cat. She had no one in her life who really cared about her, she said, and her cat, 2-year-old Sunshine, was her reason for getting up in the morning and getting through each day. Now she wanted only to dull the pain caused by her pet's death and to muster the courage to dispose of Sunshine's body in the morning.

When questioned about suicidal ideation, Nora began sobbing anew and revealed that she was losing an ongoing battle for custody of her young son, Anthony, who was currently in foster care. She reported being so tired of surviving with the bare necessities provided by welfare that she didn't feel like fighting anymore.

"What's the use?" she asked tearfully. "Nothing's ever going to change anyway." First Tony and now Sunny had been taken from her, and she believed her loneliness would prove unbearable.

The therapist attempted to extract a promise from Nora that she would not harm herself but would speak the next day with someone who would help her through the initial phases of her grief and formulate an immediate plan for getting through the difficult time she faced. She told Nora about the 24-hour mental health emergency services and provided her with the contact information.

Because she had no previous contacts with this client, the therapist did not push Nora for a "no self-harm contract." Instead, she explained that she was so concerned about Nora's well-being that she was going to request that the police perform a welfare check on Nora. She explained that the police would transport her to the mental health clinic for a thorough evaluation of her emotional status if they deemed it necessary. Although initially angered by this suggestion, Nora finally heard that her random telephone call to the therapist would be taken seriously, and that the therapist truly did not want any harm to come to her.

In this case, the therapist determined the need for immediate intervention because of the caller's alcohol consumption, grief over her current loss, absent son, and lack of hope that her situation could ever improve. Although the therapist hinted at a "no self-harm verbal contract," verbal or written contracts are of little value in the absence of a well-established client–therapist relationship.

According to Martin Rubin, medical director of Sonoma County's Mental Health Department in Santa Rosa, California, "Contracts can give a false sense of security to a therapist and can never replace a thorough evaluation for suicide risk."

In assessing a client for intent to self-harm, the following guidelines always apply:

- Ask the client directly if he or she is contemplating suicide.
- Ask if he or she has a plan.
- Establish whether the client has the means to carry out the plan (e.g., medication, a gun, a knife).

It is important to remember, also, that some factors increase the probability of suicide:

- Women are more likely to attempt suicide, but men are more likely to be successful.
- Suicide is the second leading cause of death for young adults and for adolescents between the ages of 15 and 19.
- Alcohol and substance abuse and previous suicide gestures place a client at greater risk for self-harm.
- A sense of hopelessness is a significant predictor of suicide.

According to psychiatrist Pat Hannan, clients who entertain suicidal thoughts see suicide as a means of ending their suffering, and they need to be reassured that their pain will not last forever. Things can and do change; pain eventually subsides. Anyone experiencing suicidal ideation should be reminded of the severe negative impact that this act would have upon family members and loved ones left behind.

Grieving pet parents may feel up one day and down the next; they may suddenly burst into tears, cry, and then feel better. Depressed individuals often find that formerly pleasurable activities no longer bring them joy. They become exhausted from struggling to perform day-to-day routines. As they begin to recover, they may have periods of increased physical energy even though emotionally they still feel hopeless. As energy levels increase, they may still feel depressed and anxious but now have the energy to act out their plan. In some cases of clinical depression, a referral to a psychiatrist for thorough medication evaluation is an essential part of a therapeutic treatment plan.

The therapist must recognize that the loss of a cherished pet poses the same risk for self-harm and acting-out behaviors for the pet parent as the loss through death or divorce of a human family member. Although not all who experience pet loss view their pets as family members, many do. Expressions of their pain must be taken seriously, as must declarations of intent to follow their pets in death. In a society where human life and relationships seem more vulnerable and fragile than ever, the bonds people form with their pets take on new importance. When the bond is broken, a bereaved pet parent may turn to thoughts of self-harm or suicide.

Unusual Presentations

Because any psychiatric condition—including anxiety, depression, and thought disorders—may be exacerbated by sudden loss, therapists will occasionally encounter individuals with unusual presentation in both individual and group therapy settings. Nonclinicians may experience a great deal of anxiety when confronted with unusual symptoms. It is important for therapists to accurately assess the presenting symptoms and make appropriate referrals if the required services are beyond one's scope of practice or area of expertise.

If it is determined that a grieving pet parent may need medication or a more thorough suicide assessment, the therapist should make the appointment for the client and verify his or her mode of transportation. The individual should be accompanied by a friend or family member to the appointment if possible. The therapist should contact the client by phone later the same day to reassess the situation and to reinforce the importance of the consultation. Most state laws allow for police transport of unwilling individuals to designated mental health facilities for evaluation. The police should not be called unless the individual refuses to seek recommended services and has been deemed by a therapist to be an imminent danger to him- or herself or to others.

Mr. X. One night, a disheveled, anxious young man burst through the office door demanding to see the "doctor who ran the pet group." The therapist was alone in an interior office of a three-story building. No one else had showed up for the group that night and no one was in the building. The man, about 30 years old, paced the room briskly, repeating that he needed to see the doctor. The therapist informed him that she was a licensed marriage and family counselor who conducted the group. She invited him to sit down and tell her his story. He stopped pacing, looked into the corners of the room, and cautiously took a seat opposite her.

The man refused to give his name, so the therapist labeled him Mr. X. He explained that he was a loner who spent his time traveling the country in a camper with five dogs, that he thought of as family. His permanent home was a cabin deep in the woods on a large piece of property owned by his parents. He did not support himself financially. It became apparent in the course of conversation that he lived off family money supplemented by Social Security Disability Insurance.

Mr. X reported that, six months earlier, one of his dogs had died of old age. He had brought the dog's body to his cabin, which had no electricity, and placed it in a deep freezer. He made frequent trips to town to replenish the ice that kept the body from rapid decomposition. He said that his religious beliefs prevented cremation or burial of the dog's body, and that ordinarily he would have allowed the body to decompose on the ground—but he could not do so with this dog because they had shared a special relationship.

He said that the dog continued to speak to him from the freezer at night, when Mr. X was feeling lonely. He was not troubled by the "exchange of thoughts" with the dead dog, but was concerned that keeping the animal's body in a deep freezer might be illegal. He did not want to get arrested by the police. He also was becoming weary of hauling ice to the freezer, and felt it might be time to allow the dog's body to decompose naturally, as he had always done when other pets died. Mr. X. knew that, once removed, his dog's body would decompose rapidly, and he was sad that he would lose his pet's companionship and the benefits of his wisdom, which he shared so willingly with Mr. X. from the freezer.

The therapist told Mr. X. that she didn't know the legal implications of keeping the body of a dead pet in a freezer at home. She did say that the relationship he shared with his dead pet was rather unusual and that, given the concern and anxiety this was now causing, it seemed the time had come to allow his pet's body to "move on." He acknowledged that his love and respect for animals in general, and his dogs in particular, was true and unshakable. He said that he found animals to be trustworthy, predictable, and unconditional in their return of affection and loyalty, and that this had not been his experience with people. He implored the group leader not to see him as "crazy" but as someone who revered animal life forms, who would never cause harm or pain to any animal.

As the conversation progressed, Mr. X's eye contact with the therapist improved and he seemed to physically relax. His feelings and beliefs were validated, and no value judgment related to his dog's body "on ice" was made. Mr. X. spoke convincingly of his reverence for animals both living and dead. Though exhibiting symptoms of thought disorder, Mr. X was not dangerous. He never gave his name or address to the therapist, and she saw no basis upon which to file a police report.

It is important that the therapist, either in a group or individual setting, allow space for pet parents to express feelings and points of view that may sound bizarre, outlandish, or even somewhat frightening, without concluding that an extreme intervention is required (i.e., involuntary evaluation with police facilitation). Pet parents often have the same sense of love, loyalty, and devotion to their pets as others do for spouses, children, siblings, and friends.

Those who engage in an active fantasy life with regard to the demise of a pet often need assistance in sorting out reality from fantasy. Depending upon their religious beliefs about the afterlife, pet parents may express ideas that run counter to the therapist's own beliefs.

In general, if an individual is functioning—that is, providing for his or her own food, clothing, and shelter or able to use that provided by others—and the therapist assesses that he or she is not a danger to him- or herself or to others, including pets and animals under his or her care, then the therapist's basic intervention is to support the behaviors that are working well and to validate feelings associated with the loss. Mr. X. agreed that it was time to allow his pet's body to move on. Although he claimed to be "tired of running to town for ice," he was more preoccupied with doing what was right. He did not return to group again, but he thanked the group leader for helping him make a decision with which he'd been struggling.

Clients Who Have Difficulty Letting Go of the Pet's Body

Similar to the story of Mr. X., occasionally we have assisted clients in the group setting who were experiencing difficulty in letting go of an animal's body after death. One man kept his dog's body on ice, in his home, for more than a month. Another pet loss support group attendee kept her small dog's body in her kitchen freezer for six months. Although both of these clients recognized that their pets were dead and that only the body remained, they were unwilling to surrender the body to cremation or burial. The pet loss support group leader, with the help of group members, gently and effectively assisted these clients in formulating a plan for relinquishing the bodies of their pets.

Heather, kept her dog Cuddles on a velvet pillow in her freezer. She would take Cuddles' body out of the freezer each night, hold her, and pet her on the pillow. She told the group leader that she was careful to not keep the body out too long for fear it would defrost.

Stephen, kept his dog, Pip, on ice packs in his living room. He admitted to having had difficulty letting go of other pets' bodies in the past. He shared a story of having taken his first dog's body to the humane society and witnessing the mishandling of the body. He said that a humane society worker placed the dog's body on the floor and shoved it into a corner with his foot. Stephen was horrified that the man would do this. He also shared his concern (not an uncommon one among pet parents) that if he were to have his dog cremated it would be part of a mass cremation and that his dog's ashes would become mixed with the ashes of other animals.

In both of these cases, the group leader worked with the clients to help them understand that their pet's bodies, although kept cold, would continue to decompose and that they might see something that would most likely be upsetting (like the pet's limb snapping off or other bodily decomposition). She asked them what they would like their memories of their pet to be. She also helped them to create "a plan of trust," in which they were able to let go of the body. For example, Heather allowed her sister to help with a "goodbye ceremony" and burial plan for Cuddles. It was agreed that Heather and her sister together would transfer Cuddles' body to her veterinarian's office. The office would then have Cuddles transported to a pet cemetery for a private cremation. Two weeks after the cremation, Heather received Cuddles' remains in a cedar box.

To best assist clients who are having difficulty making a decision about the disposition of their pet's body, the therapist should question the client closely about specific issues related to relinquishing the body. The client may harbor irrational fears or superstitions with regard to the physical or spiritual aspects of death. Once these issues are explored with the client and thoroughly understood, the therapist can validate the client's feelings, gain his or her trust, and be of assistance in creating a plan for surrender and disposition of the body. If the client is not forthcoming about underlying issues, various therapeutic interventions, such as art therapy and hypnosis, may be employed to assist in breaking through barriers of resistance.

The Animal Collector

Therapists may encounter an animal collector who has become sad or depressed because of the loss or anticipated loss of one or more pets in his or her care. In the course of conversation, the individual may disclose that he or she owns many pets, perhaps 20 or more. For pet collectors, reducing the overall number of pets for which they are responsible is usually not an acceptable option. Often the pet parent's self-identification is dependent upon owning and caring for more animals than he or she could possibly care for adequately. Such persons generally refuse to or are unable to acknowledge that many of the animals in their custody are victims of gross neglect.

Animal collectors proclaim themselves "animal lovers" and perceive reverence for life as synonymous with preservation of life, regardless of its quality. They have a hero–martyr complex that extols their personal sacrifices on behalf of helpless animals. They are extremely controlling of every aspect of the animals' lives, stubbornly refusing to part with any of them, be it through adoption of the relatively healthy or euthanasia of the terminally sick. Animal collectors steadfastly believe that animals can be perfectly happy in squalid surroundings, since any kind of life is preferable to death. Even after being cited for or convicted of cruelty to animals, these people often return to animal collecting (Lagoni et al., 1994, p. 19).

Animal collectors need to be helped to see that their reasoning is faulty in several areas. They need to look at their policy of "life at all costs" from the perspective of the animal and animal caregivers, who would certainly maintain a different, more humane position. They must be helped to identify the relationship between animal collecting and his or her own self-worth—which has been, "the more animals I save (collect), the better (more valuable) person I am."

The real work for therapist and animal collector lies in identifying the developmental voids and personality deficits that are being glossed over with the time-consuming care of too many animals, none of which can be truly well cared for and most of which are neglected or abused. The therapist must be prepared to encounter anger from the animal collector as his or her illusions are broken down and gradually replaced by a more realistic picture of the situation (see Chapter 1).

Conclusion

Most pet parents experiencing grief due to pet loss, whether sudden or anticipated, need a safe place to cry, to give voice to their emotions, and to have their feelings validated by someone who understands. They have lost a family member, a best friend, a constant companion, and a confidante. The loss of unconditional love can lead to a loss of hope that the void can ever be filled. Guilt feelings and the effects of compound loss undermine coping skills and may significantly lower self-esteem.

Whether seen in individual or group therapy settings, in psychiatric or medical inpatient units, or in conjunction with a hospice or animal health care agencies, therapists will have the opportunity to provide services to those whose lives have been enriched by the companionship of animals and who suffer when the bonds are broken.

The loss of a cherished pet can exacerbate preexisting psychiatric conditions, and the importance of thoroughly assessing risk for self-harm cannot be overstated. When the picture includes suspected or admitted drug or alcohol abuse, interventions should include referral to specialty programs or agencies in conjunction with specific interventions aimed at alleviating grief symptoms. Consultations for medication evaluation should be made expeditiously.

Therapists should assist with obtaining referrals for individuals in distress, verify their transportation, and make telephone contact periodically until the crisis phase has passed. Police assistance should be requested only when it is suspected that an individual poses an imminent danger to him- or herself or to others and when voluntary referrals for assistance have been refused.

9

ASSISTING ANIMAL CARE PROFESSIONALS

The very nature of the job often involves death and dying experiences. This is true of veterinarians who provide euthanasia services for their patients. During natural disasters, animal care workers are especially vulnerable to experiencing trauma when assisting in a devastating situation.

Pet loss affects not only pet parents but all people who work in the animal care profession. Like a pebble dropped in a pond, the ripple effect created by the loss can touch police, firefighters, veterinarians, their staff, humane society workers, groomers, pet shop employees, zookeepers, wildlife and domestic animal rescue volunteers, and animal trainers. It is well documented that any professional who works with animals is at risk for developing emotional attachments to them. All are vulnerable to experiencing grief and loss when the bond is broken with animals in their care.

In this chapter, we will discuss specific ways to help animal care professionals in their work environment. Therapists can help professionals avoid the burnout, so common in these occupations, by teaching stress reduction techniques and by developing inter-office support. Several case examples are included to help therapists better understand the unique stresses experienced by animal care professionals.

Helping the Veterinary Community

Veterinarians experience a stress unknown to other medical practitioners in this country: euthanasia is an acceptable and legal means of terminating an animal's life and, because pets generally live one-fifth the lifespan of people, veterinarians are faced with the deaths of their patients on a more frequent basis than most physicians.

Most people in veterinary medicine enter the field out of a love for animals. But few veterinarians and staff members consider the effect of patient loss on themselves when they decide to practice (Pettit, 1994, p. 154).

Most veterinarians and their staff have not been taught counseling skills. When helping bereaved pet parents, staff members may experience counter-transference. They may need help sorting out their emotions while responding appropriately to a client's needs. Educating veterinary medical practitioners and their staff on self-care techniques and appropriate client interventions will help them develop coping skills and maintain comfortable boundaries.

In the past several years, published material, courses, and seminars on pet loss have been made available to animal care professionals and support staff. Although not trained therapists, veterinarians and support staff often are placed in the position of offering grief counseling to pet parents. Staff who are not skilled at or comfortable with providing emotional support to their clients are at risk for feeling frustrated and burned out in their chosen profession. Therapists can provide veterinary staff with simple guidelines for establishing a supportive, caring environment for grieving clients:

- Provide facial tissues in any place a bereaved pet parent may need them.
- Schedule appointments to allow for additional time to be spent with a grieving pet parent.
- Create a brochure that includes all available support information (pet loss support groups, private therapists, hotlines, burial information, literature on pet loss, etc.). These brochures should be available to clients anticipating, as well as those experiencing a loss.
- Send a card or flower immediately after the loss. Late arrivals can be painful reminders for clients.
- Collect any fees owed before the pet is euthanized or relinquished. A client may find it awkward to have to regain composure and pay a bill after an emotional experience.
- Let their clients know that staff members are available to provide comfort before and after the loss.
- Maintain a private area where clients can say their last good-byes, grieve, or regain composure before driving home.
- Offer to call a taxi or a friend for a tearful, distraught pet parent who is unable to drive home.
- When attending to the pet, make certain that the pet parent sees that the pet is well cared for (e.g., place a towel on exam table upon which the pet may lie).

In addition, therapists can teach self-care techniques such as case-by-case debriefing that includes all available staff; pursuit of a hobby or physical fitness outlet for stress reduction; and finding and sharing humor in stressful work environments.

One veterinarian sent home a letter with his clients when he scheduled their pets for surgery, saying that he reserved the right to cancel the surgery on the scheduled day if he wasn't feeling emotionally up to performing it. He attributed this to the fact that he once had a patient die and he had found it emotionally draining. This veterinarian was in desperate need of self-care techniques. He had crossed the line between appropriate concern and emotional overload. Many of his clients left his practice because they viewed the letter as an admission of a lack of confidence in his skills as a surgeon.

Veterinary medical teams may need help in developing skills for working through their emotions and maintaining healthy perspectives on the roles they play within the practice. When working with veterinary staff, therapists should address the beliefs of each staff member and his or her feelings regarding loss. By encouraging veterinary health care professionals to work through their own feelings about loss and any unresolved personal losses, therapists can help them develop the skills they need to confront the issue of patient loss in the practice. Educating them about the process of grief and the normal parameters of emotions experienced during loss may help them deal effectively with their own emotions while assisting a grieving client.

The following guidelines are helpful for assisting veterinary medical practitioners and their staff:

- Take a team approach to cases in which euthanasia is an option. This may alleviate individual feelings of failure and grief regarding patient loss.
- Establish and participate in a grief support group for veterinary medical professionals. This is a safe place to discuss feelings about the loss of patients and to receive support from a therapist and group members.
- Refer grieving pet parents to pet loss therapists or pet loss support groups. This shows clients that the veterinary staff cares. It also takes the burden of providing emotional support off the veterinary practice. It validates the importance and significance of the loss for both pet parent and veterinary staff.
- Encourage open communication among staff members. Pet loss is an opportunity for all practice members to grow emotionally and to solidify working relationships (Pettit, 1994, p. 155).

Dealing with Patient Loss

The loss of a favorite patient may mean that a long-term relationship with a client ends too. Veterinarians and staff may miss seeing a patient and parent who once frequented their office. Losing a patient can be difficult for the entire staff, especially if the loss was unexpected. The veterinarian and staff may impose self-blame when this happens. Clients often are furious with the veterinarian and staff when their pets die in the veterinary team's care, especially if there is no reasonable explanation for the death.

Dr. Morgan. Dr. Morgan was performing a routine spay on an 18-month-old puppy. The puppy had been given a blood panel and examination prior to surgery and appeared to be in excellent health. The surgery went well. Dr. Morgan was suturing the surgery site when the puppy went into respiratory arrest. Dr. Morgan and his medical technician attempted unsuccessfully resuscitate her.

Dr. Morgan had to break the news to his clients. He felt at a loss for words. He had never experienced this type of patient loss in his 16 years of practicing medicine. He felt as if he had failed. A postmortem examination was performed and tissue samples were sent to a pathologist. The cause of death was undetermined.

For several days, Dr. Morgan's emotions fluctuated between anger and remorse. He felt depressed. He began to doubt his medical abilities. He took time off from work. At home he was unable to relate to his family. His appetite diminished and he preferred to perform solitary activities. It took several weeks before he returned to his former level of functioning. Time and consultation with colleagues finally helped to restore his confidence.

Treating "Family Members"

Sometimes veterinarians are placed in the position of performing euthanasia or lifesaving procedures on their own pets or on the pets of their colleagues. The following case depicts the issues confronting veterinarians in these situations:

Dr. Romero and Dr. Martinez. Dr. Martinez's Doberman, Max, was at the end of his life. His physical and mental functions were deteriorating rapidly; it was time to perform euthanasia. Dr. Martinez asked his associate, Dr. Romero, to perform the euthanasia. Dr. Romero agreed to carry out Dr. Martinez's wish.

When it came time to perform the euthanasia, Dr. Romero felt anxious. She wanted the process to go smoothly, and she wanted Dr. Martinez to feel that his last moments with Max were good ones. The process did go smoothly. Dr. Romero was able to relinquish Max from his suffering and to support her friend and colleague through his loss. Dr. Romero was surprised at how tearful she was feeling. She realized that she had become quite attached to Max, because he had spent so much time at the hospital recently.

For several weeks after Max's euthanasia, Dr. Romero was unable to perform this service for her patients. She requested that Dr. Martinez perform all euthanasias. The next time Dr. Romero performed euthanasia, she found herself identifying with the client's grief to the point of tears. Although the process went smoothly, Dr. Romero found herself sobbing. She was so overwrought with emotion that her client began to care for her instead of the other way around.

Dr. Romero sought the help of a therapist and learned that she was experiencing counter-transference each time she performed euthanasia. Both Dr. Romero and Dr. Martinez said that the personal experience of euthanizing Max had made them feel more compassionate and understanding toward their clients who were facing a loss.

In human medicine it is considered unethical or unwise to treat a member of your family, but these rules do not apply to veterinarians who treat their pets. Veterinarians who treat their own pets place themselves at risk for failure in their own eyes and those of their families, as the following case study illustrates:

Dr. Kent's Wife. Dr. Kent's wife rushed their rabbit, Checkers, to her husband's veterinary hospital when she noticed that he had become overheated in his cage at home. The rabbit had a cage that sat on the ground with the door left open so he could come and go as he pleased. The cage was shaded in the afternoon, but it had received direct sunlight in the morning. That morning, one of the children had latched the door when Checkers was in the cage, and Mrs. Kent hadn't noticed until she went outside to feed him. At that time, she saw that Checkers was having a seizure and that his water bottle was empty.

When Mrs. Kent arrived at the clinic, she was afraid Checkers was dying. She looked for her husband, but Dr. Kent was in an exam room with a patient. When he arrived in the treatment room a few moments later, Mrs. Kent was near panic. She wanted immediate action taken to save Checkers. Dr. Kent worked on Checkers until the nurse came in and informed him that other patients were waiting.

Dr. Kent said Checkers was stable and told his wife to stay with Checkers while the rabbit lay in a bath of cool water. Mrs. Kent had been told that the rabbit's temperature was high and that he needed to have it lowered. While Dr. Kent and the nurse went to see another patient, Mrs. Kent put ice in the water, thinking that might help lower the rabbit's temperature.

When Dr. Kent came back to check on Checkers, he saw the ice and told Mrs. Kent to take it out of the water immediately, saying that she had made the water too cold. Mrs. Kent, feeling angry and abandoned by her husband and the staff, snapped, "Well, I'm not a veterinarian, I don't know what I'm doing, and no one is helping me."

Dr. Kent asked his wife to go home, saying that he would take care of Checkers and bring him home. When Dr. Kent arrived home with Checkers, he told Mrs. Kent that the rabbit's temperature was now too low, and that he would need to spend the night on a heating pad. Mrs. Kent felt guilty. She blamed herself for not noticing that the cage door had been latched, for not placing the cage in a spot with permanent shade, and for putting ice in the water.

Checkers died the next morning. Mrs. Kent was depressed, sad, and angry at herself. The following week she still felt angry, but now her anger was directed at her husband and his staff. She was furious that she had been left alone with Checkers when he needed prompt attention, and that no one had given her good directions for the bath.

Although Dr. Kent reassured her that the ice probably hadn't caused the rabbit's death, Mrs. Kent still felt guilty and angry. She could hardly stand to be in the same room with Dr. Kent. She sought the help of a therapist, who helped her work through her anger. They discussed safe ways in which she could process her anger without allowing it to destroy her relationship with her husband. Together, Mrs. Kent and the therapist arrived at a place of acceptance and forgiveness toward both herself and her husband.

Euthanasia

It is important for clients and veterinarians to arrive at the decision to euthanize at about the same time. Sometimes veterinarians have to refuse further treatment they feel will be ineffectual in alleviating the suffering of a patient. In this case, a client may get angry with the veterinarian for not being able to do more for the pet. If the veterinarian sees there are no other options available for the patient except to alleviate the animal's suffering, he or she may feel frustrated at not being able to convince the client that this is the best course of action. The veterinarian may even view the client as selfish in his or her determination to keep the pet alive.

Moral Stress and Ethics

Sometimes clients request convenience euthanasia for pets for whom they no longer wish to provide care. If the veterinarian feels there is no compelling medical or behavioral reason for administering the euthanasia, he or she may refuse to perform the procedure. The client then may threaten to suffocate, drown, or shoot the pet. The veterinarian may be hesitant to refer a client to an already overburdened humane society. If the veterinarian administers euthanasia for these reasons, he or she must live with the decision and perhaps with the hostility of other staff members who are against the euthanasia of healthy pets.

Medical practitioners face ethical and moral decisions on a daily basis. Tensions can arise not only between the veterinarian and the client but between the veterinarian and support staff members as well. It is important to facilitate open communication within the practice and to allow for an occasional difference of opinion. In an ideal veterinary setting, all staff members would possess the same values and views, but this is not realistic.

Holly and Dr. Hunt. Holly, a veterinary assistant, was furious with Dr. Hunt for euthanizing a healthy elderly cat. The cat's parent had become incapable of caring for herself and her pet. She expressed love for the animal, but was entering a nursing facility that did not allow pets. She had no friends or family who would care for the cat, and she did not want her relinquished to the humane society, where her chances of adoption were poor due to her age. For these reasons, Dr. Hunt agreed and carried out the wishes of the pet parent. Bad feelings remained between Holly and Dr. Hunt for many weeks.

Working in a Humane Society

Of all animal health professions, humane society employees who administer euthanasia are at the greatest risk for stress and burnout. Depending on the caseload and adoption rate, the number of euthanasias performed on a monthly basis in an animal shelter can be staggering.

Monica. Monica had been trained to administer euthanasia by injection to animals whose adoption time at the animal shelter had expired. A therapist stood on the opposite side of a metal table in a small room, watching as Monica euthanized 30 animals in one day, one after another. Boxes of puppies and kittens were brought in to await their turns to die.

Having witnessed several euthanasias in veterinary practices, the therapist arrived at the shelter thinking that the procedure was one that eased an animal's suffering and was performed with kindness, respect, and thoughtfulness. She found that it is one thing to see an elderly or terminally ill pet die peacefully; it is quite another to watch healthy baby animals destroyed.

The therapist found it quite difficult to stand on the concrete floor listening to the yaps and mews of the animals as the euthanasias were performed. The room decor was depressing, with dingy walls absent of any form of poster, painting, or photo. There wasn't money available to paint the room or to provide better ventilation or lighting. As the therapist considered these things, Monica talked about how she felt. She said she had come to the conclusion that, in offering the animals a good death, she was keeping them from a life of neglect, starvation, and other abuses. She found the work depressing, and said there were few people who were willing to do it; that was why she chose to stay. She shared that sometimes she felt so depressed by her job that she contemplated suicide.

The therapist was asked by the humane society to develop a support group for the volunteers. After spending the day there, she realized that the people who volunteered at animal shelters were in desperate need of support. She recommended to Monica that she take a leave of absence from her job and explore her feelings in counseling.

Jeanne. Jeanne volunteered in a county-run shelter. She became involved in a movement to assist and promote the adoption rather than destruction of the animals relinquished to the facility. She was highly effective in promoting her cause and was able to educate people in a position to change things at the shelter.

Jeanne came to the pet loss support group when she realized that she was experiencing a lot of stress and grief from her efforts to change things at the shelter. She had been volunteering so she could meet the needs of the animals and make a difference. Jeanne had fallen in love with a kitten she had adopted from the shelter. She was upset to discover that the kitten had heart and kidney disease and would not live. She had already bonded with the kitten in hopes of having something to love when her elderly cat, Kibbles, died. To add to her stress, she had recently lost her job.

One day when she was at the shelter, Jeanne broke down in tears as she photographed the animals that needed to be adopted. She said there were so many of them who weren't going to be adopted, and she felt she understood how they must feel. Jeanne said she had been adopted as an infant. She desperately wanted to find homes for these animals.

The therapist suggested that Jeanne take a break from working at the shelter and continue with her political efforts to make changes there. Jeanne said that she would like to, but a fellow volunteer, who had been there for several years, informed her that volunteers rarely stayed. She attributed this to the stress of seeing so many animals die. The volunteer had told Jeanne that she had been praying for someone to come, and that Jeanne was the answer to her prayers. Leaving would make Jeanne feel guilty, and she didn't want to abandon the animals.

Jeanne broke down and sobbed. She had taken 30 photos of animals who needed homes, and all of those animals had been euthanized. She felt an urgency to do something so new animals would not have to perish.

The therapist talked to Jeanne about the importance of self-care. Jeanne acknowledged that if she didn't help herself, she couldn't help the animals at the shelter. The therapist encouraged her to realize her own limits. Another person who had volunteered at the shelter for many years had told Jeanne she was able to continue her work only because she detached herself from the euthanasia aspect of the environment. She never visited the animals once she received them at the front desk. The therapist asked Jeanne to consider ways in which she could emotionally detach from her work.

The therapist also encouraged Jeanne to come back to the group and to discuss ways in which she would be effective at changing things within the shelter without causing grief for herself in the process.

Like veterinary staff members, humane society staff members usually choose their work because of a love for animals. Typically, it is difficult for volunteers to listen to the stories of pet parents relinquishing their animals. Often animals are abandoned because their parents are too ashamed to bring the pet into the facility. Employees may become hardened by, or disenchanted with their work. They often feel anger toward parents who drop off boxes of puppies, kittens, and rabbits born because they neglected to spay or neuter their pets. These parents may reappear a few months later with yet another box of animals.

Staff may be called upon to counsel or assist a tearful pet parent who is relinquishing a pet to the shelter. They may not know what to do or say to the person. They may even feel callous toward all pet parents, tending to view the vast majority as people who are insensitive and uncaring toward animals.

Employees are at risk for establishing bonds with pets that are to be adopted or destroyed. Often they are overburdened by the number of animals taken in. They may feel a variety of emotions when a pet placed in their care dies or is adopted (see Chapter 2).

Animal Rescue Workers

Animal rescue workers are at risk for forming attachments to the animals that are victimized in the wake of natural and manmade disasters. In the aftermath of Hurricane Katrina, where many survivors were forced by authorities to leave companion animals behind volunteer animal search and rescue teams were mobilized. Many animals perished in the disaster, while a large number of rescued animals were emaciated and ill, beyond the help of medical intervention. For many of those who responded to care and medical treatment, reunification with their families was not possible. Well-intentioned rescue workers were horrified to discover that many of the animals they lovingly rescued were not adoptable and had been placed on euthanasia lists. As time ran out for these lonely displaced pets, rescue workers made arrangements to claim them and arrange for their care and shelter in other areas of the country. Reunification and adoption efforts continue on behalf of these relatively fortunate animals, while others remain lost and abandoned in affected areas of the Gulf Coast.

Animal rescue workers, like all those who work in emergency response fields, must be on alert for symptoms of burnout and post traumatic stress disorder (PTSD). The Red Cross and other disaster response agencies should remember that those associated with the rescue, evacuation, and shelter of animals are deeply affected by the pain and suffering of the animals whose lives they are attempting to save. Debriefing services should be offered to those on the front lines of animal rescue, just as it is offered those who work with the human population. In a group format, skilled debriefing teams, consisting of a minimum of two persons, check in with rescue workers as they come off shift to rehash events of the day and identify accompanying emotional responses. It is important that everyone be invited to speak, but open discussion is not mandatory. Debriefing staff members have the opportunity, in the space of an hour or so, to identify individuals who may be at risk for experiencing residual trauma, and who might benefit from an individual counseling referral. This format affords rescue workers the opportunity to vent emotions both positive and negative, and receive support from others who share their commitment to rescue operations. By sharing experiences of their rescue efforts, participants recognize common threads among them, helping to "normalize" their emotional responses to working under highly "abnormal" circumstances. Debriefing is not therapy, although it is therapeutic in that it affords an opportunity for rescue workers to defuse the highly charged emotions associated with working in life and death situations, often under hazardous conditions.

Other Animal Care Professionals

When pets are kept as commodities or put on display, we tend to think that the professionals who care for them see them only as objects. Recent studies have shown that this is not true. Animal caretakers can and do form deep personal attachments with their charges. In a recent study on euthanasia in zoos, Bob Szita (1988) wrote that caretakers revealed many bonding experiences and a variety of emotions when animals in their care died.

In this study, zookeepers described the animals in their care as friends and pets who brought them joy (Szita, 1988, p. 158). Zookeepers often experience grief when an animal is ill or injured, dies, or is relocated to another zoo. Not unlike animal trainers, zookeepers must face their losses alone when the bond is broken between caretaker and animal.

An animal trainer for Marine World–Africa USA shared that he has experienced grief whenever one of his tigers or lions died. He said he typically begins to experience the loss as the animal ages and he realizes that the relationship they share is about to end. He views each of his lions and tigers as having a unique personality requiring various levels of response from him. He admitted that he feels deeper attachment to some animals than to others. When the animals become too old to perform, they live on his property until they die.

People not only bond with pets, they bond with wildlife too. A volunteer from a wildlife rescue center shared her feelings about the loss of a raccoon: "I really liked this raccoon that was put in my care. It was very ill, but I was hoping my efforts would save it." She provided around-the-clock nursing care for several weeks in attempting to save its life. She was surprised at how much she grieved when the raccoon died. She said the worst part of the loss was her colleagues' lack of compassion. They said things like, "It wasn't your pet." "Get over it." "It was just a raccoon."

Janet. Janet owned a pet shop. She loved birds and had had one, Mr. Montague, for 20 years. Mr. Montague accompanied Janet to work each morning. He was a favorite of all the store employees and the customers. Mr. Montague often entertained people with his limited vocabulary and quirky behavior.

When Mr. Montague became ill, Janet took him to the veterinarian, but the staff was unable to save his life. Janet was so overcome with grief she found it impossible to go to work. Everywhere she looked, she was reminded of Mr. Montague's absence. She couldn't bear to answer customers' questions about his death. She closed her store for a week and stayed home. There she was reminded of Mr. Montague at every turn, as she encountered his toys, food, special perching places, and cage. She decided to escape her surroundings and took a vacation with her husband. On vacation she began to feel better, but when she returned home, she was grief stricken anew. She decided to sell her store and her home and she created a new life for herself and her husband. Several years later, she opened a new pet shop in a new location.

Pet losses have far-reaching effects on people who work in the animal care field. Although there have not been studies citing the bonding between medical researchers and animals, it has been noted that many researchers respect and care about the animals upon whom they are performing experiments (Koski, 1988, p. 29).

Achieving Closure

In any profession, there is a need to obtain closure when a loss occurs. Veterinary medical professionals need to know they have done all they could for the patient and the client. Grieving clients need to know there will be an end to their pain and that there is help available while they are going through a loss. Therapists can help veterinarians and humane society volunteers by encouraging them to develop and maintain a basis of support for grieving pet parents. This broadens the clients' base for emotional support, thus reducing their dependency on staff. It helps staff members to feel they are helping the clients by referring them to a place that can provide support and understanding during a difficult time.

Therapists should inform clinic and shelter staff members that it is normal to feel awkward when attending to a grieving client. Grief support can be as simple as validating the pet parents' pain and giving a referral to a pet loss therapist.

Shaylyn. Shaylyn was grief stricken when her rabbit, Jelly Belly, was euthanized. She tried to put the pain of the loss out of her mind. She was tearful at times and would frequently cry at home.

One day Shaylyn had to purchase food for her cat, Melody. She was about to pay for her purchase at the local pet shop when she saw a poster of a rabbit that looked like Jelly Belly. She burst into tears and could barely see to write the check. The store clerk knew Shaylyn and asked what was wrong. Shaylyn shared her loss with the clerk. The clerk felt awkward attending to Shaylyn as she sobbed at the checkout counter. She immediately handed Shaylyn a box of tissues and told her how sorry she was to hear about her loss. She also remembered a therapist who had come into the store and given her brochures on a local pet loss support group. She offered one of the brochures to Shaylyn.

Shaylyn called the clerk a week later to thank her for her support.

Relaxation Techniques

Therapists can teach their clients relaxation techniques that will enable them to take better care of themselves. Centering, focusing, use of visual imagery, self-hypnosis, and biofeedback are some techniques clients can use to reduce stress. Clients should be encouraged to think of relaxing techniques that they have successfully employed in the past (such as taking a hot bath, working out, going for a walk, sitting in the park, meditating, or renting comedy videos).

Therapists working with animal care professionals should also remind them to pursue relationships outside of their profession in order to achieve balance in their lives. Educating animal care professionals about various coping techniques and brainstorming on specific things they can do to reduce stress on a daily basis will empower them to cope with the unique aspects of their profession.

Education and Other Types of Training

In *The Skilled Helper*, Egan (1982) encouraged counselors to avoid burnout in their profession by "spending time upstream," suggesting that professionals apply their skills and talents in a way that brings them joy and satisfaction. To enhance job satisfaction, for example, a therapist who counsels clients on grief and loss may choose to spend part of his or her time counseling parents-to-be on coping with the birth of a child. Balancing the negative aspects of the profession with the positive can reduce stress.

In the case of the humane society employee who performed multiple euthanasias, it was recommended that she spend part of her time in the adoption center of the program. Seeing pets going home to loving and responsible homes could be a joyful balance for the negative aspects of having to end an animal's life.

Conclusion

People who work in the animal care professions may be exposed to the loss of animals on a daily basis. No one is immune to grief when a bond with a special animal is broken. Veterinarians and other animal health care workers need to learn ways to cope within their work environments. To minimize burnout, animal health care professionals must learn to detach themselves from the deep sadness experienced by grieving pet parents while still maintaining an appropriate level of empathy for their patients and clients.

Therapists working with animal health care professionals should possess a basic understanding of the unique stresses to which they are routinely exposed. Most people enter the animal health care profession out of a genuine love and concern for the welfare of animals. Grief and stress are not isolated experiences; they can affect relationships among co-workers, customers and clients, spouses, children, and extended family.

Educating animal health care professionals about the grieving process, validating their feelings, and encouraging open communication can provide a foundation of understanding, increased self-esteem, and enhanced awareness that can reduce or eliminate burnout in the profession.

10

PET LOSS DUE TO NATURAL DISASTER OR PERSONAL TRAGEDY

Dr. Pia Salk sits with a canine victim she rescued in the aftermath of Hurricane Katrina. Rescue volunteers are faced with the kind of unrelenting stress and fatigue that can result in post traumatic stress disorder.

Lessons Learned from Hurricane Katrina

As the flood waters rose in New Orleans following Hurricane Katrina and failed levees, a man and his dog were stranded on the roof of their home. They watched as a rescue boat approached. The rescuers refused to transport the dog and informed him that another rescue boat, one for animals, would soon be arriving. As the water continued to rise; the terrified man boarded the rescue boat and told his dog to sit and stay. He prayed that the rescue boat would come and find his dog soon. He tearfully promised his dog that help was on the way and that they would be reunited.

Once the man reached safety he discovered that there was no rescue boat on the way to save his dog. Ten days after his own rescue, he arranged for friends to take him back to his flooded home in their own boat to search for his beloved dog. Much to his amazement and relief, he found that his dog did indeed obey his command to "sit and stay." The dog was very thin and appeared to be ill, having had no food and only contaminated water to drink in his pet parent's absence. The dog faithfully awaited his pet parent's return and gratefully responded with love and affection.

This was just one of many stories to surface in the aftermath of Katrina disaster. Few of the stories, however, had happy endings. However, they are poignant examples of what can happen when evacuation plans make no provision for the rescue and care of animals.

Perhaps the story that touched the hearts of many was the little boy whose dog was taken out of his arms just as he boarded the evacuation bus outside of the Superdome. The boy cried, "Snowball," "Snowball," and dropped to his knees sobbing and then vomiting as his pet was carried away by a policeman. The boy and his dog had made it to the relative safety of the rescue vehicle only to be forcibly separated by authorities. Observers of this incident were horrified to witness the traumatic separation of these loving friends by rescue authorities after they had already faced so much danger together.

These stories illustrate the considerable strength of the bonds people share with their pets. Moreover, they expose a lack of sensitivity toward human–companion animal relationships and speak to the need for consideration of them in disaster plans at all levels of government. State and federal organizations are now creating disaster response plans that include the rescuing of animal family members as well as human ones. Louisiana introduced into legislation an animal evacuation bill to ensure that, in any future disaster, officials will not separate people from their household pets and service animals. It is hoped that similar bills will follow in other states, and that evacuating people with their pets will be the mandated norm in disaster response plans.

Why Pets and Their Guardians Should Be Evacuated Together in a Disaster

Victims of disaster are often accidentally or forcibly separated from their pets, sometimes permanently, just at the time when they need one another most. When faced with the horrors of losing homes, property, possessions, jobs, and loved ones, the presence of a faithful companion animal can make the difference between abject despair and digging deep to uncover strength and resolve to carry on. Disaster survivors can find strength and hope in caring for an animal that might have perished in the absence of their lifesaving interventions. The pet parents can nurture and care for their dependent animals at a time when they have lost control over so many aspects of daily living. The unconditional love that companion animals offer in return brings immeasurable comfort to individuals and families during a period of great stress and suffering.

Pet parents should never be forced to leave their pets behind at the site of a disaster. Disaster survivors will deal with many forms of grief and depression related to loss and displacement. It is a well-established fact that many pets are valued as family members. The additional trauma of leaving a pet behind to fend for itself may seriously compromise the coping mechanisms of the individual or family in facing new challenges as disaster survivors. Conversely, allowing companion animals to be rescued with their owners will strengthen the bond between them and foster a sense of hope for positive outcomes.

It is critical that legislation be enacted to honor and preserve bonds between people and companion animals in the aftermath of disaster. People and their pets should be rescued simultaneously whenever possible. Provisions for the care and shelter of these animals should be established in the same general area as their guardians are sheltered. Medical care for sick or injured animals should be provided by veterinarians designated in the local disaster response plan. Pet identification tags must be placed and cross-referenced with names of family members. Open visitation is essential and the pets should be placed back with their owners as soon as possible. Local disaster plans should clearly spell out rescue and shelter plans for all animals, and should reflect intentions to shelter pets and guardians together, whenever possible. Swift reunification of companion animals and owners in the aftermath of disaster will contribute positively to the emotional recovery of the victims, reducing the impact on already strained community resources.

Pet parents and therapists will want to familiarize themselves with their local disaster plans, which are available at county offices. Many pet parents may not know that the Red Cross does not allow animals in their shelters. However, humane societies and veterinary medical associations work with local government to establish disaster response plans for the medical care and sheltering of animals in the aftermath of disasters.

Help for Pet Parents During a Disaster

Therapists who truly wish to be of service to victims of disaster need to understand, acknowledge, and honor the importance (see Chapters 1 and 2) of companion animals. They must not just suspect that human–animal bonds are strong, but must know in their hearts, even if they don't share a fondness for animals, that these pets may be as important to these victims as are other human family members.

When interviewing disaster survivors, both in the field and in relief shelters or later in office settings, the therapist must inquire about animal family members that were lost during the evacuation process. It is important that the victim describe the situation that resulted in the separation from the pet, and that time is allotted for him or her to express emotions relative to the incident. Try to determine if there is a realistic possibility of reunification. Give the victim hope for a positive outcome only if reunification seems likely. If there is no such hope (the animal has died), then give him hope that he will make it through the process of grieving by validating the loss, acknowledging the relationship shared with the pet, and offering information about pet loss grief and local support services.

The first responder or therapist should learn the circumstances surrounding the pet's disappearance and should be familiar with the animal rescue and shelter portion of the local disaster plan. It is important to the well-being of the client that accurate information (names, addresses, phone numbers of contact agencies and individuals) be given to the client, who might have previously received sketchy or erroneous information regarding the rescue and disposition of his or her pet.

As stated, most disaster plans should team up veterinary medical associations and humane societies to provide medical care and safe housing for animal victims of disaster. Contingency plans, if the designated shelter is out of commission or overwhelmed with incoming animals, should be spelled out in the plan and may involve a cooperative effort with adjacent cities, counties, and volunteer veterinarians. Thus, through a mutual aide agreement, care and shelter for displaced pets can be assured.

In addition to being familiar with local disaster plans, pet parents need to be adequately prepared on the home front, to assure the safety of human and animal family members. Home disaster preparedness should include a minimum three-day supply of food, water, and medication for animals as well as humans. However, a seven-day supply is best. Remember to include a "pet emergency first aid book" (see reference chapter), and a standard first aid kit too. Also, keep photos of your pets on hand and make certain they have identification (tags, micro-chips, etc.) on them. Being well prepared for emergencies at home, however, does not assure preparedness for the emotional trauma that individuals and families may encounter when disaster strikes. The challenges faced by disaster victims are unique and must often be met while experiencing powerful emotions of helplessness, hopelessness, and the intense sorrow that accompanies loss of possessions and loved ones.

In the aftermath of both manmade and natural disasters, anger and frustration with rescue and evacuation procedures, as well as with subsequent shelter services, may be the prominent emotion encountered by first responders and shelter counselors. Loss of the victims' housing, possessions, and loved ones is a traumatic experience that few of us encounter in our lifetimes. Yet, in recent years, it has become apparent to all that the world can be a dangerous place. Recently, we have witnessed the destructive forces of a tsunami, several hurricanes, earthquakes, tornadoes, wild fires, a terrorist attack on the U.S., and the prospect of endless war. We are urged by our government to plan ahead. Day-to-day living has become more of a challenge for most of us, and coping with new threats seems, at times, overwhelming.

Given that our coping skills are already working overtime in today's demanding, often hectic society, it should be clear that victims of disasters will require a great deal of empathy and understanding from caregivers if they are to recover from disaster trauma. First responders to a disaster scene do not perform therapy in the field, but rather use debriefing skills to triage survivors' needs, referring them to appropriate resources (see Chapter 11). Response staff should inquire as to whether a pet was lost to the disaster and consider the impact of the loss on the victim. This affords the victim the opportunity to vent emotions related to the loss. First responders are in a position to validate these emotions and convey them to staff at the next level of intervention.

Therapists will need to further explore what the loss means to the client and attempt reunification whenever possible. If it is known that the pet has perished, the victim should be assisted through the early stages of the grief response. Past coping strengths can be identified and reinforced as the client attempts to meet new challenges and demands without the comfort and support of his companion animal. Therapists who work with disaster victims in ongoing counseling situations will need to address the long-term effects of the pet loss experience on their clients. It may take months or even years for clients to come to terms with the traumatic events of the disaster, but therapists who are knowledgeable about the roles that pets play in people's lives will be better able to serve their clients.

Survivors of disasters grieve the loss of many things at once: loved ones, their health, homes, possessions, jobs, convenience, predictability, and dignity. First responders will help survivors deal with the broader, earliest phases of the shock of loss and displacement. Subsequent assisting staff will begin to isolate and prioritize issues for the victims. It is important for the therapist, who may follow the client in an agency or office over a period of time, to understand the emotional devastation that is common to disaster survivors. Our focus here is to make sure that the importance of pet loss is understood and addressed by therapists and counselors assisting disaster victims, both in the field and in counseling relationships further down the recovery continuum. A therapist who is reluctant to recognize the pet as a family member may impede the healing process. The vast majority of survivors will place the loss of a pet high on their priority list. The therapeutic relationship between therapist and client is enhanced when the therapist acknowledges the pet as a family member and pursues appropriate interventions on the client's behalf.

Clients must feel uninhibited in sharing their feelings about their loss without fear that their emotions might be discounted, diminished, or ridiculed. Clients who are reluctant to talk about their experience will need to be reassured by the therapist that they are free to share emotions related to pet loss and that such expression is critical to attaining a positive outcome from therapy. For example, clients often share that the loss of their pet is more deeply felt than the loss of a human family member. Clients may feel hesitant in sharing this for fear of seeming shallow or not loyal to the person they loved and lost.

Post Traumatic Stress Disorder (PTSD)

PTSD can result when the person is exposed to an event that typically is outside of the range of normal human experience. Often these situations are perceived as life-threatening by the victim. They often result in powerful shocks that can have long-lasting consequences.

Both children and adults, ideally, should be assessed for PTSD after surviving a traumatic event. There are numerous therapeutic models that have been successful in assisting clients through a traumatic loss. One of the treatments discussed in Chapter 11, Therapeutic Interventions and Treatment Modalities, is eye movement desensitization and reprocessing (EMDR). This therapy, alone or combined with hypnotherapy or play therapy, can effectively treat clients with trauma. EMDR has been known to have as high as an 80% effective rate in recovery for PTSD clients.

There are teams of people skilled in this type of therapy who often avail their services to disaster victims (see Chapter 13).

Jamie and her three young children, ages 8, 10, and 12, survived a tornado that ripped through their Midwestern town one morning in mid March. Her husband, a long-distance trucker, was on the road and Jamie had to make a hasty decision regarding the safety of her children. She plucked them from their beds and herded them into the basement, sheltering them in a small room without windows. Once they were safely settled in the room they realized that one family member was missing—their dog, Andy. Jamie quickly ran up the stairs and opened the basement door. She whistled and called for Andy until she realized that she needed to return to the children. As the tornado passed through their neighborhood it destroyed their home and some of their neighbor's homes, as well as damaging property for miles around them.

Andy's body was discovered by the children two hundred yards from what had once been their home.

First responders to the disaster were primarily concerned with feeding and sheltering the people, who were coping with the immeasurable grief and loss. Jamie and her children were crowded into a high school gym. Four hundred men, women and children struggled to come to terms with the devastation and loss they had endured from the tornado.

The tornado struck with little warning. Jamie had saved the lives of her children. However, she felt that she had failed to save their dog, who had been their friend and protector for ten years.

Jamie and her husband were assisted in applying for financial aide, processing insurance claims and finding temporary housing. The family grieved their losses together, including the loss of Andy.

A couple of months later, Jamie sought counseling for depression. She shared with the therapist her guilt over Andy's loss. She also shared the fact that family and friends had told her that she should be thankful that her children were alive rather than continuing to mourn the loss of her dog.

As Jamie's story unfolded in therapy, the alert therapist watched as sadness clouded her face and her shoulders slumped at the mention of Andy. Although Jamie did not focus upon Andy's loss, the therapist accurately read her body language and encouraged her to talk about the dog, particularly her efforts to save him. Through skillful interviewing, it became apparent that Jamie's guilt about Andy was at the core of her depression. The therapist helped Jamie understand that she had done her best to save the family pet and that in the face of her best efforts, there was no blame for the outcome. Jamie was able to see that her guilt was an undeserved negative emotion that was interfering with her day-to-day ability to function. The therapist gave Jamie a safe venue for exploring her negative emotions, and helped her break through the guilt barrier that was hindering her recovery from this loss.

While disaster victims have to cope with an abundance of loss, it is difficult to know where to begin in therapy. Exploration of the role of the family pet is never to be ignored. In exposing and exploring areas of vulnerability, the skilled therapist can do much to help disaster victims identify healthy coping skills, make steady progress toward recovery, and prevent symptoms of PTSD from surfacing in the future.

While we focus on the pet parent's need in this chapter, it is also important to note that there can be another type of disaster victim—the animal rescue worker. Rescue workers who go in after a disaster and look for animal victims are vulnerable to developing PTSD. Oftentimes rescue workers witness horrific scenes in trying to find surviving pets. Many times they work long, hard hours, trying to save as many animal victims as they can. They must cope with all the inconveniences a tragedy brings (e.g., contaminated water, no electricity, hot, humid or freezing cold temperatures, etc.). They must use survival skills and stay mentally strong while trying to aide frightened, displaced, sickly animals. The sights, sounds, and smells can haunt rescue workers long after the disaster has occurred. Animal rescue workers should be prepared, as much as possible, to be willing to seek follow-up care for themselves with a therapist regarding any mental health issues that might arise from assisting in a disaster situation.

Therapists and first responders should readily make available their services for assisting animal rescue workers too. It is important that mental health first responders assess rescue workers for PTSD and provide appropriate mental health referrals and follow-up care.

Conclusion

Pet parents should consider their pet's needs when making disaster plans for the family. Food, water, and medication for both human and animal family members should be obtained and stored in sealed, shatter- and waterproof containers. Photos of the pets, in case they go missing, should be part of any home disaster preparedness kit. Pets should also be microchipped and wear a collar with tags for identification purposes. Be familiar with your local disaster plan. Review specific policies and procedures pertaining to the rescue and shelter of pets. Make note of important phone numbers that might be difficult to obtain in the aftermath of a disaster. County and state agencies offer brochures and other printed materials that address disaster preparedness and describe evacuation procedures for both people and animals, should this become necessary.

First responders and therapists must take care in identifying, acknowledging, and validating the variety of losses a disaster victim may experience. Debriefing exercises conducted by first responders allow disaster victims to express their earliest emotions related to trauma and loss. When attending to the immediate survival needs of disaster victims, it is important that an assessment of emotional needs be done and that appropriate referrals for follow-up care be made. In addition, it is important that animal rescue workers be assessed and referred to mental health services as needed.

In the aftermath of disaster, survivors often must adjust to major lifestyle changes. They may have lost homes, friends, relatives, jobs, and the sense of safety they have previously taken for granted. It is important to remember that the loss of a cherished animal companion may be equally, or even more, traumatic as the loss of a human friend for these individuals and families. Failure to acknowledge and address the effects of pet loss in the aftermath of disaster may seriously impede the process of recovery for disaster victims.

Disaster victims and animal rescue workers should receive information for appropriate follow-up care. This should include contact information for pet loss support (see Chapter 13).

In a disaster, victims and their pets should be evacuated together. Visitation on a daily basis should be allowed and encouraged at pet shelters. Every precaution possible should be taken to cross-reference pets with their human families. Not allowing pets to be evacuated with their pet parents can interfere with the emotional recovery by compromising the coping mechanisms of the victims.

11

THERAPEUTIC INTERVENTIONS AND TREATMENT MODALITIES

Pets help us to feel good and may help to normalize an unusual experience. Murphy, a feline friend of Savannah's, comforts her in the hospital after she experienced a traumatic accident.

Clients who are experiencing the grief associated with pet loss can benefit from a variety of therapeutic interventions. They run a spectrum from initial debriefing efforts by first responders to multiple therapy sessions for the treatment of depression and post traumatic stress disorder (PTSD). Clients should seek out therapists who have an understanding of the issues that are unique to grieving pet parents and are trained in treatment modalities that are effective in the treatment of associated symptoms.

Many pet loss clients respond favorably to a brief therapy format, where they are seen in therapy for six to eight weekly sessions. Therapists help the client to see that their grief response to the loss of their pet is normal, although friends and co-workers may not readily relate to the depth of their grief.

Once the client's feelings are acknowledged and validated in a safe therapeutic setting, he or she is helped to develop new skills to cope more effectively with troubling symptoms. The client is directed to employ new coping techniques at home and report back to the therapist at the next session. For example, when people tell the client to get a new pet to get over the loss, the client may be instructed to respond by saying, "You wouldn't advise me to go out and get a new best friend or child, so it's clear to me that you've never experienced the loss of a pet you've truly loved." This empowers the clients to deal with people who may inadvertently trivialize the loss. For many clients, working through a heartfelt pet loss with like-minded individuals is the best therapeutic approach.

One therapeutic model that works well alone or as an adjunct to other therapies is the *pet loss support group*. Such support groups validate and help to normalize the client's grief experience. This is important in a society that tends to minimize the significance of a bereaved pet parent's grief.

A pet loss support group can provide people with a safe and understanding place to express their feelings. In a support group setting, clients discover that their losses are not unique. Much of the healing that can come out of participating in a group is in the fact that pet parents discover they are not alone.

Clients are educated about the grief process and about the human–companion animal bond. They take comfort in knowing that others share similar feelings for their pets and they learn new, effective coping skills from the experiences of other group members. This is especially true for clients who attend a group prior to the loss of their pet. Ideally, clients should be referred to a group when they first learn that there pet has died or when a terminal diagnosis has been made. Ideally, clients who receive support prior to the loss of their pets are able to move more readily through the grief continuum.

Sometimes clients who need therapy do not seek it until they experience the loss of a pet. This can happen for two reasons. First, a client who has used his or her relationship with a pet as a form of therapy and support may not feel the need to see a therapist until the pet dies.

Second, clients who feel uncomfortable about seeking out professional support may not do so until they are faced with a crisis such as losing a pet.

Attending a pet loss support group may be a client's first step toward seeking help. That is why a competent therapist—one who can assess clients for various mental and behavioral disorders—should lead the group. Often clients attend a group to discuss their loss and end up sharing other unresolved issues, stressors, and even alcoholism or drug abuse. Once a resistant client has taken the initial step of seeking support for a pet loss, he or she often is willing to follow the group leader's advice in obtaining a referral to work on other issues. Sometimes a client will ask to see the group leader on a one-on-one basis outside of the support group as well.

Pet loss support groups can operate in conjunction with other types of therapies. Clients who attend support groups may also want to continue with private counseling, which allows clients to meet their needs in a variety of ways. A competent support group leader will refer the client back to the client's therapist as problems arise that cannot be appropriately handled in the group setting. This is especially important for clients who exhibit symptoms of clinical depression or express suicidal ideation within the group framework.

Therapists who lack experience in the specialty area of pet loss and grief do their clients a service by referring them to a pet loss support group. The group can see such clients through the crisis phase of their grief while offering a shared, empathetic perspective on this special type of loss. It can also work to normalize their grief response as they interact with other pet parents.

Establishing a Support Group

Pet loss support groups have been established throughout the United States by both therapists and lay persons (i.e., pet owners who have experienced a loss). Some groups are sponsored by humane societies, veterinary medical associations, and other animal concern agencies. Some therapists establish groups that meet out of their offices and charge an attendance fee. Others create workshops and teach clients common, expected stages of grief, human–animal bonding, and the unique aspects of this type of loss. There is no one particular formula for establishing such a group. Some support groups are up and running in a matter of weeks; others may take longer. There are also online pet loss support groups that may be helpful to clients who do not have access to a group that meets in person. In our experience, face-to-face contact with pet parents affords the best opportunity for validating and working through a pet loss.

Over the years, we have helped therapists establish support groups throughout the United States. The common element we have found that ensures a group's success is a competent professional group leader who has knowledge and experience in the field of human–animal bonding and pet loss. Groups should be structured to run between an hour and 90 minutes, and should always include education about the normal grief process that accompanies the loss of a valued companion animal. The group leader should be competent in diffusing anger and in allowing each participant a turn to speak, and should be able to provide intervention for clients who are suicidal, abusing substances, or mentally ill.

Many nonprofit groups, often depend on donations to meet their budget needs, cannot afford to meet weekly due to a lack of funding. They also may be the first groups to be cut when working under umbrella organizations that are downsizing or reconstructing to meet their own budget needs. Counselor fees and facility usage fees limit the number of times a group can afford to meet.

Although many nonprofit groups cannot afford to meet weekly, this opens the door to clients who are in urgent need of support. If a client has to wait more than a week to join the group, he or she may be less likely to attend, because the initial impact of the loss has dissipated somewhat. Holding the group offsite away from a veterinary office, animal shelter, or other facility where animals reside, may make it less painful for clients attending. The group leader should establish referral links with other mental health care providers so that other needs of group members can be met.

Printed materials on pet loss support and the grief process should be made available, referring not only to staff members but to clients as well. Handouts on how parents can help their children through a loss are useful, as are those describing the practice of euthanasia and burial options. Handouts should be available at any pet health care provider or pet business (e.g., veterinary offices, groomers, pet shops, the Humane Society, and even in therapists' offices) or where people would seek grief support services.

Our pet loss support group is sponsored by the local veterinary medical association. The group leader is a psychiatric registered nurse and a licensed marriage, family, and child counselor. She has extensive training in grief counseling and human–animal bonding and carries her own malpractice insurance. She also is skilled at assessing various mental disorders and substance abuse. The veterinarians make an annual donation to the association to offset therapist fees and printing costs and the facility use is donated. The group has proven to be a valuable extension of local veterinary medical practices. Local veterinarians refer their clients to the group, for which there is no cost to clients. The group is available to all ages and is run on a drop-in basis. It has been our experience that clients attend an average of three times. Some clients return to group the following year on the anniversary of their pet's death. Most group members eventually adopt and successfully bond with new pets.

When parents bring children, we encourage their participation by making the group a comfortable environment for them as well. Young children often do not express their feelings verbally. We provide crayons, paper, and toy animals to encourage expression. Children often draw a picture of their pets or write a story about them. They share with the group through their art, stories, and poetry (see Chapter 5).

When new groups form, the initial turnout can be expected to be small. It is not uncommon to get only one or two people at first. As information about the group is given through professional referrals, the media, and word of mouth, more people will attend. The group's founders should create an attractive brochure that outlines the focus of the group and gives details on meeting dates, times, location, and a phone number to call for more information.

Seeking Referrals

Pet loss support group facilitators shouldn't overlook any possibility for referrals. Personal introductions can be made to humane societies, county shelters, veterinary medical associations, individual veterinarians, therapists, family practitioners, clergy members, teachers, hospice volunteers, groomers, animal rescue organizations, animal service organizations, and breeders. Letters introducing the group can also be sent. Anyone who comes into contact with grieving pet parents should be made aware of the group. Offering to give a presentation on pet loss and the benefits of group support is another good way to inform people about the importance of referring to a support group or therapist trained in pet loss.

Consider aligning with a veterinary medical practice or with several smaller practices. Therapists would then be on call on- or off-site to assist clients who are experiencing or anticipating the loss of their pets. When a pet parent is first told that his or her pet is terminally ill, will require extensive treatment, has died suddenly, or should be euthanized, the therapist would be called to guide the client through the initial intense grief response.

Because pet loss experiences may not happen on a daily basis in a veterinary practice, therapists might want to offer their services to veterinarians on several levels—providing staff training on human–companion animal bonds and pet loss response, for example. Offering phone counseling, crisis intervention, and educational materials on human–animal bonds and grief, as well as support for bereaved pet parents in the form of individual counseling or support group sessions is also helpful.

Veterinarians and other animal care professionals may need guidance on when and how to make appropriate mental health referrals. A veterinarian who would readily refer a fatigued, underweight, agitated client to his or her family physician for a checkup might hesitate to refer the same client to a mental health professional, even when symptoms of anxiety are apparent. Because of the stigma attached to mental and emotional illness, a veterinarian may fear reprisals for suggesting that a client might benefit from a therapeutic intervention. Others believe it is not their place to suggest therapy for clients.

Therapists can encourage referrals by reminding veterinarians that clients who need grief support may burden the practice with their requests for help, resulting in costly delays in service delivery. Clients may call frequently or stop by the clinic to relive the course of events with the veterinarian. Point out the beneficial aspects of referring bereaved clients to your group instead.

Rhonda. Rhonda's cat, Nelson, died after getting tangled in the telephone cord and strangling. Rhonda discovered his body with the cord wound tightly around his neck. Although it had been several weeks since Nelson had died, Rhonda was agitated, depressed, and guilty. She imagined how Nelson must have struggled to free himself. She thought that if she had come home directly from work, instead of going out to dinner with friends, she might have saved Nelson's life.

Rhonda had been seeing a psychiatrist for treatment of anxiety. She asked the doctor for an alternative to drug treatment, telling him that she was feeling more agitated since Nelson's death. The doctor suggested a self-hypnosis relaxation technique Rhonda could use any time. While she was hypnotized, the doctor gave Rhonda a post-hypnotic suggestion: Anytime she felt anxious, she could use the following imagery: the doctor described a beautiful meadow in the middle of which stood a "safe" tree. Rhonda could sit by the tree until she felt calm and able to function again. Rhonda used this technique whenever she was feeling anxious. Her doctor encouraged her to meditate on a daily basis as an to adjunct self-hypnosis and imagery.

Self-hypnosis helped Rhonda lessen the anxiety she felt by giving her a safe place to retreat to when she felt anxious. In addition to hypnosis, the therapist used other techniques such as cognitive therapy and behavior modification. After a year of therapy, Rhonda was able to overcome her depression and significantly reduce her anxiety while she resolved her loss. Two years after Nelson's death, Rhonda adopted another pet.

Family Therapy

While it is often beneficial for families to attend a pet loss support group, some families might prefer to work with an individual therapist who is knowledgeable about pet loss issues. Because family members often react to the loss in different ways, counseling can be beneficial in making certain that everyone's feelings are expressed and acknowledged. Once the degree of loss is identified for each family member, the therapist can effectively integrate treatment to address the varying degrees of attachment to the family pet. Family members learn to appreciate and respect each other's feelings regarding the loss. The loss, and how the family members support each other through it, can help them grow stronger as a family.

The therapist can also devise individual treatment approaches for family members who were most traumatized by the loss. A particular challenge to a therapist is the client who has witnessed the traumatic accidental death of a pet. In such cases there is no time to say goodbye. It is difficult, if not impossible, to arrive at a reasonable explanation for the pet's death. In one such case, the family dog was run over by a speeding truck on the road in front of the house. Two children in the family witnessed the events and were severely traumatized:

The Family. An entire family came to the pet loss support group: mother, father, son, and daughters ages eleven and nine. They wept openly for their German shepherd, Tuffy, and talked about how empty their home seemed without him. The children had seen the dog hit by a truck speeding down the road, and they were angry that the truck driver had not stopped to help Tuffy. They all spoke about the blood-soaked asphalt in front of their house. The father reported weeping each time he drove into the driveway, and the mother described her repeated attempts at washing the spot off the asphalt.

The family worked hard on their grief issues in the group. They finally made the decision to move from their home. Although this seems like an extreme measure, for this family it had therapeutic value. Their attempts to "wash away" the memory of the accident had failed. They believed that a physical move from the site would give them their best chance at resolution. That decision was supported by the group leader, because the family had worked hard to arrive at a solution that would work for everyone.

Art Therapy

Art therapy is a tool that can be used when a client appears to be "stuck" somewhere along the grief continuum. He may be unable to express negative emotions attached to a certain aspect of a traumatic event. For example, a survivor of a flood may not be able to recall the emotions he felt at boarding a rescue helicopter while his loyal dog remained on the porch, flood waters rising around him. The client's ability to clearly recall the event and associated feelings may serve as a defense mechanism, warding off the enormity of anger, frustration, and horror that might threaten to overwhelm him once the memory surfaces. At the same time, the client cannot proceed toward a healthy resolution of his grief until the event is revisited and the accompanying emotions released.

From the more tangible memories available to him, a client can be directed to make a drawing of a certain aspect of the traumatic event. The drawing may be crude or refined, and a variety of colors should be available to enhance the client's self-expression. The therapist, noting major themes and background fills, will make assumptions about the client's feelings from the content and colors incorporated into the drawing. The therapist will question the client about the validity of these assumptions and draw him into a dialog about specific aspects of the picture and their meaning to the client. In this way, the client can use the drawing as a springboard to exploring emotions that could not be otherwise coaxed into consciousness.

A single session utilizing this approach may be successful and the therapist must be prepared to deal with an outpouring of negative emotions that may become "unstuck" all at once. Art therapy can be utilized as a primary or complementary treatment modality, depending upon the degree of trauma and degree to which undesirable emotions have been buried and kept at bay.

Once the client is able to recall and examine the entire event and the accompanying emotions, cognitive therapy, hypnotherapy, and eye movement desensitization therapy (EMDR) may be useful in assisting the client to view his actions and responses in the best possible light, freeing him from the anger, frustration and nagging guilt that can impede progress toward resolution of grief.

Cognitive Behavioral Therapy

Cognitive therapy is a popular and effective therapy tool that works well with families and individuals by changing the way clients look at various aspects of a pet loss. Cognitive therapy examines the client's belief system regarding events and their role in the outcome of a loss. A client whose perception, thinking, reasoning, attention, and judgment, (cognition) are rooted in self-blame, guilt, and anger will harbor a great deal of negativity regarding all aspects of the event. The therapist's job is to alter the negative thoughts, beliefs, assumptions, and attitudes attributed to the client's behavioral response to the pet loss.

Clients may exhibit an all or none type of thinking, looking at all events and actions as "good" or "bad," with no middle ground. For example, a client who is guilt-ridden over postponing euthanasia and causing unnecessary suffering to a pet can best be helped if the therapist reframes the events to show that the client made the best possible choice within the context of the time and resources available.

Lynne. Lynne's Pomeranian, Misty, was 18 years old at the time of her euthanasia. For four years Lynne had curtailed her social life to accommodate Misty's need for around-the-clock eye medication. Lynne administered the eye drops in the morning before she went to work, came home at noon to administer more drops, and returned home by 6 p.m. to repeat the process. She had many acquaintances but few social friends because her daily activities revolved around Misty's nursing care. As Misty grew older, she showed signs of arthritis as her vision worsened and her hearing failed.

Finally, Misty was diagnosed with inoperable cancer and was given three to six months to live. Three months later a large tumor could be palpated on Misty's neck. Lynne knew it was time to consider euthanasia, but she wasn't ready to let go of her pet. Misty had become incontinent, unable to bear her own weight most of the time, and completely dependent on Lynne. Finally, the tumor beneath the skin ruptured and Lynne was forced to take action.

When she arrived at group, Lynne was distraught with grief over having waited so long to euthanize Misty. She said she had kept Misty alive for her own selfish reasons long after the dog's quality of life had declined. Upon questioning, Lynne revealed that she had acquired Misty with her former husband, Bob, early in their relationship. Misty was their "only child" and Lynne and Bob had both loved and pampered her.

When Lynne and Bob divorced, Misty moved to another state with Bob. This left a giant void in Lynne's life. Recognizing that Misty would be better off with Lynne, Bob later returned the dog to her. As Lynne talked, it became apparent that Misty represented the good times she and her husband had shared. They were a family. As Misty's health declined, Lynne relived her marriage and divorce. To lose Misty was to lose her link to a happier past. She fought tenaciously for Misty's life and well-being.

The group leader helped Lynne to see that each decision she made had been out of love, concern, and devotion for Misty. What seemed in retrospect to have been motivated by selfishness was really about preserving the life of a pet that meant a great deal to her. The group leader reminded Lynne of the nursing care she had unselfishly bestowed upon Misty and the quality of life Misty had enjoyed for years.

Lynne finally accepted that the choices she had made for Misty were motivated by love and concern and so could not be wrong or bad. Reframing the intense experience preceding Misty's death allowed Lynne to overcome her guilt and proceed along the grief continuum toward resolution.

Biofeedback

Another therapeutic technique that can assist clients with "all or none" type of thinking and help them to overcome the anxiety associated with loss is biofeedback. Behavioral techniques include relaxation training, cognitive restructuring, and biofeedback. Biofeedback helps clients reduce and control their anxiety by assisting them in becoming aware of their physiological responses as their anxiety overcomes them and can teach them to learn to relax.

While most clients experience anxiety from time to time, treatment is called for if the anxiety is out of proportion to the event experienced or is unduly prolonged. Biofeedback is often employed in conjunction with other forms of therapy, and is reported to be as effective as other behavioral types of therapy in many cases.

When faced with a real or perceived threat, the body's sympathetic nervous system prepares the individual for "flight or fight." The typical response includes dilated pupils, diaphoresis, superficial vasoconstriction, vasodilatation to heart and muscles, reduction in gastrointestinal activity, increased pulse and blood pressure. Response to stress, as might be seen with a prolonged grief response, can activate some or all parts of the response. Whether the symptoms are isolated or clustered, they can become habitual, eventually causing physical harm to the individual.

Biofeedback is aimed at changing habitual reactions to stress that can cause damage to body tissue. This is achieved through implementation of learned and practiced feedback loops designed to promote relaxation within the mind and body. Clients learn to pay attention to the onset of unpleasant symptoms, and then employ various techniques to direct "relaxation messages" to various parts of the body. In the office or clinic setting, physical responses are electronically monitored and measured to determine the effectiveness of the intervention. Once clients demonstrate success in interrupting negative feedback loops, they are able to utilize these techniques at will, relieving the stress associated with physical and emotional discomfort.

Traumatic Loss

Following the sudden accidental death of a pet, therapists can best assist clients by allowing them time and space to emote the deep feelings associated with witnessing the traumatic event. Horrific images and disturbing thoughts may intrude upon the client's day-to-day functioning. These thoughts and images may be ones actually witnessed by the client, or may be imagined. Pet parents who are forced to abandon their pets during a disaster may experience anger at the "powers-that–be" that forced the separation from the animal, anger internalized in which the client feels a deep sense of guilt and regret for having to abandon their pet when its well-being was dependent upon them. After learning of the horrific damage a disaster caused, pet parents often fear for their pet's safety and imagine the worst. They may create disturbing mental images of their pets trying to flee a home in which they were trapped and imagine the rising water, accompanying mud, and how the pet may have suffered in its last few moments before death, not unlike clients who actually witness their pets being hit by a car, accidentally closing the garage door on them, drowning, etc., may be tormented by these mental tapes replaying in their mind. This is especially true for disaster volunteers who rescued the animals that survived Hurricane Katrina.

Many volunteers witnessed the horrific scenes of the last moments of an animal's life as they entered homes in New Orleans to rescue the pets that might still be alive. Pet parents had left pet's tied up or in cages and crates, with a few days supply of food and water, thinking that once the stormed had passed, they would be able to return to them. Most pet parents never considered that the levees would break and their homes would flood, leaving their pets helpless victims, trapped inside cages filled with water and toxic mud. Many volunteers saw the desperate scratchmarks on the insides of the cages of dead animals as they tried in vain to escape the rising water.

One rescue worker said that she had comforted co-workers who ran screaming from homes, imagining the horrific attempts of the animals to survive in the last few moments of their lives. In a disaster situation, ideally, these rescue workers would have been debriefed. Unfortunately, debriefing services weren't available to them and a significant number of them later developed PTSD (see Chapter 10).

Hypnotherapy

When a traumatic event cannot easily be recalled, hypnosis can be used to uncover the traumatic event. Clients are directed to envision a safe, comfortable place that they have visited or would like to visit. For example, one might envision walking on a deserted sandy beach, sitting beneath a giant oak tree in a meadow, on a lovely spring morning, or resting beside a waterfall in a shady glen. The therapist uses guided imagery to take them to their safe place, where they remain in a highly relaxed state and vulnerable to suggestion. Once in this state, the therapist can safely assist the client in recalling the traumatic events they experienced. During the session the client is able to release deep felt emotions, receive support and validation, and is encouraged to let go of the negative images that intrude upon their thoughts. The therapist then assists the client in returning to consciousness. Clients usually report that they feel relaxed, peaceful, and comfortable. Some find that they are able to let go and say goodbye to their pets while under hypnosis, something they weren't able to consciously do on their own.

Eye Movement Desensitization and Reprocessing (EMDR Therapy)

Francine Shapiro, Ph.D., the originator and developer of EMDR, stumbled upon this psychotherapeutic approach when investigating treatments for PTSD. Since then, EMDR therapy has been discovered to have a markedly, high success rate in treating trauma.

The EMDR therapist assists the client's healing process by becoming a partner on a journey that the client feels about himself or herself. The therapist gently guides the client to pinpointing a problem, emotion, or event that becomes the target of treatment. For example, a client accidentally crushed his dog beneath the wheels of his car. After a couple of months, although this traumatic event was in his past, the client could not think about the event without experiencing the emotions associated with the loss. He still had feelings of guilt, helplessness, anger, and sadness. After receiving EMDR therapy from a trained and qualified therapist, he was able to recall the event without experiencing the intense emotions associated with it.

How EMDR Works

The therapist talks to the client and obtains a personal history. The therapist and client work together to construct a description of the problem and the negative perceptions the client has about himself relative to this event (e.g. "I felt frightened," "I felt helpless," "I am a bad person because I killed my dog"), and emotions and physical sensations associated with event. The therapist asks the client to rate numerically the degree of upset and credibility of positive beliefs so that the client's progress can be monitored. Once this protocol is established, the therapist and client begin the processing phase of the procedure by using the eye movements (or other kinds of attentional stimulation such as TheraTapper, a light bar, or recordings for auditory bilateral stimulation).

Although there are a variety of ways in which a therapist incorporates EMDR into therapy, a typical session lasts between 60 and 90 minutes. During this treatment, the therapist is facing the client and asks him or her to bring to mind the picture of the experience that is bothering him or her and any negative self-statements, emotions, and physical sensations associated with the traumatic experience. The client is asked to hold these images in mind while watching the therapist's hand moving rapidly back and forth (or receiving any other type of bilateral stimulation by the therapist). After a series of roughly 30–50 eye movements (or more), the therapist asks the client to stop, let go of the image or thought for a second, take a deep breath, and then notice and describe what thoughts, feelings, or images arose. The therapist might ask the client to continue to his or her same thoughts, feelings, or images. The therapist then performs the bilateral stimulation process again. By stimulating the left and right sides of the brain simultaneously, the therapist enables the client to process the traumatic event so it no longer impedes daily functioning. As the thoughts, images, feelings, and physical sensations become less distressing, the therapist asks the client to bring up a positive self-statement (e.g., "I loved my dog and would never intentionally harm him."). The positive statement combined with the EMDR helps the client to associate this new way of thinking about him- or herself without the original troubling image. Relief from symptoms can be obtained in one to six sessions, or EMDR can be a procedure the therapist uses alone or as part of a longer-term therapy such as combining it with the use of hypnotherapy. When a traumatic event cannot easily be recalled or the client has resistance to recalling it, hypnosis can be used to uncover the event. R.S. Isaac Gardner, M.D., was one of the first therapists to use hypnotherapy and EMDR therapy together. He has found this treatment to be highly effective in helping clients work through traumatic experiences.

Kathy McBeth, M.A., at the Institute for Children and Families in Westchester, PA, describes the goals of EMDR:

- Focus attention on a specific memory, thought, image or emotion.
- Unravel strings of disturbing, traumatic experiences, possibly providing missing details or data toward resolution.

- Eliminate irrational components of fears to allow other expressed or hidden affect to be processed.
- Reinforce more adaptive behaviors.
- Build positive, realistic beliefs.
- Strengthen ego and instill inner resources to build self-esteem.

Brainspotting™

A more specific type of EMDR therapy is called "Brainspotting." Deborah Antinori, M.A., provides us with an in-depth look into this type of therapy. Brainspotting, she says, was created and continues to be developed by EMDR therapist David Grand, Ph.D. By fixing the gaze on a particular spot determined by the client and therapist and simultaneously locating and focusing on the client's bodily sensations corresponding to his or her particular distress, Dr. Grand has found that clients are able to experience the "dismantling" of the source of the distress. Brainspotting processes at a deep level that goes to one's reflexive core, which resides in the deep unconscious brain/body. Dr. Grand finds that this deep aspect of our physiology/psychology is capable of healing our brain/body's fixated response to trauma. This healing capacity that Brainspotting facilitates is out of our awareness, as are respiration, circulation, and digestion. The deeply focused internal processing activated by Brainspotting far exceeds what our frontal cortex or reasoning brain can offer as rationalizations to "just snap out of it". As many clients report, they already know what their problem is, they just cannot get themselves out of the maze of old negative patterning, nor can they stop disturbing intrusive thoughts, feelings and images. Brainspotting catalyzes processing at the brain/body's foundational level leading to profound healing.

In Brainspotting therapy, the client's recall of a traumatic event triggers responses in the brain/body that is located and processed through the corresponding optimal eye position or "brainspot." The client's affective and somatic "felt sense" guides them to the optimal brainspot, which is the focused point at which the eye gazes. This felt sense corresponds to the trauma in its emotional and somatic feeling tone, and directs the eye to the optimal location for deep processing.

There are two approaches, termed "inside window" and "outside window," to finding brainspots. For both approaches, the distress side corresponding to the trauma can be located with greater focus by isolating one eye and then the other. By covering one eye at a time, the client finds which one has the felt sense of higher distress in relation to the trauma. Once this distress side is located, the client puts on goggles that are constructed with a clear lens to be used on the activated distress side. The opposite side, which has a darkened lens, tends to be the client's positive resource state, or lower distress. The goggles help to further the locating and focusing on brainspots, with light activating the opposite hemisphere of the brain.

Applying the inside window approach, the therapist and client together locate the brainspot, first on the "x" (vertical) and then on the "y" (horizontal) axis. The therapist uses an ordinary telescoping pointer that is moved slowly while the client tracks its movement with his or her eye guided by bodily felt sense. First working with the x axis, the highest intensity of distress is located above, at, or below eye level as the therapist moves the pointer up and down. The level of the highest intensity determined on the x axis by the client's felt sense is then used to explore the y axis location, and the therapist now moves the pointer horizontally at the level just determined. The intersection of the x (height) and y (left/right horizontal) axis points locates the most highly charged position or brainspot, where the client then gazes and the Brainspotting therapy proceeds with progressively deep internal processing. The details of this processing will be described after the outside window approach is illustrated below.

In the outside window approach, the therapist explores the horizontal y axis only for the sake of time and simplicity, and observes the reflexive responses in the client while the client tracks the micro-slow horizontal movements of the pointer. The therapist looks for reflexive movements in the client's eyes including perceptible blinks, wobbles (eye moves in a shaking manner rapidly left to right), and freezes (like a rabbit in the headlights). Reflexive moments of the body also indicate the location of brainspots and can include twitches, jerks, swallows, or sniffs. All of these reflexive movements of the client's eyes and body signal areas where the body holds and is attempting to process significant emotional material. When the optimal brainspot is located, utilizing either or both inside and outside window approaches, the client's gaze at this spot produces an inside/outside concentrated focus that leads to feelings, memories, and images relevant to the trauma that processes in a progressively deep manner. It is important to note that the client's bodily sensations are integral to finding and processing the brainspot that resonates most clearly with the client's experience of trauma. It is possible that trauma involving a specific part of the body may not yield that same area of the body as the client's felt sense relating to the trauma. For example, the client may have experienced injury to his or her head during a trauma, but in recalling that accident, a tightness in the chest or some other sensation in another part of the body may be reported as the area most accurately corresponding to the trauma. It is important to ask the clients where they experience feelings in the body in order to locate the appropriate areas of somatic activation. Also, these areas of activation may shift in location during a session, so that the therapist should not make any assumptions regarding where in the client's body memories lie, but rather continue to track the client using the outside window technique and to ask for feedback regarding the location of bodily sensations throughout the session.

As previously stated, in Brainspotting sessions, trauma, or other negative experiences, the attendant bodily sensations and the corresponding "felt sense" are identified and utilized throughout a session. The eye position that is most resonant is then located with inside and/or outside window approaches. To track the progress in Brainspotting work, a rating scale is used as in EMDR—the SUDs (subjective units of disturbance) level is taken with 10 being the most intense distress and 0 being neutral. Clients usually report a high distress number at the beginning of a session (a 6 or higher), and a lower number (or sometimes a 0) by the end as the events are processed by the brain/body's ability to regain homeostasis. The distress is processed to the core with Brainspotting therapy and clients feel a dramatic change in their subjective experience of their distress by the end of a session.

Processing involves quiet time, where the client focuses in a laser-like fashion to the core of the issue, which lies in the deep body consciousness and the innate intelligence of the body's system to repair and rebalance itself.

Aspects of somatic experiencing (Peter Levine's work) are similar to Brainspotting, as both are founded in neurophysiological studies of the brain and body's fight-or-flight and freeze survival responses. Somatic experiencing and Brainspotting therapies access our innate blueprint for homeostasis, which is a part of all living creatures' genetic constitutions. Dr. Levine notes that when prey animals can neither fight nor flee life threatening encounters with predators, they respond by freezing. This is a part of the instinctive system that improves chances for survival in life-threatening situations. The instinctive impulse to freeze simulates being dead, resulting in the predator's losing interest in what appears to be dead prey. These prey animals may be threatened several times a day yet remain untraumatized. Animals transition from the freeze response back to homeostasis through a shaking-off sequence. Muscular trembling and vibrations follow an observable head-to-hindquarter pattern that results in the animal's return to normal activities and relaxation. This freeze/shake-off sequence constitutes nature's internal hard-wiring for prey animals to go about the business of animal life again untraumatized (Levine, 1997). In a similar manner, Dr. Grand finds that Brainspotting therapy effectively dismantles the unreleased freeze response and attendant PTSD symptoms that remain from the trauma. The deep processing of Brainspotting allows for the human version of releasing the freeze state and the resumption of daily life again free from intrusive images, feelings or memories. The laser-like focus provided by the Brainspot facilitates deep internal processing which goes to the foundation of the offending issues and utilizes our innate genetic healing mechanisms promoting optimal homeostasis.

BioLateral recordings are helpful tools that facilitate the deep processing of Brainspotting. These CDs feature music and natural sounds such as waves, rain, or running water that have been sound engineered by Dr. Grand to produce alternating left/right audio through the use of a CD player and headphones. Auditory bilateral stimulation activates both hemispheres of the brain, which has been found to maximize deep processing of traumatic material.

Pet Loss and Brainspotting Therapy

A pet loss client came into therapy with disturbing images and a tremendous sense of guilt following the euthanasia of her cat. These intrusive images were getting in the way of her daily functioning and she felt torturous guilt about the decision to euthanize her pet. As this client held her gaze at a brainspot point above her head and to her right (established by both inside- and outside-window approaches), she spent time in deep processing. There were tears and, after some time of quiet processing, she told of the death of her brother when she was young. Her experience of feeling overburdened by responsibility for her brother when they were young had made her feel guilty about his death. To further define this newly emerging material, the therapist asked the client to locate where in her body she felt the sense of being overburdened by responsibility in relation to her brother. She voiced that she felt a clenching in her stomach. The therapist then asked her to identify a shape, object or color associated with the clenching sensation in her stomach. She sensed a deep purple color in the shape of a rectangular steel cage encasing her stomach. The therapist suggested that she focus on the bodily felt sense of being overburdened with responsibility and the attendant image of the deep purple steel cage encasing her clenching stomach, and allow the processing to continue from that point.

The client continued to gaze at the Brainspot while being aware of these bodily sensations and images, and allowed the deep processing to occur. Key to Brainspotting work is allowing the processing, internal movement unique to each person to be spontaneous and authentic. It is not the cognitive portion of the brain analyzing what makes sense, but rather the deep brain/body's inner wisdom and physiology at work carrying the client to memories, associations, and images that relate directly to the traumatic material that lead to homeostasis.

These additions to the Brainspotting therapy—the use of shape, color, or image associated to the felt sense—can assist the client in further defining the body's sensations that ultimately guide the processing to positive resolution. The aforementioned client had other pertinent associations to her pattern of taking on too much responsibility, including a "deep searing pain" in her heart whenever she thought of her brother. Again, the suggestion was made by the therapist for a color, shape, or image that corresponded to the pain in her heart as she remembered her brother.

After describing a black color and the image of a locked door in her chest, she spent time in processing, gazing at the brainspot location previously located, voicing some of her associations, and letting others process quietly. As noted earlier, quiet time is important in Brainspotting work as words can get in the way of the deep processing at the reflexive core. Pertinent history was uncovered involving her mother's leaving her to care for her brother, often when he was quite ill. She felt intense panic and distress at these times, yet would carry bravely on at the expense of her own needs at such a young age—only 10 years old.

The client made an immediate present-day connection to being "left alone" with the decision to euthanize her cat. Feelings of helplessness and panic surfaced and she reported a "re-visiting" of the searing pain in her chest that she had felt in relation to her brother. Now the color relating to that pain was bright orange and a diamond shape was felt in her chest. More processing occurred as she gazed at the brainspot while tears ran down her cheeks and she expressed how sad she felt that her cat had become sick enough to require euthanasia. After some more processing, the client was able to feel a significantly lower level of distress (3) than when she began (10).

Now more images of her cat came up and she felt a hollowness in her stomach that was colorless—more processing occurred as she gazed at the brainspot. At the end of the session, her stomach felt neutral and she reported a light pink glow. Her SUD's level was now down to a 1. In the following weeks, her SUDs level was down to 0 when she brought up the death of her brother as well as the euthanasia of her cat. She felt sad about her losses, which is a natural feeling to have, but the repeating PTSD symptoms she had felt initially regarding the cat's euthanasia had ceased and were replaced with a sense of calm she had not experienced before. She now realized she made the appropriate decision for euthanasia at the right time. A newfound sense of relief came to this client, who experienced a tremendous sense of freedom as the love and happy memories of her cat were becoming available to her again. She was also able to let go of the feelings of overburdened responsibility she had had for the death of her brother.

The two events, her cat's euthanasia and her brother's death, had been tied together and the Brainspotting sessions revealed, and processed through to resolution, this client's chronic sense of responsibility for others. The death of her brother was now experienced as an event that had been out of her control. Remarkably, she felt her ability to remember her brother without the "deep searing pain" in her heart was a gift she could never have dreamed of receiving. She now experienced a connection to her brother and felt the blessing of having him back in her heart without the attendant pain her lifelong sense of over-responsibly had wrought.

In these latter sessions, we utilized the resource side eye (alternate eye to the distress side) to install more deeply the positive feelings, new decisions, wisdom, and awareness the client was experiencing. Using inner window approach, we located the brainspot that corresponded to her new sense of relief regarding both her cat and her brother, and she spent time in gazing at this point, with the attendant bodily sensations corresponding to the relief. A kind of "Zen" state was reported by the client that felt very good to her.

Pesso Boyden System Psychomotor Therapy (PBSP)

According to Antinori, who has worked closely with the PBSP developers, this therapy was developed by Albert Pesso and Diane Boyden-Pesso over the past 45 years. They began their professional careers as dancers. In the late 1950s, when Al and Diane were choreographers, they noticed that their students and dance company members often had difficulties with some qualities of movement. When they examined that phenomenon closely they discovered that what were thought of as extraneous tensions often had specific emotional meanings for each individual. From this (simply described) beginning, they went on to develop the very sophisticated and remarkable therapy known today as Pesso Boyden System Psychomotor Therapy.

PBSP is a mind/body therapy that begins with the therapist "micro-tracking" the client's present consciousness, i.e. their affect, thoughts, strategies, and values. This information is reflected back to the client using symbolic role-played figures: a Witness Figure, who labels the emotion and the context within which they are felt; and a Voice Figure, who speaks the thoughts and words spoken by the client regarding strategies and values as if they were commands coming from an outside authority. Micro-tracking includes watching the subtle changes in expression on the client's face combined with the gestalt of his or her posture, gesture, and emotional tones as he or she speaks about feelings and thoughts.

For example, the therapist might posit a Witness Figure to say something like, "I see how anguished you feel as you recall the fight with your wife this morning." Here, the client's present-moment experience is captured (and fed back to the client) by the Witness Figure, who sees and gives place for the client's feeling of anguish within the context of the fight reported by the client with his wife that morning. Thus, PBSP utilizes this and other highly specified role playing figures (or objects in individual therapy) and accurate verbiage (following exactly the client's words, affect, and feeling tone) to map a client's current reality. The micro-tracking process generally leads to associated childhood memories of unresolved developmental conflicts. These deficits are satisfied through the use of Ideal Figures who, had they been in the client's past, would have provided him or her with the wished for interactions that would result in the satisfaction of mature needs.

The client's present values and strategies might be symbolized by "Voice Figures," which are developed from the client's exact words and experience, for example a Voice of Truth ("Who do you think you are?"), a Voice of Judgment ("You can never get anything right"), or a Voice of Negative Prediction ("There will never be any hope for you"). These figures contribute to the realization of the past underpinnings of the client's current distress, which can lead to some aspect of a parent, teacher, sibling, or other important figure in the client's life as a child. Some examples are the negative aspects of Mother/ Father/or anyone in a client's life, loved aspects of Grandmother/Sister, etc., or any other aspects of a significant figure in the client's life. Role playing figures in a group setting or objects in individual sessions give place (the first developmental need) for the client's experience of reality. It is amazing to see how clearly representing what is held in the client's mind by the use of these symbolic figures can allow for a significant shift in the client's experience of what feels possible, where formerly only negative possibilities prevailed. When the content of the mind/body system is located outside the client with these role playing figures, clients can interact with these introjects from their early years and ultimately come to a more satisfying conclusion in the structure work.

As discussed above, with mapping of the True Scene (present-moment experience), the client's history usually becomes evident to them. The precursors to their current distress are usually located in the past traumas, deficits in parenting, emotional inconsistency in childhood, abuse or neglect. The building of ideal figures (ideal parents, ideal support figure, etc.) is done creatively by the client and therapist together to offset or negate what was toxic or traumatic in the client's original experience. The creation of a "new synthetic memory" awakens previously dormant abilities, knowing, and other awareness in the client.

Functional magnetic resonance imaging (FMRI) brain scans have been conducted to show the change in brain activity before and after a structure, showing more cognitive and control areas of the brain being activated after a structure. Positive changes in life are reported by clients as well as an increase in their abilities to resolve long-standing difficult issues, and to respond proactively to past traumas and other disturbing experiences that originally brought them into therapy.

PBSP and Pet Loss Therapy

Several months after the death of her elderly pet, a client came into individual therapy complaining of disturbing images after having found her dog dead one morning. She could not get the disturbing image out of her mind—how the lifeless body lay, so different from the alive and wonderful creature she had known for more than 16 years. This client found that her daily functioning was compromised, that she had nightmares about not being able to save her dog in all kinds of situations. She had a very supportive husband, adult children, and friends who understood her connection to the dog and tried to reassure her that the dog had lived a very good long life and had even spared her and the family the euthanasia decision. The client remained traumatized and inconsolable.

In our working together in individual therapy, this beloved pet was finally found to have represented an ideal parent figure for the client, providing a sense of home, safety, and security for her unlike any other person had been able to give her. This woman felt that all was right in life as long as her dog was around. In our work together, several structures were done to explore her feelings of loss and to deal with the intrusive nature of the disturbing image of her dog when he was dead. In the beginning of one structure, this client found an object to represent the loved aspect of her dog which brought forth how she had never had that kind of unconditional love from any one person. This is representing the true scene in PBSP, the client's current reality. Now she remembered the confusing childhood she had experienced, wherein her parents provided a stable home, yet were emotionally distant. This client was the youngest of three children and born to her parents, both accomplished medical researchers, quite late in their lives. The client put out both the loved aspects of each parent and then the limited aspects of them in different sessions. She felt that her parents were always "somewhere else in their heads" working out problems from the research lab and not aware of her need for them emotionally. Yet the client reported that her parents provided her with many opportunities for expression of her talents—piano lessons, horseback riding lessons, and private school that she loved and where she excelled. This client discovered she had much unexpressed anger and sadness as well as longing for her parents' attention.

She also found that she wanted to express her love and gratitude to her parents for the educational background and other privileged opportunities she had enjoyed in her childhood. Working with objects enrolled as limited and loved aspects, respectively, she was able to give place and voice to her formerly silent feelings.

The client used the same object to represent the loved aspect of her dog in many sessions, finally making a bridge to ideal parents who had qualities similar to her dog's in his constant love for her and his available presence. With the ideal parent figures, she was able to feel the unconditional love, constancy, and emotional dependability she wished for through statements the ideal parents made to her (using only the therapist's voice enrolled as their voices, not the therapist enrolled as the ideal parents) and took these statements and the feeling of warmth and comfort she felt from the ideal parents down to the child inside of her. (Note: She had rolled up two large cushions and placed them on either side as ideal mother and ideal father. In a group setting, group members would play these roles, and would say only what the client wanted to hear at a time directed by the therapist. This is different from psychodrama, where the role playing figures improvise.) The new experience of the client as a child with an ideal family is very helpful for a client who was neglected, abused, or traumatized as a child and creates a "new synthetic memory" of what should have been for the child who stills lives inside the adult. The image of the child with her ideal parents becomes the new model for the client to go to rather than the negative introjects she took in from the toxic or absent, etc., parenting of the negative aspects of her biological parents.

At the end of our work together, this client was able to feel relief when she thought of the death of her dog, which had actually been peaceful—he had gone in his sleep. No autopsy was done, but the vet suspected a stroke or heart attack, and from the position and expression of the dog, he had most likely died peacefully and quickly. The growing symbol and the usable tool of the ideal parents clearly facilitated a resolution to the issue of the client's perception of the traumatic loss of the dog. She still missed him greatly, but the intrusive disturbing images and rescue nightmares ceased. Additionally, the client was able to feel gratitude for the ways her parents had expressed love to her—by sending her to private schools and attending all of her piano recitals. The client was able to feel that this was their way of loving her. Work with the ideal parent figures facilitated her being able not only to feel the positive aspects of her parents' love for her and her love for them, but also gave place and expression for her angry and disappointed feelings at their limitations. Finally, the ideal parents provided the new tool for her to utilize as a model for self love and appreciation in revisiting the internalized symbol of herself as a child with the ideal parents and their unconditional love for her.

Conclusion

Recent tragic events in the United States (9/11, Gulf Coast flooding and Midwest tornadoes) have highlighted the roles of animals in our lives and the need for society to accept pet companions as valued family members. These events have made us even more acutely aware of the fact that pet loss is often associated with trauma. Pet parents often witness their pets being run over by cars, closed in dryers or garage doors, drowned in swimming pools, and unforeseen natural and manmade disasters.

Not long ago many people in society didn't give much thought to the loss of a pet. Pets were something that could be replaced or didn't "count" as much on the emotional loss scale as a human being. Slowly, views are changing, and therapists are seeking education and acquiring skills that will help them guide grieving clients through the pet loss grief continuum. A multitude of therapy options are now available and have been successfully used, both singularly and in combination, at resolving the emotional pain encountered by clients when the human–animal bond is broken. Many of these therapies, either alone or in conjunction with other therapies, assist the client in relieving the stress, anxiety, emotional and physical pain that can accompany a loss.

Pet loss support groups can offer clients a form of support that may be unavailable in one-to-one counseling sessions. In the group setting, clients benefit from the shared experiences of other members and learn that they are not isolated in their losses—that others feel the same way they do. Their loss is acknowledged and validated, and their progress through the grief continuum is enhanced by sharing traumatic experiences, emotional responses, and coping strategies. Often a support group is best used in conjunction with other types of therapy. Clients who attend group should be assessed and referred to the appropriate mental health services, so that additional treatment approaches can be utilized if necessary.

Regardless of age, social status, and family membership, all those who love animals are impacted negatively by the loss of a pet. Many are unprepared for the degree of loneliness experienced when their animal friend dies, is lost, stolen, or runs away. Loneliness can occur even when one is surrounded by family members, co-workers, or friends. It is intensified by the fact that society in general does not acknowledge the bonds that humans share with companion animals. Although some of the loneliness may be alleviated by adopting another pet, it is important to remember that the unique bond shared with the lost pet cannot be replaced. To bond successfully with a new pet the previous loss needs to be resolved.

Health care professionals are in a position to acknowledge the grief felt by clients for the loss of a pet. The aim of treatment is to normalize their grief experience through acceptance and validation of their feelings while guiding them safely through predictable stages of the grief process. By understanding the unique relationships clients may have with their pets, therapists are in a position to offer them a safe haven to express the anger, fear, sadness, and loneliness that make up the grief process.

12

THOUGHTS ABOUT LOVING AND LOSING COMPANION ANIMALS

Animals may accompany us through many of life's experiences and challenges. There are many, many types of bonds people share with pets. These are as unique as the stories people share about their companion animals. Barrett's study companion is his dog Molly.

There is a time for everything, a season for every activity under heaven. A time to reap, a time to sow, a time to gather together and a time to let go, a time to be born and a time to die.

—Ecclesiastes 3:1

Death leaves a heartache no one can heal
Love leaves a memory no one can steal

—Author Unknown

The poems and stories in this chapter tell about the bonds and love pet parents have experienced and the depth of pain that loss often brings. Sometimes people assume that grief for an animal is only experienced if that animal is a long-time pet. This is not true. Loving relationships and deep feelings can develop for any animal, for working dogs, zoo animals, wildlife, and farm animals. People can deeply love and care for an animal they've only known for a short time too.

It is with great respect that we include the stories of people who loved and lost their animal friends. We hope that the sharing of their stories not only honor and remember their animals, but will help to create more understanding about the bonds humans and animals can share.

A Letter of Thanks to My Fellow Rescuers—Hurricane Katrina

Dr. Pia Salk, co-founder of Animal Rescue New Orleans, began her work in the Gulf Coast as one of the many volunteers who just got on a plane and showed up despite rumors that they were not needed or that they might not be allowed admission to the Lamar-Dixon Expo Center in Gonzales, Louisiana, where rescued animals were sheltered following rescue after Hurricane Katrina. She gives this account of her experience:

It is March 31, 2006, 7 months and 2 days after Hurricane Katrina hit. Just today I have spoken separately to six volunteers who I met down in Louisiana who have now come to be good friends. We chatted, exchanged e-mails about rescue workshops to attend and just shared that thing that we each need so to share right now—that which it seems no one other than those who witnessed the fallout from this awful tragedy can share. It's hard to explain. One fellow rescuer stated that she had wished there had been some sort of exit process for volunteers to help them deal with the thoughts, feelings, images that they were now left with. I agreed, and it has been something I have thought about many times—often thinking that, as a trained clinical psychologist who is supposed to know how to offer comfort in such a case, I should do something.

As I think of the clinical side of all this—that many among us are suffering from signs of post traumatic stress symptoms that many of us are likely to meet the criteria for diagnoses of bereavement, adjustment disorder, or a situational depression, I can't help but hear blah blah blah. I do not mean to make light or dismiss anything here, I am just potently aware that what I have studied in textbooks for years surrounds me and is real and felt and not a part of academia. It is part of life. It is part of myself and of the people I have come to know and love through this. And it is life itself. These symptoms, these feelings of despair—they are life itself. They are very real reactions to real events. And they need to be tended to as such. And while I absolutely encourage those among us who are having prolonged difficulties functioning or feeling suicidal to seek professional help—to share these feelings with others—I also want to acknowledge that many of these feelings are to be expected.

I, a psychologist myself, have cried many tears about this in my own therapist's office and she has cried with me. Some might see this as strange or somehow unprofessional but I do not. I am quick to say that no one understands unless they were there. But there are many who do. What they share may not be an understanding of what we witnessed and the depth of the pain that has resulted from this, but they share an understanding of the injustice and a belief that these animals deserved so much more. They love their own animals and are thankful for what we did to help. While it is likely you will find more solace with those who also took direct action in this effort, try to remain open to the comfort offered by those offering it. And seek it out—personally, professionally—do not isolate yourself from connection. Connection is what got us involved, whether it was connection to a friend who was going to the region, connection to your own animal, whatever it was, it was about connection and kinship. That is what motivated us to take action and it is that spirit that we must rekindle as we struggle now.

So, my friend's words motivated me to write tonight. I feel a profound kinship with my fellow rescuers, one that has tears streaming down my face as I write to all of you—those I have met and those I have not. I feel a deep love and appreciation for each and every one of you. You, the person who took a stand for the animals, you, the person who took the time, made the sacrifice and by so doing defined who you are. Some of you helped from afar—reuniting animals, helping those on the ground navigate, sending out alerts, and so much more. Others of you helped at Lamar Dixon, Winn Dixie, Tyler Town, Pasado, Waveland, or the like—cleaning stalls, alerting vets to those who needed immediate care, sitting with and stroking a scared dog covered in mange with no concern for what you might catch. You were the eyes, ears, and voice for the animals. Others of you were breaking down doors and fiercely searching for that stranded little creature who might now be too weak to call out. Others of you set traps and returned time and again to get every last puppy or the bonded mate of the creature you were sent to trap.

I have a quote on my fridge that reads, "You are not truly alive until you have found something that you are willing to die for (Martin Luther King). Well, for so many of us, this was that "something."

You are my heroes, each and every one of you, and while I feel so alone in many ways—embedded in a world that does little to understand, help, and honor our fellow creatures, a world that sees Katrina as the distant past. I also feel a kinship with all of you and I am so honored to have been a part of this effort with you.

We live in a constructed reality, where animals are considered below us in some silly hierarchical order and where deep feelings are often pathologized and dismissed. What we witnessed in the Gulf Coast was truly tragic. We arrived ready to help and get dirty but found little order or direction. This left us feeling even more helpless and confused. There was no formula, no real plan, and what was most disturbing was that there was no real sense of urgency among those running the show. We looked for guidance, but once we realized that we needed no one's permission to do what was right and urgently needed, we quickly mobilized and drew on both internal resources and each other to get to work.

Our adrenaline helped get us through. But now is a different story. There is no adrenaline driving us to get that injured kitten out from under a house, or that snarling pit bull out from the drainpipe of a canal. There are no authorities we have to get past as we try to enter a restricted parish, or curfews we need to be concerned with as the day closes on a rescue we have been working on for hours. Now it is just each of us back home attending to our daily lives. And it is hard. I know for me the sadness and the rage is just below the surface and I carry it with me each day. I feel a sense of pride on some days and tremendous guilt that I did not do enough on others. It is an emotional roller coaster, but one on which I know I have many other co-travelers riding along in my roller car. I am plagued by images of certain animals that got away, that I left behind, that I pray were somehow saved. I will not recount any specifics here, as we each have our own versions of this and need not add more to the mix.

But for all of this, regardless of how much time we spent there, or if we even got there at all because we were instead assisting from afar, it was hard, and in some ways it is now even harder to tolerate. We heard stories, we saw images, and we faced obstacles that we will never forget. For some, this was more of the despair we have come to know regarding the world's treatment of animals. For others, this was new and an awakening of a sort. One woman recently said to me that she was never an "animal person," but as she saw the heart-wrenching images on TV, she had to go help—and that she has now found her calling. I am not surprised.

As we each try to reintegrate ourselves into our normal lives we face much despair. The despair comes in many forms—rage for what we saw, for how it was handled, for how it continues to be handled; rage at the people who left their animals or the people who forced them to do so; rage at the injustice of it all—that's what gets me. And then we also feel deep sadness and compassion—compassion for the same people who had to leave their animals, imagining what it would be like, what we would do, and compassion for the animals who perished, the ones who suffered so, whose suffering we could see live or could only imagine given the signs left by their lifeless little bodies. "Oh, to turn back the clock, is what we thought. How?! Why?! This cannot be!" And the feelings are too much to bear.

There seems no consolation, nothing that we can convince ourselves of to make the pain go away. And I offer none here. With the years of academic training I have endured in this sort of matter, I can offer no remedy, no potion, no salve. It is something we must simply sit with and allow its due place in the space of our emotional lives. It is something that is now within us and has come to define each of us. And it will motivate us all the more the next time around. For many, it is fueling efforts at reform, continued work at reunification, spurring ideas for new rescue groups that will help in the future. It is organic and real and living itself out in these ways. The only comfort I can attempt to offer or suggest comes in the form of kinship and in the form of action.

With regard to kinship, I'm thinking of that sort of Eastern Zen concept that, as a Jew from New York City I have little experience with, but I have come to discover that there is something to it. It is the feeling of kinship with others who share this plight. And kinship with the animals, the lovely creatures, some so fierce they evaded capture, others so weak they simply collapsed in our arms. And the ones with whom we share our homes and who live in our local communities, the ones who need us every day.

And as for action, my second suggestion for comfort: continue to take action in your daily lives. I know we are all tired and we must replenish ourselves and rest for sure. But action can play a role in this. The injustices we saw in the Gulf Coast and the actions we can take to oppose them are not limited to the fall of 2005 in that geographical region. They span the spectrum from rubbing the belly of the pound pup in our home to writing letters on matters of injustice to modeling a compassionate lifestyle that others can draw inspiration from and replicate. Personally, I try to draw the connection for people between the social injustices enacted upon animals and those from which marginalized people have suffered. They are one and the same—all resulting from the misuse of power.

We were all a part of ... well, no, ... we composed the largest animal rescue of all time and now it is we who need rescue. All that we knew before, the priorities of daily life, evade our attention as we search for some comfort and a sense of where to file this massive experience. At times, I get this strange sense that the animals who perished have our backs on this, that they are watching from afar and will ensure that we will be all right. We must stay connected to them and to each other. And let this be the impetus to think outside of the box, to shake things up for the sake of the animals, for ourselves, and for the future of social justice. As Margaret Mead once said, "Never doubt that a small group of concerned committed citizens can change the world." We are those concerned citizens and we must applaud ourselves and each other.

I applaud you. I give you a standing ovation. You are my kind of people. The people who know what is right and what is important, the people who take action, who are not afraid to get dirty physically or emotionally. You feel deeply; it is what defines you. You are extraordinary and deserve the comfort that you so crave. Take a moment to close your eyes and summon the animals who died—those who perished in Katrina or those that shared your life in other ways and have now also died. Connect with them as a great force of compassion and love that is accessible to you, that is part of you—that may sound hokey, but I find it helpful. Find ways to access comfort and share those ways with others.

I have great love and appreciation for each and every one of you and am proud to have you as kin.

Katrina Dogs

Much of the comfort I crave these days comes from my two Katrina dogs—a term that has come to be like a brand name for the newest, chicest trend in animal welfare.

I am so full of love for these creatures, it is unimaginable. There is Luna, the feral one who was so traumatized upon her arrival at Lamar Dixon I had never seen such a sight—her eyes filled with pus, deemed aggressive for snapping at the catchpole, and essentially doomed because of her spirit to live. And there is Sweetie, the little skeleton pit bull my friend Megan and I rescued from a porch in the upper 9th ward. Upon her rescue, she crawled right passed the food we put out for her and into my lap. She was starving when we found her but craved human touch and comfort more than the food. She just sat still in my lap with her face pressed up against mine for the longest time. It was on a day that we were not supposed to bring animals back because Lamar Dixon was full and would take only criticals. This pair *was* critical in our book.

Luna has transformed. The moment I set eyes on her a switch flipped and I silently conveyed to her that I had her covered. In the days at Lamar Dixon, I would often sneak off to sit with her and try to get her eating from my hand—my only real respite in the time spent there.

After I jumped through the bureaucratic hoops and got her cage tagged for adoption I felt relieved, only to find one day that she had been loaded on a transport to a public shelter in Iowa. I was livid, and that was the first moment in my initial weeks there that I said, "No more; I can't do it anymore." But, like so many of you, I found a way and kept on with the work. I frantically contacted the shelter in Iowa and was able to have her shipped to me in Los Angeles when I returned. I set her up in her own room, where she would not leave her crate while I was around for more than three months. She would eat out of my hand occasionally, but that was it. If she heard a sudden noise, she would literally try to climb the walls like a wild animal as if attempting to escape for her life. My vet and others confirmed that she was feral and they were dubious about her ability to become less fearful. I was torn about how best to care for her. I would fill the room with the smell of lavender, as it's supposed to be calming. I bought a CD with calming music specifically for animals and I would sometimes nap on the floor by her crate to convey some sense that I would be vulnerable near her and she could trust me. I became a flower child temporarily.

There seemed to be little change as the time passed, but I then began to notice the subtle things—like her tail was now straight down and not between her legs. Her ears were different; they seemed to square off her little Labrador head and not be angled downward. And I'll never forget seeing her sleep deeply for the first time—that really got me. I sobbed quietly as I witnessed her get what was likely the first restful, deep sleep she may have ever had. And to think she allowed herself to let go enough to do so in my presence. So I became grateful for the little changes and I let her know that whatever she did was okay.

A few months after receiving Luna, Sweetie, the pit bull, now joined us. She was transported to me from my new friend Adrianne's care. Adrianne had taken her from Lamar Dixon with a lot of other special-needs pups. I couldn't get her out of my mind, so I called to adopt her. She was driven across country by two people I had never met who answered the call and another friend who had wanted so to help but had not been able to go to New Orleans herself. I feel much gratitude toward all of them.

When Sweetie arrived she was a playful bundle of love. She came complete with heartworm, home-crafted clipped ears and what looked like the udders of a cow—the result of many litters. Sweetie and I would roll and play as Luna watched quietly from her crate, which I had now opened so it was only a place for her to sit in. I watched her, wondering what she thought of this, and then, it was almost as if a switch now flipped in her. Her tail began to wag for about a second at a time. I sent word out to all of my friends, alerting them to this news. I was ecstatic. The e-mails I had been sending were typically one liners: "Luna ate from my hand today, Luna took a nap in front of me." Now they were, "Luna wagged her tail today!!!!!, Luna licked my hand, Luna jumped on to the couch with me!!!!" It was thrilling.

This was a dog that had likely never been touched by a human hand prior to Katrina and was so traumatized by her capture. Now she had decided to step outside of what she knew—to take a huge risk and to trust me. What a gift. One I thank her for each day. She taught me so much—patience, acceptance, true kinship. I had surrendered to her, deciding I would likely never really get to pet her or kiss her little black muzzle. I accepted that we would live together in kinship, not needing anything from each other, just sharing space and an occasional glance. But as I accepted this, she gave me so much more—a miracle of sorts.

Now she runs and plays and rolls over so I can bury my face in her tummy. She licks my face and wags her whole body. We take naps on the couch either spooning each other or fully entwined with Sweetie, and all with our faces pressed up against each other. I look at these guys when they are sleeping and wonder what they went through, what they saw, how they felt, and I am thankful that they are here with me now, and safe. The love I feel for them is so very pure, and I share this with you all simply because I want to share something that might uplift you for a moment. Something that speaks to the kinship we need to cultivate with each other, a kinship born of pure love and respect, the kind of love that needs nothing in return.

One of you rescued Luna. I may have met you, I may not have. It need not matter as we each play a role in this collective. But I deeply thank you for the role you have chosen and I re-commit to mine.

Pets and the Agony of Separation

Tamra Teig Kjos

I never really considered myself a "dog person." I had grown up with a family cat in the house and I was fond of her soft, quiet presence. As an adult, unfortunate experiences with neighbors' dogs made me view cats as the infinitely superior pet choice. Cats, I argued, did not bark in the middle of the night and they discreetly buried their excrement, rather than rudely depositing it on neighbors' lawns. I liked to joke that I even made a verbal prenuptial agreement with my husband that I could have a cat. I realize it was no small sacrifice for him, as he is decidedly not a "cat person" and even claims to be allergic to them.

Over the years my husband, who had fond memories of growing up with a family dog, suggested that it would be nice to get a dog "for the kids." Our children would even ask now and then if they could have a dog (usually prompted by hearing his request), but I had always held firm. I argued that we wouldn't be able to take spontaneous weekend trips like we could with the cats. I said that, as a freelance writer and mom of three kids, I was already too busy to take care of another living thing. Besides, with a husband who traveled extensively and kids busy with all their activities, I knew who would end up taking care of the dog, regardless of the promises pouring forth to the contrary.

My final argument was that our three-story house in Portland, Oregon was not very dog friendly. Although we had a large wooded lot, the house was built into a hill and it took two flights of stairs to get down to the back yard. The front of the house was close to the street, and none of the yard was fenced—it was no place for a dog.

Fortunately, the entire family was distracted from the whole puppy issue after our young cat Trixie escaped for a romantic interlude one evening. I had been putting off the vet appointment to get her spayed, because she was an indoor cat, but her animal instinct proved to be a powerful and fruitful force. A few months later, Trixie was the proud mother of four adorable kittens. Two of them found a loving home with some neighbors who had two children. Thanks to strong lobbying by my children, and my own weakness for kittens, the other two (soon named Cricket and Bear) became members of our family. The children and I were delighted, and my husband was resigned. Our family was complete—or so I thought until one fateful trip to the grocery store to buy milk.

It was a beautiful Saturday evening in May—and almost closing time at the supermarket. I parked next to the entrance and hustled my eight-year-old daughter Elena out of the car. As we approached the entrance, we saw an older woman standing by the door, holding the cutest, fluffiest, black puppy I had ever seen. While I paused to allow

Elena to pet it, the woman told me that she was selling it for a friend of hers, and this female was the last of a litter of nine. Perhaps sensing an interested customer, she added that the father was a nice black lab and the mother a very sweet Australian shepherd.

Although Elena wanted to linger, I was in a hurry to get home and the woman smelled strongly of alcohol. Besides, I most certainly wasn't interested in what she was selling. "We are not getting a dog," I told Elena firmly, as I tried to ignore the pleading look in her big blue eyes.

Just then, a grocery clerk came out of the exit and approached us. "Are you the lady who's selling the puppies?" she asked the woman.

"Yes," the woman answered.

"Well, your mom's on the phone, and wants to talk to you," the clerk replied. The woman hurriedly followed her inside, still clutching the puppy.

"Good luck," I called after her, and took Elena's hand to enter the store.

A few minutes later, as we exited the store, we saw the woman again. She had a box in one hand and the puppy in the other. Something made me stop and ask, "Is everything okay with your mom?"

"She's sick," the woman replied, as she set the box on the ground. "I have to get home right away."

"What are you going to do with the puppy?" I asked. My question surprised me—it seemed to pop out on its own when I saw, with mounting concern, that the woman was putting the puppy into the box. "Oh, I'll just leave her here in this box," she said rather distractedly, "I'm sure somebody will take her."

It was almost dark now, and my motherly instinct emerged. I turned to Elena, who was silently but intently observing our exchange. "I need you to wait in the car for me for just a minute, okay?" I walked with her the few steps to our van, deposited the grocery bag on the floor and settled her into the back seat. "I'll be right back," I said. Then I paused, and looked intently into her hopeful eyes, "But we're not getting a dog."

My mind raced as I turned back to the woman. Our good friends, who lived just around the corner from us, had a Welsh Corgi. "I'm sure they'll take her just for a day or two, until I can find a home for her," I thought to myself, "or maybe they'll even want to keep her; she's awfully cute."

The woman had paused when she saw me returning, and I hurried up to her, my words spilling out. "Wait a minute," I said to her, "I just can't leave her here—I'll take her. How much are you selling her for?"

"Well," the woman hesitated, "I sold the others for $10 apiece …"

I rifled through my wallet and pulled out a $20 bill. "Here," I said, figuring she probably needed it more than I knew. "And thank you."

The woman watched as I carefully lifted the puppy out of the box and held her warm body firmly to my chest. "No, thank *you*," she replied. "I gotta get home … 'bye."

"Goodbye," I replied, and I turned back to the van and my waiting daughter.

Elena's eyes widened when I opened the door and placed the plump bundle into her arms. "We're just rescuing her, honey," I stated gently but firmly, "we can't keep her." My daughter merely nodded her head slightly as she gazed down in wonder at the squirming puppy she held in her lap.

Maybe it was fate that my neighbors with the dog weren't home when I stopped at their house. All I know is, as soon as I walked into our house holding that puppy, there was no turning back. My husband even suggested that, deep down inside, I really did want a dog, no matter how much I protested.

As it turns out, I'm grateful for the turn of events that day. Our dog Pepper is now almost five, and I'm still amazed at what an ideal dog she turned out to be. She's gentle and loving without being too demanding of our attention; she hardly barks, she doesn't dig, and even as a puppy she never chewed on something that wasn't hers. The cats don't even seem to mind her so much, now that she's learned not to chase them. And I still think she's the cutest dog I've ever seen.

She loves to accompany my husband on walks and all his outside chores and she'll play with the kids until they drop from exhaustion. But, as far as I'm concerned, she's really my dog. I think there's a special bond between us because I rescued her. She's my constant companion whenever I'm at home—lying at my feet when I'm working at the computer, following me around the house as I do household chores, even riding in the back seat when I run errands.

Okay, I'll admit it: I probably sound like a typical "dog person" who loves her dog wholeheartedly and thinks her dog is the best dog ever. Actually, I think the fact that Pepper won over a stalwart "cat person" like me makes her even more special; which is why a recent positive life change for our family has one aspect that I find agonizing.

Just a few months ago, my husband was offered a unique opportunity with his company that involved a move to Paris, France for two to three years. We had discussed the idea of living abroad before and we agreed it would be a great experience for the entire family, especially the opportunities to travel all over Europe and beyond. The only problem was, what do we do with three cats and a dog if we end up in an apartment and when we go on trips for three weeks at a time?

Although it was one of the most painful decisions I'd ever had to make, I agreed with my husband that it would be too difficult to take our pets with us. As much as we would miss them, we felt it would be too hard on them to make such a long trip and be faced with so many unknown factors. We came to this conclusion after already moving them once, from Portland to Minneapolis, Minnesota. The cats took months to adjust, and were skittish even after a year. After what was probably a loud, dark, terrifying plane ride, we couldn't get Pepper anywhere near her kennel.

Her one experience being boarded at a kennel proved to be even worse. A small, bandaged wound on her tail wasn't kept clean and dry, and the resulting infection was so severe that her tail had to be docked. It was such a horrendous experience for Pepper that I felt she would be too traumatized ever to go to a kennel again.

Once the decision was made to find new homes for the pets, an even more difficult task began—the search for new parents. I made flyers with their pictures on them, describing their personalities in detail. I requested that the three cats be adopted together, or at least the two siblings, and I asked for a family with a large yard to adopt Pepper so she could have the space to run that she was accustomed to. The kids and I talked to our friends and neighbors and I distributed the flyers at our children's schools and at our vet's office, because I hoped to give them to someone I knew or who could be vouched for by our veterinarian. We prayed together that we would find the perfect families for our beloved pets; but as the weeks went by, and our deadline got closer, we had no suitable responses. I was actually nurturing a secret hope that nobody acceptable would come forward so I could argue that we would just have to find a way to take them, even though I knew that wouldn't be in their best interest.

When my husband mentioned we might have to resort to taking them to a shelter and hope they would be adopted, I started asking everyone I talked to if they knew someone who would be interested. The stress of trying to find homes for pets that I loved so much while making all the complex moving arrangements took its toll. I started having trouble sleeping, and I often found myself choking back tears as I explained my plight to a sympathetic listener.

Fortunately for all of us, our prayers were answered in two very different ways. My mom and dad, who live on a farm in Iowa, agreed to take care of Pepper until we returned. They had a dog years ago, but now that they were older they liked being without any pets so they could take extended trips in the winter. But my mom convinced my dad that it would make our long-distance separation easier for her if she could take care of the canine member of our family. We were all so happy, knowing Pepper would have her "grandma and grandpa" and we could even see her when we flew back to visit once a year.

Now there was just the issue of our cats, which seemed to be a more difficult proposition, because there were fewer cat lovers than someone interested in having a dog. It seemed that people were either allergic to cats, didn't like cats, or already had cats. Just at the point where I was prepared to beg my husband to take them with, I got a call from my vet's office. They had a long-time client whose cats were very old, and she was looking for some kittens or younger cats. Surprisingly, they told me she was willing to take all three of ours.

My hope surged as I called Valerie and chatted with her on the phone. Her cats were indeed older; one was 17 and had several medical issues that required almost constant attention. Valerie had also taken in several dogs that could no longer be cared for by their parents, and she spoke of them all so lovingly that I could tell she was a kind, devoted pet parent.

As I told Valerie my story, and tearfully told her how unbearably painful it was for me to part with them, I was shocked when she said, and "I could give them back to you when you move back, if you still wanted them."

I couldn't believe that she would be willing to be a foster mother for *three years;* it was so much more than I could have hoped for. The kids were overjoyed when I told them, and after going to Valerie's home to see how accommodating she was, I knew that Trixie, Bear, and Cricket would have a good home with her and her husband.

We've been in Paris almost three months now, and I miss our pets every day. Photographs are in almost every room; a picture of Pepper is on my cell phone screen, and Bear is this month's screen saver on my laptop computer. Sometimes, I imagine a movement out of the corner of my eye—a dark blur, like one of the cats is scampering by. And the dreams ... one night I dreamed my parents had just come to Paris for a visit and had brought Pepper with them. It seemed so real, as I knelt down and hugged her strong, warm body and she wriggled with happiness. Just last night I dreamed I was lying on my daughter Elena's bed cuddling with all three cats, as I did so often back home. Just as I was burying my face into Trixie's fluffy, purring side, I woke up—the warm scent of her still in my nostrils.

Having to give up my pets, even temporarily, has been one of the most emotionally painful things I have ever done. But I try to focus on my family and our busy lives here in France, knowing that the time will go by very quickly. I cherish the photographs and memories; I look forward to visiting and, most of all, I dream of the happy reunion we'll have with Trixie, Cricket, Bear, and Pepper when we return. I want our family all together again.

Two Poems

The following two poems commemorate the cat Simon Hughes, written by his parent, Chuck.

Sir Simon

On the warming hearth he recovers
solemn and still,
The old pearl gray cat with coat sleek as a seal.

His purring gaze a gift received
one Christmas Eve long ago:
   olympic dare diva,
    stand-up comic mime,
     Quan Yin of the museful smile;
my secret paramour now warming by the fire.
And forget not the brave knight
and soldier for my fears,
steady guide by the looking glass
reflecting now my immense unease.
I cannot see his breathing—
but I know he rests
softly and still.

Continuative Friend

Was that you that visited me
the other night in bed?
a certain pressure noticeable
a steady pressure downward on my head.
An uncanny weight, a weight that conjured dread,
but only for a moment …
I was observing dawn through a glass door,
so how could you—three days dead and
resting deep beside the wisdom cedar,
now be perched upon my head …
But the touch so spoke to me of you,
soft ribbons of fur caressed my face
a bright mug of your gray imp danced
between my eyes, the pressure downward
now strangely reassuring ….
To confirm this verisimilitude
I slowly reached a timorous hand up.
My hand was graced by the momentary touch
of the soft warmth of what felt like
a smaller you.
A vivid longing found root in that touch.

A moment later, now wide awake
the spectral weight had vanished.
An exhilarant hand lay empty at my side
and deep within my breast
a vernal brook surrounds my heart.

Beloved Friend Facing Euthanasia

Annette Grimaldi

My beloved cat Freckles came to live with me during a time when I was not fully prepared to accept a new pet into my life. I was not certain whether I was ready to have another pet, as my cat Roxanne had just died and I was in the midst of dealing with the emotions from her sudden loss, when my sister phoned and asked me if I would like to adopt a cat named Freckles that she had at her home. It happened that Freckles was not getting along with my sister's current cat, and so she was trying to find a good home for Freckles where she would be given lots of attention and love. In fact, my sister had adopted Freckles from a couple who could not keep this cat because she was not getting along with their current cat. Apparently, Freckles needed to live in a home in which she would be the only pet, and because I no longer had any pets of my own, my home would possibly be the right type of place for Freckles to live.

A bit reluctantly, I agreed that I would stop by my sister's house to meet Freckles. I remember when I first laid eyes on Freckles how I thought she was an unusually beautiful cat: a long-haired tortoiseshell with distinct markings on her face and a tail with fur that flowed like a full plume of feathers. I understood why someone named this cat Freckles, as she actually did have some freckles on her body, especially one noticeable one near her mouth. Freckles was born in October, and her fur truly resembled the season of autumn with the leaves turning bright colors. She was an autumn cat.

Besides Freckles' outer beauty, she had an inner gentleness and sweetness that made my heart melt. As I sat on my sister's basement floor, Freckles rolled over onto her back with her legs fully outstretched and allowed me to pet and tickle her tummy. Her body language was saying "I like you … I feel comfortable with you." Freckles really captured my heart, and I felt that there was something indescribably unique about her. My decision was easy...Freckles would be coming home with me.

Over the next fifteen years that Freckles was in my life, she and I developed a bond that grew stronger with each passing year and with all of the many special experiences we shared together in the human–pet relationship. Although she was friendly to other family members and friends, and she let others show affection toward her, Freckles never developed as strong of a level of attachment with anyone else as with me, as though she adopted me as her surrogate mom.

Freckles brought an incredible amount of joy and enrichment to my life. She was unconditional love. I have always thought about the way Freckles ended up being in my life, that somehow fate had something to do with how she came to live with me. For if Freckles had gotten along with the first couple's cat, they would have never placed an adoption advertisement in the paper that my sister just happened to notice. Or if Freckles and my sister's cat had gotten along together well, my sister never would have tried to find a new home for Freckles. Or if I had a cat at the time, I would have never been able to adopt Freckles from my sister. The more I think about it, the more I feel that Freckles was meant to be with me.

Not too long after I brought her home with me, I almost lost her to a careless roommate who left an empty box out on the bedroom floor after unpacking, and Freckles jumped into the deep box to take a nap. When my roommate lifted the box to carry it to the garbage bin, suddenly Freckles jumped out, shocking my roommate. It was Freckles' good fortune that she woke up when the box was being moved because I am not so sure that my roommate would have noticed her, as the box was so deep, and Freckles might have been lost outdoors. This incident made me immediately realize how much I would miss her if she disappeared from my life.

I have many wonderful memories of Freckles that will stay in my heart forever. Freckles loved rolling around in catnip, and the crazy cat in her would emerge when I sprinkled some catnip on the floor. You could never touch Freckles when she was having her catnip fix, though. Freckles loved chasing the beam of a flashlight or running after a ribbon or a string. In the winter, when fluffy white snowflakes fell from the sky, she would sit on the windowsill and try to "catch" the snowflakes, her head shaking with excitement. When I placed one of my feet in front of her paws, she would gently put one of her paws on top of my foot and keep it perched there until I pulled my foot too far away from her so that her paw would slip off my foot. She taught me early that I must never go into a room and close the door on her so that she could not be in the same room as me. If I did, she would lie on the other side of the door and slide one of her paws under the door and pull so that the door would make banging noises. I taught Freckles how to "sit" for a treat; she learned this trick quite easily. Freckles loved to have me sing to her as she sat on my lap. As I would sing, I would rub her tummy and she would bury her entire head in my arm and purr. Her favorite song for me to sing was "Mr. Sandman" (Mr. Sandman, dream me a dream ...).

I had several nicknames that I came up with over the years for Freckles, and many are simply too silly and probably do not make much sense. Freckles was my sweefur, piteau, pumpkin-eater, frankenpuff, dog-e-dog, love bug, Christmas cat, tigger, freekles, pookie, frankenfurter, peekachue, bootes of the booteses variety, and my nurse-cat. The nickname nurse-cat was very fitting for Freckles because if ever I was sick, Freckles would always be by my side seemingly watching over me ... her mere presence was a great comfort.

One fact that is extremely difficult to face about loving a pet that is very close and dear to our hearts is that eventually the pet will die and we will have to find a way within ourselves to let go and say goodbye. In November 2005, I had to face this awful reality when Freckles was diagnosed with lymphoma. The diagnosis was a great shock to me, and I was hoping that something could be done to improve her condition and prolong her life. However, each day that went by, her quality of life was diminishing further.

I promised myself that I would not let Freckles suffer in any way or allow her last few days on this earth to be spent in the care of a veterinarian, because her visits to the vet were usually stressful to her. Therefore, I tried to make her last few days with me as peaceful, loving, and comfortable as possible in the comfort of my home. The decision to euthanize Freckles was one of the most difficult decisions of my life, for I was letting go of a wonderful cat, and I knew how sad it would be that she would no longer be physically with me. But I had to put aside my own feelings and needs so that Freckles would not have to suffer any longer. She died peacefully at the age of seventeen. The feeling that surrounded me on that sad day was her love.

I miss Freckles beyond words every single day, as she was such a bright light in my life, and she was really one in a million. The transition I have had to make from Freckles being with me almost every single day for fifteen years to her being physically absent all of a sudden was very difficult. When she died, she took a big piece of my heart with her, yet in turn she left a big piece of her own heart with me. I have come to understand the special human–pet relationship and that there is a grieving process to go through, just as when a human close to us dies. I sense that Freckles is with me in spirit and that she is my little angel in fur. I have hope and faith that I will be reunited with her one day, in God's time. Love you forever, Freckles.

My son, Leaffy

Suzanne Mackey

My beloved Leaffy, you were a marvelous gift from God that I was fortunate enough to share for four beautiful years. During that time, you brought me tremendous joy and happiness that I'll always treasure. It was an honor and privilege having shared my life with you. Thank you from the bottom of my heart for having been the light of my life.

Without you, the house is so quiet, at times it's unbearable. I miss our daily walks, running errands, and snuggling when we took our naps, but most of all, I miss hugging and kissing you and letting you know how much I love you. I remember how fond you were of the simple pleasures in life: treats, tummy rubs, being brushed and massaged, playing with your ball, and roughhousing on the couch. Whenever I come home now, I long for your wonderful greeting; you always made me laugh because you'd run around with joy, and jump up and down with a warm-hearted smile while your tail wagged a mile a minute. You made me feel loved, appreciated, and special.

You were an extraordinary teacher who taught me some of life's most memorable lessons, such as enjoying life to the fullest, being patient, and living in the moment. More importantly, you were my best friend, who loved me unconditionally no matter what—you never judged, criticized, or belittled me. Your heart was filled only with the purest love. In addition, you were my constant companion, confidante, an exceptional listener (you were intent on my every word as if you understood everything), and above all, you comforted me in difficult times and celebrated with me in happy times. Last, you were my little shadow who followed me everywhere, and now you are my special guardian angel watching over me from above.

You were so selfless that you waited until the day after my birthday to become gravely ill. You were very brave and courageous through it all. Oh, how I had prayed for a miracle, but it wasn't meant to be because God was calling you home. I didn't want to lose my precious teenage son, but I knew it was time for you to go to Heaven. On your last day, I was blessed to have been able to spend a few hours alone with you before your journey. It was a time of heartfelt tears, immense gratitude for the love, support, and comfort you had given me throughout the years, and the sorrow of having to say goodbye. I wanted to run away with you because bringing you to the vet's office was the hardest thing I have ever had to do. I stayed with you until the bitter end, stroking your silky fur and comforting you with words of love because how could I not be there for my best friend when you had always been by my side.

My heart aches for you, but I realize that you are a free-spirit— happy, healthy, and peaceful in Heaven now. I love you so much my dear, sweet Leaffy and you'll remain in my heart forever. Please remember me and wait for me in Heaven. Oh, what a joyous day it will be when we are reunited. Take care, my pumpkin boy.

Willie

Laurel Lagoni

The first time I saw Willie, he was slinking around our neighborhood, fending for himself after his parents had moved away and abandoned him. The last time I saw Willie, he had scooted out my back door and through the rails of the gate that separates our deck from the bigger yard beyond.

It was 9:30 on a Saturday night. We had guests. I was distracted by the conversation inside and didn't go after him. I remember thinking," I'll find him in a little while."

Willie was basically an indoor cat, 18 years old, and struggling with kidney failure. However, at night, he often spent a half hour sampling the sights and smells of outside. He never wandered far. Whenever I called for him, he appeared: a pitch-black cat materializing out of the night. He would meow, the dogs would race to greet him and celebrate his return, and I would close and lock the door, content that all the members of my little family were tucked in for the night.

But this Saturday night, Willie did not return—not the usual half hour later, not at midnight, not a 4 a.m., when I woke my husband and asked him to help me look. Next morning, when my daughters began to tearfully search the neighborhood, there was no sign of Willie.

I, of all people, should have known better. As the former director of the Argus Institute for Families and Veterinary Medication at Colorado State University's Veterinary Teaching Hospital, I've listened to hundreds of parents relate stories of losing a pet abruptly and unexpectedly. I'm familiar with the guilt, anxiety, the what-if's and the if-only's. Yet I succumbed to a situation many other pet parents find themselves in: My cat loved getting a taste of the natural world and I wanted to make him happy.

His outdoor needs were simple. Just a few sniffs of fresh air, a couple of rolls in the dust of our gravel driveway, time enough to catch the cool night breeze and feel the wind ruffle the fur along his back. So I let him out, telling myself that if something happened to him, at least he would die happy.

But that was my head rationalizing the decision. Now that something *has* happened, my heart is not so accepting.

I feel guilty that I didn't look harder for him before I went to bed. I feel anxious about stopping our search, even though several weeks have gone by. I worry that he's trapped somewhere or that he's injured and in need of help.

I am painfully aware that if I'd taken any of several small steps—going after Willie right away, for instance—the outcome might have been different. These what-if thoughts are hard to bear: What if he needed me and wondered why I didn't come? What if a wild animal chased him and … well, anyone who's been through this knows how it goes. Horrible images run through my mind. They make my throat and stomach tighten, my heart beat faster, and my eyes fill with tears.

I know my remorse and sadness are normal. I know I can't make the feelings go away, and I also know that I shouldn't try to. I need to grieve, to feel guilty, and to cry. I have lost a cat who saw me through graduate school, the births of my daughters, and the deaths of my dogs. I have also lost a buddy, a member of my family, and a familiar, supportive presence.

Willie was always there. We understood one another, respected one another. He wasn't like a child to me. He was an adult cat when I adopted him. He was my peer. He was wise and independent in his way as I am in mine. Because of this, I didn't quite feel I had the right to dictate how or where he spent his time. He was his own cat. He chose to live with me. And that Saturday night, he chose to go outside.

I find it very hard to accept that I will probably never know how Willie died. However he met his end, it isn't the one I would have chosen for him. And it's not the goodbye I would have chosen for my daughters.

But whether a pet dies suddenly or is compassionately euthanized after a long illness, the grief of the parent is mostly the same. It's a process. It doesn't go away in a day or two. It demands expression—lots of crying, talking with people who understand and will listen. And it hurts. No matter what the circumstances of loss, that never changes.

Police Dog, Reflections of Czecky

Diane

I was told he was an escapee from the "Iron Curtain," a dog smuggled out of then-Czechoslovakia by his trainers that could fetch a better price across the border in Germany. I only knew that the dark-faced 18-month-old German shepherd stole my heart the day we met.

I reported for three weeks of intensive police dog handler training and met my future partner. His papers said his name was "Sparo," but we called him the Czecky dog because of his homeland. The nickname stuck and he was forever "Czecky." Little did I know this was the beginning of the most unusual partnership of my life. This dog would be my constant companion, my trusted partner, and friend.

The city where Czecky and I worked was busy and tested his skills from the beginning. We were constantly called upon to search for suspects who had fled from officers and were in hiding. Czecky had to be tough and aggressive at times, yet loved to hop out of the patrol car, flop onto his back in what I called his "public relations" pose, and allow children to rub his belly. Czecky was well known by many of the school-age children for his visits to their classrooms as part of the drug abuse resistance education (D.A.R.E.) program. We would assemble a large group on the playground near the closed patrol car. I would instruct them to say "Hi Czecky" and told them if they were loud enough to awaken him, he would open the door and come out to see them. After several loud attempts, I would surreptitiously use my remote control to open the door. Czecky would run to my side with a big dog smile on his face. He loved the attention poured onto him by large groups of children.

I have often been questioned by others about why I wanted to work "alone" rather than with a human partner in a high crime area. Some could not understand that I would choose my four-legged partner over the best of cops every time. My answer was that my partner's devotion knew no bounds. My partner was never tired or distracted by what had happened in his personal life prior to the shift. He never let his emotions interfere with his actions or decision-making. I was always in awe of my furry partner's ability to read body language and situations. He spent 100 percent of his time watching people's body language, mine included. I might have initially been casually talking to someone I contacted, and Czecky would be sitting quietly watching. If my voice changed, or the body language of the person became aggressive, Czecky would instantly become more agitated and bark. His mere presence was enough to prevent some situations from escalating into violence or a foot pursuit. Suspects who might have been inclined to challenge or flee from an officer were less inclined to try the same tactic with a police dog present.

I also noticed Czecky's ability to single out the suspect, no matter what the environment. On many occasions I would return to the police station to complete paperwork in the briefing room. This room was used for briefings at the start of a shift and by officers to compete paperwork. The door at the front of the room led to the carport/jail area and officers who had juvenile suspects in custody were required to bring them into the station via the briefing room, not the jail. Czecky would sleep at my feet while I completed my paperwork as officers came and went by this door. If, however, a juvenile suspect entered with the officer, Czecky immediately snapped to attention, his eyes trained on the individual. Rarely would the situation call any more attention than the other groups of officers, but Czecky always knew. He could pick up on their anxiety from across the room the moment they entered.

The police station was Czecky's home away from home and he and the other police dogs were favorites among most of those working there. Czecky knew the location of every dog-cookie-containing desk and would occasionally slip into the watch commander's officer for his expected reward. His patrol car was another safe haven for him and he never needed encouragement to hop in the car to go to work. He quickly learned what things triggered contact with people, and when I would turn on the overhead lights for a traffic stop he would bark happily. He frequently looked over my shoulder as we drove and would watch people we passed on the street. Sometimes, he would bark at a person we were passing and I have always wondered if he knew something that I didn't, as if he had a sense that person was in need of contact with the police. I could never conduct the experiment—could you imagine the courtroom testimony ..."Officer, why did you stop my client?" "Well, you see my police dog told me to." But I always felt that he was sensing something beyond my ability to see.

Even police work can have humorous moments and police dogs have theirs also. If I were ever to ask Czecky what his most embarrassing moment was, he might have told the following story. Our department was working a kidnap-for-ransom case and the suspect had picked up the money at the money drop and fled. The suspect was under surveillance by officers on the ground and in the air and the case had drawn in other law enforcement agencies, such as the FBI. When the suspect crashed his car and fled on foot, a several-block perimeter was established and Czecky and I were called in to search. I remember that the first yard we were to search was surrounded by a tall cinder-block wall and we had to enter via a side gate. Czecky knew what all the activity was about and loved to search. When I sent him into the yard he took off across the concrete and rounded the corner of the house. I followed more slowly and heard his nails scratching on the concrete followed by a loud splash. Unfortunately for Czecky, this back yard contained a pool, and he had rounded the corner with enough speed to be unable to stop himself from falling into the water. The sight that met me as I got to the corner was one very wet shepherd swimming to the side of the pool. I remember thinking that we might be able to find the suspect by following the sounds of laughter, but fortunately the suspect was not in the first yard. We found him several homes away and I often wonder if he was surprised by how wet the police dog was. Czecky always gave swimming pools a wider berth after that incident.

Part of the relationship that officers form with a police K-9 comes from living together away from the job. Czecky became part of the family for my husband and two stepdaughters. Later, when I had my first child, Czecky became a self appointed guardian and would quietly slip himself in between my daughter and anyone who might be near her. He would then lean quietly against their legs as if to say, "You are too close, please back away." My husband, never really a dog person, grew to love him as well. In early discussions about this dog that was going to live with us I would try to minimize the impact on my husband with statements like, "Well, he can probably sleep in the kitchen." Suffice it to say that in no time my poor husband learned to accept (and enjoy) allowing a 90-pound shepherd on the bed to say good morning (placing himself in the middle of course). Czecky was never far from my side, even while asleep.

Czecky's training was later expanded to include disaster-type searches among the rubble of collapsed buildings. He tackled this task with great aplomb and was the first police canine in California certified for urban search and rescue. He even received training in avalanche searches and was called upon in several incidents. He looked truly happy riding on chair lifts or in helicopters—as long as he got the window seat. He had a wonderful sense of adventure and seemed to rise to the challenge of whatever task was presented.

As Czecky grew older I advanced to a position in the detective bureau. Czecky had served the city well and was granted his retirement. I would have to say that he did not like being left at home every day, but we still enjoyed our daily runs together. As time passed, he was no longer able to run without becoming exhausted but the vet could pinpoint no specific reason. When he developed a mass on his chest, tests were inconclusive. A few short weeks later I awakened one morning to find him in terrible distress. A trip to the emergency vet revealed that he was bleeding into the heart sac from the cancer that had been growing in his heart. I always felt that it was the cruelest blow that his great heart could be his downfall. We at least had our goodbye, and he died quietly and humanely in my arms. As hard as the decision was to make, he had been dying before my eyes and could not be saved. It was my last gift to a dog that gave me many. Czecky was cremated and returned to me. I thought I might bury him here where I live but feel somehow we would not be connected enough. I want him to remain with me forever, so perhaps someday we can be scattered to the winds together.

Remembering Siam

Nancy Miller

Siam Miller, sometimes called Sammers by me in private, came to me a little more than two years ago and left this plane of existence on Sunday, October 31, 2004 in my arms, in our home in Prescott, Arizona, after a long illness.

During this time with me Siam taught me more about giving and receiving unconditional love than anyone, including family, friends, husbands and lovers, had in my life before. He opened my heart.

The first thing anyone noticed about Siam was how handsome he was with his long beige hair in many shades; his very expressive large brown face; his loving clear blue eyes; his perky brown ears that heard everything, said or unsaid; his amazingly long striped whiskers; his strong brown legs and paws; and his wonderful bushy brown tail, which he held high as he strolled through life. He was a big boy (probably 18–20 solid pounds of cat), very long and tall, yet as gentle as could be. There was a little nip there though, sometimes a love bite and sometimes when he was not pleased. At times he meowed to himself when walking around the house, sort of like muttering. I loved hearing it. It was low and almost musical.

He loved to sleep on the stool in front of my chair while I watched TV. After a long while, when he finally decided it might be OK to come into my lap, he first put one foot forward and then the other came on very gently, curling up once he was there. I think his former parent was a frail older lady and he was afraid of hurting me. I loved having him there.

During the day he slept on the bed, on the stool near my chair, in various places on the floor, on the trunk at the top of the stairs where he could watch everything going on in the house, on the couch, and sometimes curled up in a chair in the back hall. In the morning he would often sunbathe, stretched out with feet in front and back on either his stomach or back, like a bathing beauty. When stretched out he was VERY long.

He spent the nights on my bed, always way in the corner near my feet so he wouldn't disturb me while I was sleeping. Every now and then, very slowly and gently and shyly, watching for my reaction, he would walk up alongside of me to be petted. I always welcomed him and felt it was an honor to be visited by him. When I fell asleep he'd walk back down to the foot of the bed. (Sometimes) he would climb up onto my stomach while I was lying in bed. For me that was wonderful.

At mealtimes he came to the kitchen and looked at me, sometimes meowing, reminding me it was time to be fed. He had a hearty appetite and loved most of the food I gave him, especially the large shrimp I gave him for lunch.

He was always respectful of his parakeet brothers and sisters ... sitting and watching, and talking with them. He never tried to jump up onto their shelf. Once or twice he gently touched the bottom of the cage with his paw.

Despite his size, he was incredibly graceful. He could walk across a table or windowsill full of delicate knick-knacks and not disturb one.

(Sometimes) he would have what I called a "cat fit." He'd run from the far corner of the upstairs to the corner of the downstairs next to the birds and back up again, and then over to the dining room, where he'd jump up on the counter and then to the top of the cabinet/room divider, and so on, around and around. It was pretty amazing how strong and agile he was. He loved sniffing the firewood I brought in from outdoors—lots of interesting critter smells.

He loved his house and got very upset when I planned to sell it and move to another one. The people coming through to look at it upset him even more. That's when his decline started, with his appetite beginning to lessen.

He taught me a lot about loving and caring about and caring for and asking for help during the six months he was ill. Toward the end I even got over my fear of needles so that I could give him sub Q fluids three times a day…

Farewell Siam. I still love you and love the visits you have been making to your house since you left.

A Little Dog Whose Name was Joe

Joyce Gillespie

> We lost a real good friend today,
> And a truer one we'll never know.
> He wasn't famous, but we won't forget,
> A little dog whose name was Joe.
>
> He was fuzzy and brown, a poodle by breed,
> With a heart just filled with love.
> As a protector he was fierce as a lion,
> As a friend, he was gentle as a dove.
>
> He could do all the tricks that most dogs do,
> And some that were all his own.
> He seemed almost human, and with him around,
> You never felt alone.
>
> He loved to eat cookies and table scraps,
> He loved to go "Bye-Bye" too.
> And to get you to rub his tummy for him,
> He'd try all the tricks he knew.
>
> Oh, he climbed on the couch and slept on the bed,
> And sometimes made all kinds of noise.
> And chasing cats and other dogs,
> Was one of his favorite joys.

One time he was lost in Canada,
And for weeks we searched in vain.
And when our hope was almost gone,
Joe Brown came home again.

He was sometimes clever and sometimes dumb,
And sometimes merely a clown.
But the love we felt was reflected there,
In his eyes so soft and brown.

For eleven years his place in our lives,
Was companion, protector and friend.
And now this 24th day of May,
Joe Brown's life comes to an end.

And yet, in our hearts, he'll still live on,
Though years may come and go.
There'll always be a special place
For a little dog whose name was Joe.

And if God has provided a heaven for dogs,
There's one thing I surely know.
A special place there is being filled,
By a little dog whose name was Joe.

Murphy, a Friend Through Many of Life's Changes

Jennifer Anders

Murphy came into my life at a particularly vulnerable time. My marriage was on the rocks; I had an infant son and had lost my beloved orange tabby, Toby, a few months earlier.

My son, Sean, and I went to the humane society to just *look* at cats. It was springtime, so kittens were plentiful. As I looked at all of the little bundles of fur stumbling around in their cages, the decision was made—there would be a new addition to our house. They were all so cute it was almost impossible to decide. Murphy was in a cage with several other babies. He was small, round, and adorable. I took him out to show Sean and the little ball of fluff crawled up my arm and fell asleep. I was hooked.

Murphy saw me through a great many things in the seventeen years we shared. He was my constant loving companion. Murphy was a large cat but he didn't, or maybe couldn't, meow. He made a sort of coughing sound when he tried. It was his loud, deep purring that was his signature trademark. I used to tell him I was afraid he'd explode if he purred any louder.

"Murph" was a house cat but did like to occasionally "graze" outside in the summertime. He never ran off or wandered much farther away than one of the neighbors' yards. His marking were almost "cow-like" and his belly hung lower and lower over the years, which made his grazing look even cuter.

Murphy patiently put up with a lot of other animals coming and going over the years. He didn't much like the dogs that came to live with us, but tolerated their presence. Murph and the other long-time cats that lived with us were close companions. They loved the old gentleman.

The last few years of Murphy's life we had our ritual. Each morning he would sit on the edge of my bed and wait until I came out from my bath. Then I was to sit next to him and pet him. He sat in the same spot every day. And no matter how late I was running, I would sit down and pet my dear old friend ... it's something I still dearly miss.

Men came and went in my life after my divorce, but Murphy's love never waned. Even at the end he tried to be near me and cuddle each night—even if it was only for a while.

In the last days he grew very weak, and yet at the end, he somehow managed to get down the basement stairs to find a private place to leave this world.

I knew the end was coming but I didn't want to believe it. My dad had died suddenly only a few months earlier and I had yet to come to grips with that. How could this dear furry soul leave me too? But I knew it was his time to go and took some comfort that he would be with my dad. When I found him in the basement he looked at peace but my tears just wouldn't stop flowing for my dear friend.

The next morning, as I sadly carried him from the house, there sat Toots and Marlow, his feline companions, one on the TV and one on the stereo, as if "at attention" watching us leave.

It was a fitting tribute to my dear Murphy.

Memories of Cotton

Diane Whitney

The rescue center that placed Cotton with me said they had never met a kitten quite like him and I soon learned what they meant. Cotton was quite a character, full of life and full of mischief. I think he thought he was a dog as he followed me everywhere, waited for me at the door when I came home and never said no when I wanted to pick him up and cuddle. As one friend put it, Cotton didn't know that he was supposed to be aloof.

He also didn't seem to know he was supposed to sleep a lot as he was always underfoot wanting to know what was going on and getting into absolutely everything. He was a perpetual baby, who often had to be protected from his own goofy antics. As an example, he once managed to get a drapery cord wrapped around his back paw then bungee jumped off the back of a chair and ended up swinging upside down through the air. Another time I found him sitting quietly and contentedly on the dining room table with a toothpick sticking out of each corner of his mouth. Cotton had the loudest purr I ever heard and loved to come to my parties and go from lap to lap for hugs. He also loved to play hide and seek when I changed the bedding, diving under the sheets and then waiting there perfectly still while I pretended to be frantic looking for him. When I would finally peek under the sheets and spot him, he would quickly scramble out, looking ever so proud of himself.

Cotton made me laugh all the time and gave me endless love and affection. Most of all, he made me a better person by always reminding me of the softer and sweeter side of life.

A Tribute to Madam Houdini, a Beloved Horse

J. Suzanne King

Our Texas quarter horse arrived with papers, sorrel coat and soft eyes.
Quickly we knew on her gentle nature we could rely.
From the onset she stood above the average steed
Picking door locks and breaking boy horse hearts, to name some deeds.

Jen, Many, and Dini enjoyed the equestrian groove.
Blue ribbons, shows, bunny ears, with pictures to prove.
Through trials with hurt hooves, colic, and horse couches,
The fun of being together outweighed all those slouches.

The girls grew up and entered a new stage,
Jen promised her loyalty would hold,
Our girl, Dini, golden one would never be sold.
Kimmy, Dylan, and Tyler came on the scene,
Now they too could play with our horse queen.

After earthly time had run its course,
She dreamed of Valhalla and new dimensions to horse.
With the grace that she lived, Dini broke through her fence,
And sped joyfully to familiar realms not so dense.

Not to some distant star did she go,
But close by, where, for a thought she would show.
Until future time to reemerge as new.
And continue the bond through eons true.
We honor the children caretakers and Jen.
We honor this horse who showed love doesn't end.

Losing Fannie Brice, Our Funny Girl

Multiple Losses and Life's Lessons

Debbie Antinori

Sometimes I feel like it's just enough already. Enough loss, enough illness, etc., etc. I'm in that middle life area where things start to change really fast all around and I can get very scared. Fannie's death is part of this fast change that creeps up like a riptide or tornado. Shih-tzus are supposed to live to be 15–17; everyone knows that. So what went wrong with Fannie? She was so very healthy and full of life. She was never sick and never missed a meal until that last week.

Fannie was our first experience with euthanasia. She developed difficultly breathing suddenly one night and within four days we had to have her euthanized. We took her to a specialist who determined the difficulty with her breathing was neither viral nor bacterial from which she might have been able to recover. It was most likely ARDS—acute respiratory distress syndrome—something that Shih-tzus can be prone to, but it seems that many breeders don't know this. It really is that rare. So why Fannie? Why her? These were the same questions I asked myself four years earlier when we got the terminal diagnosis on my mother—liver cancer, it'll go fast. They weren't kidding (oncologists usually don't)—it was 19 days of hospice and my mom died. She had had cancer six years before, but had just gotten an "all clear" in July. By mid-August, she just didn't look right and went downhill from there. No amount of testing could produce any results until December 8, 2001, when we got that terminal diagnosis. Then we got 19 days to be with her and say goodbye—"we" being my dad and me—and to be very present with her and alternately walk around like zombies, in shock, trying to absorb the enormity of it. Or just to survive it. Again, I wrote poetry, and it has sat waiting for me to write around it and do something with it. It's just still too huge to go there.

Before Fannie I did lose a pet, my little parakeet. Mr. Derby died about 10 months after my mother. That was very hard. It is really hard to have multiple losses. You feel like you just can't get your head above water and another wave smacks you in the head and the undertow is especially strong. In many ways, I feel I never really fully grieved Mr. Derby—that undertow from losing my mother was all-consuming. It's the biggest loss I have ever had.

And now, four years later, another one leaves—little Fannie. I immediately turned my attention to her "life partner," Pimpernel, our other Shih-Tzu. He was devastated without her. She was the alpha. Fannie was the smaller of the two, about 10 pounds, a little black and white cracker-jack, quick, smart, funny—Funny Girl, Fannie Brice. Pimpernel is bigger, 14 pounds (now become 17 pounds at age 10), a little younger than Fannie, a retired show dog, but definitely the fan club to Fannie. She shone and he followed in her shadow. Even though he became a champion and even went to Westminster, Fannie was the little star and she loved everyone she met, drawing their attention first. Now Pimpernel was sullen and disoriented without her, and I was really worried. However, Pimpernel has found his place as an "only dog" in this last year. Both were therapy dogs in my private practice and now he is enjoying the attention of all the clients, who find him so special and deep and dear. Those clients and friends who knew Fannie see the change in Pimpernel since her loss and think it is remarkable. When Fannie was around, Pimpernel just wasn't as people oriented. He was second-string therapy dog, and now he is a true champion once again—not in the ring this time, but in people's hearts.

I have dreams about Fannie: she returns and I know she cannot stay. I had dreams like this about my mother too, soon after she died. Recently, one of these dreams about Fannie was so REAL. It was such a clear and enjoyable dream, even though I knew she'd disappear again when I woke up. I even felt in the dream that I could bear her leave-taking better now—I've come a long way. Sometimes I just shake my head—my mother and Fannie are the two who just really shouldn't have gone when they did. My mom was 76 going on 50. She loved life. Fannie was the most exuberant little creature I've ever known. She loved life, too. Was it just enough for them? Did they not want to get old and deal with all that elder years bring? Do accidents happen? Whatever the reason, I know that what *is*, is. I trust that, on some level, it was their time. I know they are together and can feel this in very poignant ways at times. That doesn't mean I wouldn't make a bargain with the devil to get them back if I could (especially if he really was Al Pacino—you remember that movie?). But seriously, I am aware of some kind of reason for these very difficult things. I know my father better than I ever have before. We are so close. I know Pimpernel in a different way. I appreciate things much much more, even though I've been through a lot of loss in my life and think that I really have always appreciated things. There's something very humbling and stark about losing your mom, and about losing the one who seemed like she'd keep on being there to help me deal with being without my mom. I talk to my mom and to Fannie, especially when I walk Pimpernel outside. I am sure all my neighbors think I'm crazy. But I don't care. Something about being outside feels closer to God to me, to nature too, of course—and to where they must be somehow. So I talk a lot when I'm outside.

We were all together as a family for Fannie's euthanasia—Paul (my husband), Pimpernel and me. I held Fannie in my arms. Her gaze never left mine as she went where she had to go. I had cried a lot about four days before, when we could see how sick she had become so rapidly. I didn't cry a lot after she died, although I'm a big-time crier. I felt a lot—a whole lot. I still do, though it is more bearable.

I will write more. I have plans for that. It was good to write this. It is an unusual style for me. I am aware of the cryptic conversational style, and my sense of humor that I fear seems almost irreverent at times. Fannie Brice, Funny Girl—she just won't let me get too deep or heavy here. She was a bundle of joy and it is my responsibility to find that joy inside myself now that she is gone. She came to enjoy her life and to teach me something. I had better learn it. This is how I feel about loss in general and certainly about pet loss. So let me ask you as you are reading along here: what do you experience because of your loss? What is it that you are learning about yourself? How was your pet with you and how can you have something of that special quality in your life now, or if not now, in the future? How can you honor the time spent together by making meaning in your own unique way because your pet died or was lost? That is my orientation. For me, it doesn't come all at once, all the answers to those questions. But it does come—what is my reaction to this loss and what is my soul pushing toward, who am I becoming in this journey of life when things are totally out of my control? I'm still working on it. I hope you are, too.

Our Bodies, Our Bug Selves

Keldin Holler (Coya Steele Silverlake)

> We never know who or what we're going to love, especially if we remain open to love.

She'd elongated and stretched out her perfectly segmented body while suspended upside down from the top of the glass enclosure where she lived, her backwardly curved silhouette now resembling a crescent quarter moon.

She is the younger of the two Indian walking sticks I adopted just after Hurricanes Rita and Katrina ripped over the Gulf Coast. I guess I could have named them after those storms but they wanted their own names with some quirkiness thrown in. They are pretty quirky creatures as far as bugs go. There is a bit of New Orleans here, but this one was named Tiptina Thimbleina after the famous music club in New Orleans and for her tiny size. Her older sister was named Ogrebrite Thunderbite. The quirky irony here is that these insects look like they have a tremendous underbite, rather like some bulldogs. You might say, "That's a face only a mother could love." Well, when adoptees show up, regardless of looks, somewhere along the way the heart takes over ... even if it's resonating with a pumping organ that's more like an undulating tube (with green blood in it) that runs the length of the body. What can I say? I love my bugs. But then, I've always had a soft spot in my head for insects.

Back to the molting: I'd noticed a piece of exuvium (the remains left from the molt) on the bottom of their bug box in the past, but had never witnessed the event. They tend to be nocturnal creatures, this family of insects know as phasmids or walking sticks. So, most activity, including eating leaves, occurs at night. This night, I'd stayed up late just to watch "Mrs. Doubtfire" again. It's been a few years and I needed a fix. When the movie was over, I checked on the "girls" and noticed Tippy was looking odd and pale. She was unusually bowed backward in her upside-down position. Upon further inspection, I noticed she was literally coming apart at the seams. What unfolded in the next 30–40 minutes was nothing short of an exquisite orchestration. I have found myself spellbound by the delicate webmaking of many a spider, dumbfounded at the marking and movements of brilliantly colored and tufted caterpillars, awestruck at the tiny translucence of freshly hatched garden spiders (orphaned eggs I'd brought in for the winter) and, of course, wowed by an emerging tiger swallowtail from its cocoon, but never had I been so "included" and viscerally in sync with an insect or arachnid metamorphosis.

I had lost my feline companion of 13 years only weeks before. Her long illness and ultimate euthanasia took stores of vitality from within me. Now, I was grieving with the holidays happening all around me and "Mrs. Doubtfire" was granting me some reprieve, but Tiptina opened a different door for me in the wee hours of that December morning: New life, life again. Shedding the old, releasing the weariness; the hurt, the pain, the deadness that tugged at me ... and it all comes in waves. She showed me that. "When you get too tired, STOP, rest for a while, then start again." In the blues, it's called "the turnaround"—

that's what great music is about; the build-up and the resolve. Nature mimics this in many forms and proportions. Waves—undulations—cycles. Or better, maybe we're all part of the same pulse.

When Tippy was in the last stanza of her "shedding song," Ogrebite moved into place so Tip could flip around under her, grab on and pull the last segments of her abdomen out of her "old house." By this time, I think I was having a total *kundalini* experience—full body tingling, lights, color. Just as mice have been recently recorded singing very high-pitched songs, I wonder what the melody of a molting walking stick would sound like. Well, even though my ears did not hear her or Ogrebite doing her midwife bug part, the cells in my body heard them, resonated, responded and mimicked.

When I got up the next morning, they had eaten all the exuvium. Somehow, I think this "skeleton eating" physiologically gave rise to the next phase: egg-laying or "dropping." Required hormones kicked in. It's the second week of February and easily 100 eggs have been dropped.

It's so hard to watch them grow up and leave home. These insects only live about a year, then the next generation is hatched. They come here, they have different appearances and markings from each other, with independent "quirky" personalities, likes and dislikes, and life-spans. One of a kind, never two alike.

13

PET LOSS RESOURCES

Jessamine and Stephanie play with Bonita, a snake. There are many places to turn for support when the bonds with companion animals are broken.

Knowing where, and whom, to turn to during a time of loss can provide us with the tools to assist in our recovery. Reaching out to others in times of distress is not only wise, it is healthy and helps us to work through heartfelt emotions. Provided in this chapter is information about pet loss support for pet parents, therapists, animal health care professionals, and others.

Resources

American Psychological Association: http://www.apa.org/

American Animal Hospital Association
12575 W. Bayaud Ave.
Lakewood, CO 80228
303-986-2800
info@aahanet.org

Pet Loss Support Hotlines and Grief Counselor Referral Websites

University of Illinois at Urbana-Champaign
College of Veterinary Medicine
C.A.R.E. Pet Loss Helpline
1-877-394-2273
griefhelp@cvm.uiuc.edu

Delta Society
580 Naches Avenue SW, Suite 101
Renton, WA 98055-2297
425-226-7357
info@deltasociety.org
www.deltasociety.org

University of California Davis
School of Veterinary Medicine
Center for Companion Animal Behavior
Lists memorials, hotlines, organizational and web resources
for companion animal loss
http://www.vetmed.ucdavis.edu/ccab/petloss.html

Pet People Help, World by the Tail, Inc.
126 W. Harvard St., Suite 5
Fort Collins, CO 80525
Toll free: 888-271-8444
Local: 970-223-5753

President and CEO laurel.lagoni@wbtt.com
Customer Service Manager patricia.nay@wbtt.com
http://www.petpeoplehelp.com

International association of Pet Cemeteries
Pet Loss Support Hotline
518-594-3000

Washington State University
College of Veterinary Medicine,
Pullman, VA
509-335-5704
Trained WSU veterinary student volunteers staff phones as compassionate listeners—6:30–9:00 p.m. Mon.–Thurs.; 1:00–3:00 p.m. Sat. (PST)

Pacific Animal Therapy Society (P.A.T.S.)
Pet Loss Support Line
9412 Lauries Lane
Sidney, BC, V8L 4L2
250-389-8047
patspets@shaw.ca

Iowa State University
Pet Loss Support Hotline
2116 College of Veterinary Medicine
Ames, IA 50011
888-478-7574

University of Floridav
College of Veterinary Medicine
Gainesville, FL.
Pet Loss Support Hotline
352-392-4700, ext. 4080

Tufts University
Boston, MA
Pet Loss Support Hotline
508-839-7966
www.tufts.edu/vet/petloss/

Cornell University Pet Loss Support Hotline
College of Veterinary Medicine
Companion Animal Hospital
Box 35, Ithaca, NY 14853-6401
607-253-3932
www.vet.cornell.edu/public/petloss/

The Ohio State University
Pet Loss Hotline
614-292-1823

Virginia-Maryland Regional College of Veterinary Medicine
Pet Loss Support Hotline
540-231-8038

Companion Animal Association of Arizona Inc.
P.O. Box 5006
Scottsdale, AZ
Pet Grief Support Service/Helpline: 602-995-5885

Michigan State University
College of Veterinary Medicine
Clinical Center C-100
East Lansing, MI 48824
517-353-5064

The Chicago Veterinary Medical Association
Pet Loss Support Helpline
630-325-1600

The Redwood Empire Veterinary Medical Association
Pet Loss Support Group
Santa Rosa, CA
707-573-9803

Colorado State University
College of Veterinary Medicine & Biomedical Sciences
Argus Institute for Families and Veterinary Medicine
970-297-4143

Hawaiian Humane Society
http://www.hawaiianhumane.org

University of Minnesota
School of Veterinary Medicine
Pet Loss Support Hotline
612-625-3770

The Association for Pet Loss Bereavement (APLB)
P.O. Box 106
Brooklyn, NY 11230
718-382-0690
http://www.aplb.org/
Maintains a comprehensive directory of therapists with special
training or interest in pet loss

The University of Pennsylvania
School of Veterinary Medicine
Philadelphia, PA
212-898-4529

The Rainbow Passage Pet Loss Support and Bereavement Center
Grafton, WI
414-376-0340

The Australian Center for Companion Animals in Society
Hotline (02) 9746 1911

Pet Bereavement Support Service (England)
0800-096-6606

Super Dog Pet Loss Support and Grief Counseling
Http://www.superdog.com/petloss/counsel.htm
Lists grief counselors throughout the U.S.

The Iams Pet Loss Support Center and Hotline
888-332-7738

American Veterinary Medical Association
Pet Loss Resources
http://www.avma.org/care4pets/avmaloss.htm

For support groups and hotlines not listed in your area contact your local or state veterinary medical association.

EMDR Resources

David Grand, Ph.D.,
2415 Jerusalem Avenue
Suite 105
Bellmore, NY 11710
516-785-0460
Dgrand1952@aol.com
http://www.biolateral.com/bio.htm

Francine Shapiro, Ph.D.,
http://www.emdr.com/shapiro.htm

EMDR: A Closer Look (A Guilford Press Video, New York)
Http://www.guilford.com

Other Therapeutic Resources

Pesso Boyden System Psychomotor International Office
Strolling Woods on Webster Lake
Lake Shore Drive
Franklin, NH 03235
603- 934-5548 (9am-5pm EST)
www.pbsp.com
pbsp1@aol.com or pbsp@pbsp.com

Antinori, D., Journey through Pet Loss (2000), Yoko Spirit Publishers, audiobook. www.petlossaudio.com.

Bibliography

Allen, K. and Blascovich, J. (1996). The value of service dogs for people with severe ambulatory disabilities: A randomized controlled trial. *Journal of the American Medical Association*, *275*(13), 1001–1006.

Axline, V.M. (1947). *Play therapy*, NYC: Ballantine Books.

Barba, B. (1995). The positive influence of animals: Animal-assisted therapy in acute care. *CNS: Journal for Advanced Nursing Practices*, *9*(4), 199–202.

Brockmeier, J. (1990, October). A practical approach to managing stress. *Veterinary Forum*, 30–31.

Bustad, L. K. (1990). *Compassion: Our last great hope*. Renton, WA: Delta Society.

Carmack, B. J. (2003). *Grieving the death of a pet*, Minneapolis, MN: Augsberg Fortress (publishing house of the Evangelical Lutheran Church in America).

Carmack, B. J. (1991). The role of companion animals for persons with AIDS/HIV. *Holistic Nurse Practitioner*, *5*(2):21–31.

Cawley, R. (1994). Therapeutic horseback riding and self-concept in adolescents with special educational needs. *Anthrozoos*, *7*(2), 129–134.

Church, J. A. (1987). *Joy in a wooly coat*. Tiburon, CA: H. J. Kramer.

Friedman, E. (1980, July–August). Animal companions and one year survival of patients after discharge from a coronary care unit. *Public Health Reports*, 307–312.

Goldman, L. (1996). *Breaking the silence*, NYC: Taylor & Francis.

Goldman, L. (1994). *Life and loss, a guide to help grieving children*, NYC: Taylor & Francis.

Gorczyca, K. (1990). Special needs for the pet owner with AIDS/HIV. *The Latham Letter*, *11*(4), 1, 18–19.

Hall, E., Lamb, M., and Perlmutter, M. (1986). *Child psychology today* (2nd ed.). New York: Random House.

Hart, L. A. (1989). Aquarium fish for recovery of coronary patients in intensive care. Davis, CA: Final report on a study funded by the Delta Society Human Animal Program, School of Veterinary Medicine, University of California.

Kale, M. (1992). Kids and animals: A comforting hospital combination. *Inter Actions*, *10*(3), 17–21.

Kale, M. (1992). Losing their pets would kill them … literally: Animals and AIDS patients. *Inter Actions*, *10*(2), 9–12.

Kay, W.J. (1984). *Pet loss and human bereavement*, Ames, IA: Iowa State University Press.

Lagoni, L. and Butler, C. (1994). *The human–animal bond and grief*, Elsevier.

Levy, T. and Orlans, M. (1998). *Attachment, trauma, and healing: Understanding and treating attachment disorder in children and families*, Washington, D.C.: CWLA Press.

McCulloch, M. (1996). Psychiatrist discusses emotional problems brought on by death of a loved animal. *DVM 11*(5), 32–34.

McElroy, S. (1996). *Animals as teachers and healers*, NYC: Ballantine Books.

Nieberg, H.A. and Fisher, A. (1982). Pet Loss: A thoughtful guide for adults and children, NYC: Harper & Row.

Niego, M. (1992, Summer). Rx: Animals: Prescriptions of animals in goal-directed rehabilitation and motivational therapy are becoming more common. *ASPCA Animal Watch*, 9–13.

Polland, B. (1997). Feelings inside and outloud too, Berkeley, CA, Ten Speed Press.

Ross, C. (2005). *Pet Loss and Children: Establishing a Healthy Foundation,* NYC: Routledge.

Ross, C., Sorensen, J. (1998) *Pet Loss and Human Emotion, Guiding Clients Through Grief,* NYC: Routledge.

Ryan, T., Hines, L. M., and Bustad, L. K. (not dated). Hearing dogs: An experiment in training. *PAL Digest.*

Tousley, M., (1996), Children and Pet Loss: A Guide for Helping, Phoenix: Companion Animal Association of Arizona, Our Pals Publishing Company (booklet).

Shapiro, F. (2002). *EMDR as an integrative psychotherapy approach: Experts of diverse orientations explore the paradigm prism*, Washington, D.C.: American Psychological Association Books.

Shapiro, F. (2001). *EMDR: Eye movement desensitization and reprocessing: Basic principles, protocols and procedures*, NYC: Guilford Press.

Shapiro, F. (1997). *EMDR: The breakthrough therapy for overcoming anxiety, stress and trauma*, NYC: Basic Books.

Traisman, E. (1996). *My personal pet remembrance journal*, ISBN# 0-9651131-0-8, Direct Book Services, 800-776-2665.

Voelker, R. (1995). Puppy love can be therapeutic, too. *Journal of the American Medical Association, 274*(24), 1897–1899.

Walsh, P. G. and Mertin, P. G. (1994). The training of pets as therapy dogs in a women's prison: A pilot study. *Anthrozoos, 7*(2), 124–128.

Warner, D. (1987) Good grief: Education support system for bereaved children and teens. Santa Rosa, CA: Santa Rosa Memorial Hospital Health and Wellness Education Services.

Whyham, M. C. (1993). The role of companion animals in prisons. Paper presented at the First International Congress on Human-Animal Companionship: Health Benefits, Cuauhtemoc, Mexico.

Wolfelt, A. (1983). *Children and grief,* Philadelphia, PA: Accelerated Development.

Books for Children

Blain, M. (2002). *Jasper's day*, Toronto, ON: Kids Can Press.

Rylant, C. (1997). *Dog heaven*, The Blue Sky Press/Scholastic Books.(ISBN: 0590417010).

Rylant, C. (1995). *Cat heaven*, The Blue Sky Press/ Scholastic Books. (ISBN: 0590100548).

Viorst, J. (1971). *The tenth good thing about Barney*, NYC: Aladdin Paperbacks, Simon & Schuster.

Rogers, F. (1988). *When a pet dies*, NYC: G.P. Putnam's Sons.

References

American Pet Products Manufacturers' Association. (2006). Pet owner survey. Greenwich, CT.

Arkow, P. (1987). *The loving bond: Companion animals in the helping professions.* Saratoga, CA: R & E Publishers.

Baker, E. (1988). Pet loss and separation: A mutlifactorial problem. In W. J. Kay, S. P. Cohen, C. E. Fudin, A. H. Kutscher, H. A. Nieburg, R. E. Grey, and M. M. Osman (Eds.), *Euthanasia of the companion animal* (p. 102). Philadelphia: Charles Press.

Boulden, J. (1994). *Saying good-bye activity book.* Santa Rosa, CA: Jim Boulden Publications.

Bowlby, J. (1969). *Attachment and loss.* New York: Basic Books.

Bowlby, J. (1973). *Attachment and loss* (2nd ed.). New York: Basic Books.

Bowlby, J. (1980). *Attachment and loss* (3rd ed.). New York: Basic Books.

Brown, M. (1990). *The dead bird.* New York: Harper Junior.

Buscaglia, L. (1992). *The fall of Freddie the leaf: A story for all ages.* New York: Slack Book Division.

Carrick, C. (1981). *The accident.* New York: Clarion.

Castro, S. L. (1990). Animal collectors. Paper presented at the Delta Society Ninth Annual Conference, October 11–13, Rochester, New York. Center for Applied Psychology. (1992). The Angry Monster Machine (game). King of Prussia, PA: Author.

Ciba Seminar. (1996, June). San Rafael, CA.

Egan, G. (1982). *The skilled helper* (2nd ed.). Belmont, CA: Brooks/Cole.

Fudin, C. E. and Cohen, S. P. (1988). Helping children and adolescents cope with the euthanasia of a pet. In W. J. Kay, S. P. Cohen, C. E. Fudin, A. H. Kutscher, H. A. Nieburg, R. E. Grey, and M. M. Osman (Eds.), *Euthanasia of the companion animal* (pp. 80–84). Philadelphia: Charles Press.

Gentry, A. (1987). The human–animal connections: Are our pets as important to our well-being as we are to theirs? *Sacramento Bee,* April 11.

Grollman, E. (1990). *Talking about death: A dialogue between parent and child.* Boston: Beacon Press.

Hannan, P. (1996). Personal interview, November 5, Santa Rosa, California.

Hart, B. and Hart, L. (1988). *The perfect puppy: How to choose your dog by its behavior.* New York: W. H. Freeman.

Heegaard, M. (1988). *When someone very special dies: Children can learn to cope with grief.* Minneapolis, MN: Woodland Press.

Herek, G. M., and Berrill, K. T. (1992). *Hate crimes: Confronting violence against lesbians and gay men.* Newbury Park, CA: Sage.

Hodges, W. F. (1991). *Interventions for children of divorce: Custody, access, and psychotherapy.* New York: Wiley.

Kay, W. J., Cohen, S. P., Fudin, C. E., Kutscher, A. H., Nieburg, H. A., Grey, R. E., and Osman, M. M. (1988). *Euthanasia of the companion animal.* Philadelphia: Charles Press.

Kidd, A. (1982, fall). Human benefits from the human/companion animal bond. *The Latham Letter*, pp. 1, 7–9.

Kidd, H., and Kidd, R. M. (1990). Factors in children's attitudes toward pets. *The Latham Letter, 11*(4), 1 & 13.

Koski, E. (1988). The use of animals in research: Attitudes among research workers. In W. J. Kubler-Ross, E. (1969). *On death and dying.* New York: Collier.

Lagoni, L., Butler, C., and Hetts, S. (1994). *The human–animal bond and grief.* Philadelphia: W. B. Saunders.

Levinson, B. (1982). The future of research into relationships between people and their animal companions. *Animal Problems 3*(4), 283–292.

Levy, B. (1981, August). Exploring the bond between people and their pets. *Dog Fancy*, pp. 34–35.

McElroy, S. C. (1996). *Animals as teachers and healers.* Troutdale, OR: New Sage Press.

Montagu, A. (1986). *Touching: The human significance of the skin.* New York: Harper & Row.

Mooney, S. (1983). *A snowflake in my hand.* New York: Delacorte.

Mugford, R. (1977). The contributions of pets to human development: A review of literature from the social sciences portraying the role of pets in society. England: Pedigree Pet Foods.

Newman, N. (1980). *That dog!* New York: Crowell Junior Books.

Nieburg, H. A., and Fischer, A. (1982). *Pet loss: A thoughtful guide for adults and children.* New York: Harper & Row.

The People–Pet Partnership, (not dated). *How to start a pet loss support group.* Pulman, WA: Author.

Pettit, T. H. (1994). Hospital administration for veterinary staff. Goleta, CA: American Veterinary Publications.

Polland, B. K. (1975). *Feelings inside you & outloud too.* Berkeley, CA: Celestial Arts.

Quackenbush, J., and Graveline, D. (1985). *When your pet dies: How to cope with your feelings.* New York: Simon & Schuster.

Rando, T. (1984). *Grief, dying, and death: Clinical interventions for caregivers.* Campaign, IL: Research Press.

Rogers, F. (1988). *When a pet dies.* New York: Putnam.

Ross, C. B. (1987). Pet loss and the human–companion animal bond. Master's thesis, Sonoma State University.

Ross, C. B. (1995, April). Cats and dogs combat AIDS depression. *Sonoma Business Magazine*, p. 38.

Ross, C. B., and Sorenson, J. B. (1994). Grief counseling: Hospital administration for veterinary staff. Goleta, CA: American Veterinary Publications.

Ross, C.B., (2005) *Pet Loss and Children, Establishing a Healthy Foundation.* New York: Routledge.

Ross, C.B., and Sorensen, J. B. (1998) *Pet Loss and Human Emotion, Guiding Clients Through Grief.* New York: Routledge.

Rubin, M. (1996). Personal interview, November 20, Sonoma County Mental Health Services, Santa Rosa, California.

Rush, S. (1983). *Tiffany: The elegant cat.* Santa Rosa, CA: unpublished work.

Savishinsky, J. S. (1988). The meanings of loss: Human and pet death in the lives of the elderly. In W. J. Kay, S. P. Cohen, C. E. Fudin, A. H. Kutscher, H. A. Nieburg, R. E. Grey, and M. M. Osman (Eds.), *Euthanasia of the companion animal* (pp. 143–144). Philadelphia: Charles Press.

Schell, R. and Hall, E. (1983). *Developmental psychology today* (4th ed.). New York: Random House.

Sibbitt, S. (1991). *Oh where has my pet gone?* Wayzata, MN: B. Libby Press.

Sipchen, B. (1977). Divided on divorce. *Los Angeles Times*, February 24, Sec. E.

Stein, S. B. (1990). *About dying: An open family book for parents and children together.* Boston: Beacon Press.

Stevenson, R. G. (1988). Euthanasia of pets: The impact on children. In W. J. Kay, S. P. Cohen, C. E. Fudin, A. H. Kutscher, H. A. Nieburg, R. E. Grey, and M. M. Osman (Eds.), *Euthanasia of the companion animal* (p. 75). Philadelphia: Charles Press.

Szita, B. (1988). Euthanasia in zoos: Issues of attachment and separation. In W. J. Kay, S. P. Cohen, C. E. Fudin, A. H. Kutscher, H. A. Nieburg, R. E. Grey, and M. M. Osman (Eds.), *Euthanasia of the companion animal* (p. 158). Philadelphia: Charles Press.

Tebault, H. (1997). Telephone interview with President of the Latham Foundation, August 6, Alameda City, CA.

Vaillant, G. E. (1996). John Bowlby. *American Journal of Psychiatry*, 153(11), 148.

Viorst, J. (1971). *The tenth good thing about Barney.* New York: Atheneum.

White, E. B. (1952). *Charlotte's web.* New York: Harper Junior.

Wilhelm, H. (1985). *I'll always love you.* New York: Crown.

Wolfelt, A. (1983). *Helping children cope with grief.* Muncie, IN: Accelerated Development, Inc.

Worden, W. J. (1982), *Grief counseling and grief therapy: A handbook for the mental health practitioner.* New York: Springer.

Worden, J. W., and Silverman, P. R. (1196 November 15). Parental death and the adjustment of school-age children. *Omega: The Journal of Death and Dying*, *33*(2), 91.

About the Authors

Cheri Barton Ross, M.A., C.T., is author of *Pet Loss and Children, Establishing a Healthy Foundation* (Routledge, 2005). A journalist, editor, and playwright, she is also founder of the Redwood Empire Veterinary Medical Association Pet Loss Support Group in Santa Rosa, California.

Jane Baron-Sorensen, R.N., MFT, has recently retired as the patient care manager for Psychiatric Emergency Services, a division of Sonoma County's Department of Health Services, in Santa Rosa, California. She led the Redwood Empire Veterinary Medical Association Pet Loss Support Group for 15 years.

Index